D1058179

THE
COLD
VANISH

THE
COLD
VANISH

Seeking the Missing in
North America's Wildlands

JON BILLMAN

GRAND CENTRAL
PUBLISHING

NEW YORK   BOSTON

Grand Central Publishing
Hachette Book Group
1290 Avenue of the Americas, New York, NY 10104
grandcentralpublishing.com
twitter.com/grandcentralpub

First Edition: July 2020

Grand Central Publishing is a division of Hachette Book Group, Inc. The Grand Central Publishing name and logo is a trademark of Hachette Book Group, Inc.

The publisher is not responsible for websites (or their content) that are not owned by the publisher.

The Hachette Speakers Bureau provides a wide range of authors for speaking events. To find out more, go to www.hachettespeakersbureau.com or call (866) 376-6591.

"What Happened to Jacob Gray?" piece originally published by *Bicycling*.

"How 1,600 People Went Missing from Our Public Lands Without a Trace" piece originally published by *Outside* magazine, reprinted with permission.

"Race for the Plane" piece originally published by *Outside* magazine, reprinted with permission.

"Squaring The Legend of Troy James Knapp" piece originally published by *Outside* magazine, reprinted with permission.

"Hunting Down the Alaska Highway Murderers" piece originally published by *Outside* magazine, reprinted with permission.

"How Maui Volunteers Found Two Missing Hikers in a Week" piece originally published by *Outside* magazine.

"Long Gone Girl" published by *Runner's World* magazine, August 2016. Written by Jon Billman.

LCCN: 2020933587

ISBNs: 978-1-5387-4757-5 (hardcover), 978-1-5387-4756-8 (ebook), 978-1-5387-5324-8 (Can. pbk.)

Printed in the United States of America

LSC-C

10 9 8 7 6 5 4 3 2 1

For Hilary

CONTENTS

CONTENTS

CONTENTS

MISSING
Jacob Gray

Age: 22
Height: 5'11
Weight: 145 lbs
Features:
-Brown Hair
-Brown Eyes
-Caucasian

Camping Gear Found On April 6, 2017
Sol Duc Road, Olympic National Park, Washington

Clothing:
-Blue MontBell Thunder Pass jacket
-Charcoal MontBell Thunder Pass pants
-Green hooded Duffle coat with long toggle buttons
-Rust Carhartt dungaree pants
-Tan knit hat

If you have information call
Santa Cruz CA PD (831) 420-5820
Case number: 17S-01626

A vanish:
A magicians' trick.
In mathematics, arriving at zero.

AUTHOR'S NOTE

YOU DREAM ABOUT missing persons, even though the nightmares don't belong to you.

Rational professionals I've met in my research—law enforcement and search-and-rescue personnel—tend to believe that our world is still a big, wild, and remote place, and logic and reason are at the core of missing persons cases. A very difficult puzzle laid out on a massive table, but there are rules and clues, and the puzzle can be solved. I agree with them most of the time.

I've been obsessed with writing about missing persons in wild places. In the April 2017 issue of *Outside* magazine, I wrote a feature about a college student, a runner missing in southern Colorado, that attempted to answer questions about who goes missing, why, how many are out there, and what the hell happens once you're gone. That story elicited more feedback—much of it polarizing—than anything I'd ever written.

You can't discuss missing persons in the wild without broaching the subjects of conspiracy theories and the paranormal. Though many do, I'm not advocating for Bigfoot as an explanation for any of these cases. Same goes for UFOs and portals to hidden dimensions. What I am insisting is that rhyme and reason so often fly out the window when someone vanishes in the wild. So many cases defy explanation, and often dumb luck is as useful a tool as a

FLIR (Forward-Looking Infrared Radar)–equipped helicopter and a team of trained tracking dogs when someone—or a body—does get found.

In early April 2017, a young touring cyclist named Jacob Gray stepped off his bike and disappeared in the northern district of Olympic National Park in northwestern Washington. What ensued was a mystery that echoed other cases I'd researched. What was different for me is that Randy Gray, Jacob's father, allowed me unlimited access into the courageous search to find his son. The feature I wrote on Jacob Gray for *Bicycling* magazine was the catalyst for meeting Jacob's family, but it soon became apparent that their generosity, and the huge, strange purgatorial underworld of the vanished, deserved a book.

The *Outside* story was a work of investigative journalism; Jacob and Randy Gray's story is more personal to me than most of the reporting I've done, and in more than a few places I fail at journalistic objectivity. I made four trips out west to rendezvous with Randy. He invited me to his hometown of Santa Cruz, California, on Christmas Day 2017, and we loaded up his Arctic Fox slide-in camper with food and gear and lit out in search of Jacob. We spent days and weeks together living out of the Arctic Fox, as well as a barn on the Olympic Peninsula of Washington used as a home base for Bigfoot researchers, a Native American reservation on the Strait of San Juan de Fuca, a cult compound in Canada, and an illegal wilderness tent site on a mountain in Olympic National Park. We napped on ferries, on beaches, and on Sitka spruce logs. We talked with heroin junkies living in Port Angeles, Washington, and on the fringes of Chilliwack, British Columbia. We went swimming in the Pacific Ocean and the Sol Duc River. We stumbled across three brand-new missing persons cases on Vancouver Island.

I couldn't help but become Randy's friend. It's infectious when, sitting around the little galley table in the Arctic Fox, eating tacos,

Randy would map plans to help the search for other missing persons, like Kris Fowler, who went missing on the Pacific Crest Trail in 2016. Or Randy would sketch designs for a new type of swiftwater rescue tool based on a type of lifeguard surfboard he'd seen in Hawaii; some days the current and boulders in the Sol Duc River nearly beat him to death, and he designed a rescue boogie board to help mitigate that. He bought and installed a new toilet in the Bigfoot Barn because the old one wasn't flushing quite right, and it was *the least he could do* in exchange for free rent. He spent hours on his phone helping friends and family with *their* problems. All this positive energy while shouldering what many psychologists believe is the heaviest burden a human can bear.

I don't think I could rise to the occasion to find my missing son the way Randy Gray has, to be as open-minded and full of generosity, love, and optimism while bushwhacking through a dense level of hell.

The disappearance of Jacob Gray in the wild represents one of hundreds—thousands—of persons who have vanished in remote places. Trying to find them often leads to a clusterfuck, and we don't even know how many of the vanished are out there. There are more every day.

Jon Billman
Marquette, Michigan
February 2020

THE
COLD
VANISH

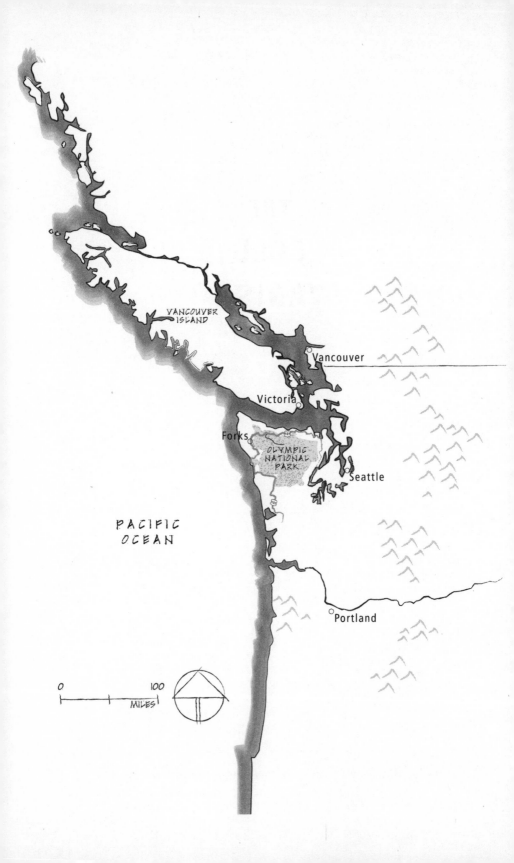

CHAPTER 1

THE OLYMPIC PENINSULA

Jacob answered, "My life of wandering has lasted a hundred and thirty years. Those years have been few and difficult, unlike the long years of my ancestors in their wanderings."
                                                                          —Genesis 47:9–11

MUCH DEPENDS ON a red bicycle. The bike is heavy and too small for Jacob's athletic five-foot, eleven-inch frame. Ideally for a journey of this scale he'd ride a *large*, but the *medium* is what he has to roll with. After all, he figures, bikes are like surfboards—you don't always have the perfect one for every condition. The important thing is the wave, the ride. And this one was free. The red Specialized Hardrock says *Milwaukee Tools* on it because his dad, Randy Gray, age sixty-three, won it in a raffle. Jacob—like his house-builder father, handy with a Skilsaw—fashioned a plywood rack behind the seat and bolted two milk crates to it side-by-side.

Instead of cycling-specific shoes with stiff soles and ski-binding-like clipped-in pedals favored by seasoned touring cyclists to allow for more power transfer to the cranks, Jacob's bike is outfitted with stock flat BMX-style rattrap pedals that accommodate his running shoes and hiking boots. Not built for speed, not lithe, not pretty, a size too small, but hell-for-stout, as the builders say. And as utilitarian as a pickup truck. He'd recently sold his Volkswagen sedan and now the bike is his transportation, which suits him just fine.

Jacob's preferred gear shop is the Port Townsend, Washington, Goodwill. He loaded his third-hand yellow-and-red Burley child trailer with pots and pans that still have the thrift-store price tags on them. His grandfather's wool Hudson's Bay blanket is heavy but warm, even when wet. A full roll of duct tape, a toolbox, camp stove, deck of cards, a Holman Bible, a tent, fuel bottles, a case of vintage Mountain House dehydrated meals, two first-aid kits, carabiners, climbing crampons, a bow and a quiver of arrows, a rain poncho, a sleeping bag, spin-cast fishing rod and reel, and enough tarps, rope, and bungee cords for a one-ring circus. The bike, trailer, and supplies weigh as much as the 145-pound twenty-two-year-old does soaking wet. Which he is.

The weather is snotty, which it never *isn't* in northwestern Washington in early April, but that doesn't slow him down. Jacob, a keen surfer who grew up on the beach in Santa Cruz, California, is ionized by water, as Randy puts it—whether surfing on it or riding in it. His dad talks of getting a dose of negative ions via whitewater, no matter how cold. Jacob is known to frequently trunk it—not don a wetsuit even when conditions warrant, which in the cold currents off Santa Cruz is most of the time. Jacob loves water, the colder the better.

What Randy's ion theory lacks in scientific proof, it more than makes up for in *shaka* vibes. "Even if we don't go surfing, we'll get a mocha and go down to the beach and watch the sunrise," Randy says. "That's our thing, Jacob and me." The two will sometimes sleep on the beach, with no sleeping bag, just watch the sunset and curl up in the sand like sea turtles until dawn.

Jacob has nowhere he has to be, and all the time in the world to pedal there. He doesn't tell anyone where he's going, not even Wyoma Clair, his grandmother, whom he'd been temporarily living with in Port Townsend. On April 4, 2017, he quietly leaves Wyoma fifty bucks on the table and heads out into the headwind and rain in the middle of the night.

When it hits social media that a cyclist is missing, there are reported sightings, few and mostly credible, but not very helpful. The cycle touring season hasn't ramped up yet, as most cyclists wait for the weather to temper. Car and truck traffic is light on Highway 101 at night. So it's logical that no more than a couple motorists report seeing a young man on an overloaded bike pulling a trailer westbound through the driving rain. A man claims to have seen Jacob twice on April fifth, in Indian Valley and along Lake Crescent. On Thursday, April sixth, a woman reports having seen a man towing "a red trailer" climbing Fairholm Hill at one o'clock in the morning.

No one gives it much thought. Touring cyclists are legion here soon, and Jacob is just the first robin of spring.

Later that morning, a local Port Angeles woman named Stacey passes Jacob as he churns up the Sol Duc Hot Springs Road, about two miles upriver from the 101. The park entrance shack is closed for the season, but the steel gate is open because the park itself is open, as is the Sol Duc Hot Springs Resort. Coming down-mountain later that afternoon, Stacey notices the rig, laid down 6.3 miles upriver from the 101; she's curious enough that she snaps a quick photo of the abandoned contraption, a flash of red-and-yellow aluminum and nylon against the lush universe of rainforest greens. It isn't a good place to camp or stash a bike for long, highly visible there under a Sitka spruce tree, not ten yards from the road, twenty yards from the river.

On the afternoon of April 6, an Olympic National Park worker radios his dispatch. *"Dispatch, 7-4-1 Ron on North Plain. I've got a bicycle that has went off the Sol Duc Road about, ah, mile marker 7, and I can't find anyone around it. You might want to send a ranger up here so we can see what's going on."*

ONP Dispatch: *"Copy, thanks for the info, 16:30."*

Dispatch connects him to Ranger John Bowie.

Ranger: *"Ron, I'll head that way. Is that bicycle down the bank a ways, or is it easy to get to?"*

"It's easy to get to. It's got a little carrier on the back of it too. It looks like it crashed off the road."

"Okay, so it didn't look like maybe somebody hid it there to go off for a hike?"

"It doesn't look like anybody's hit it, he just went off the road. I'm gonna stay here until you get up this way."

Ranger: *"Okay."*

Employee sign-out.

Standing next to the bike, which is just off the tarmac, Ranger Bowie can hear the roiling Sol Duc River even though he can't see it. There is a recurve bow and some target arrows poking out of the trailer. He sees four arrows stuck in the ground between the road and the bike and trailer; the arrows seem stuck there deliberately, in a row. A little strange, but he's seen it all, probably meaningless. Bowie does a quick look-around and doesn't find the cyclist. At six p.m. he calls Ranger Brian Wray and asks him to check it out in the morning.

On Friday, April 7, just before nine a.m., Ranger Wray arrives at the bike. No cyclist. No anyone. The four arrows are still there, stuck in the ground. No sounds but the rush of the Sol Duc River and spring birds—you could lie in the middle of the road and it's more likely you'd die of cold exposure before getting run over by a car.

Rangers perform what's called a "hasty search." Some search-

and-rescue personnel hate the term *hasty search*, preferring to call it the *Reflex Phase* of a search. "Hasty" implies half-assed, a lazy afterthought. At any rate, rangers don't find anything other than the bike, trailer, and gear; they don't know anything more than anyone else about where the cyclist could be. This is becoming a head-scratcher even to trained rangers.

Searchers use the acronym POS and sometimes joke that it stands for "piece of shit." It stands for *probability of success*, finding the missing. At this point the POS still remains high—the bike's owner will come walking out of the bush and greet them with a hello.

But what nags at the rangers is the positioning of the bike, trailer, and gear. Nothing is locked up or secured. There seems to have been no attempt to hide anything from the infrequent motorists. Rangers don't think there's much they can do other than kick through the ferns for evidence of any sort, and walk the riverbanks, looking for something washed up on the bank or snagged on one of several logjams. Still, is anyone even *missing,* just because they aren't, at the moment, logically, where they should be?

Searchers speak of "scenario"—why and how did the target come to be missing? It appears that Jacob—or someone—has been organizing gear. A tarp is partially spread out. But no logic points them in any one direction.

The four arrows are puzzling to the rangers. A bow and practice arrows are quite the tools to pack on a bicycle outfitted for a multi-day tour. They ponder the significance of the number, four— the four arrows stuck in the ground in a line, when the remainder stay in the quiver, next to his recurve bow and fishing rod, are a head-scratcher.

Wray photographs the scene. It's time to more closely inspect the cyclist's belongings. Wray secures the bow and arrows in his duty SUV. At approximately 9:20 a.m. he calls the district ranger, Michael Siler, to get one of his bosses up to speed. The ranger looks through the other gear in the trailer. It's surprising he doesn't find a kitchen sink.

Wray finds some iodine tablets—good for emergency water purification—but figures this cyclist would have a water filter and bottles, which are not there. Logic points him toward the river, twenty yards or so away. It makes sense that the cyclist bushwhacked to the river for water. He—it's assumed the cyclist is a *he*—slips on a rock and ends up in the cold, swift current. He can't swim, or he hit his head and is unconscious, drowns. Or the current is such he can't get out and succumbs to hypothermia in the thirty-something-degree water.

Or, he hitched a ride up to the lodge where he could soak his damp bones for an hour before catching a ride back to his bike.

Mountain lions live in the park, but an attack on a human would leave messy evidence. Same with a black bear, though a bear attack on a human is extremely rare here. More probable is an abduction, but that doesn't make the top of any lists.

Park rangers see the full spectrum of human behavior—it's possible the rider decided bike touring is not for him or met someone interesting and caught a lift to Seattle.

Though it's more probable than human abduction, it's less likely that the owner abandoned the bike to go on a trail hike—there isn't a trailhead in the immediate vicinity, he didn't secure his gear, and a hiker won't get very far before hitting snow.

The bike, trailer, and gear along the Sol Duc Road is now what searchers call the "LKP"—Last Known Position. Rangers do not find a phone among the gear, but do find a paper list of phone numbers—they're on to whose stuff this is. And they know where he was; now where the hell is Jacob Randall Gray?

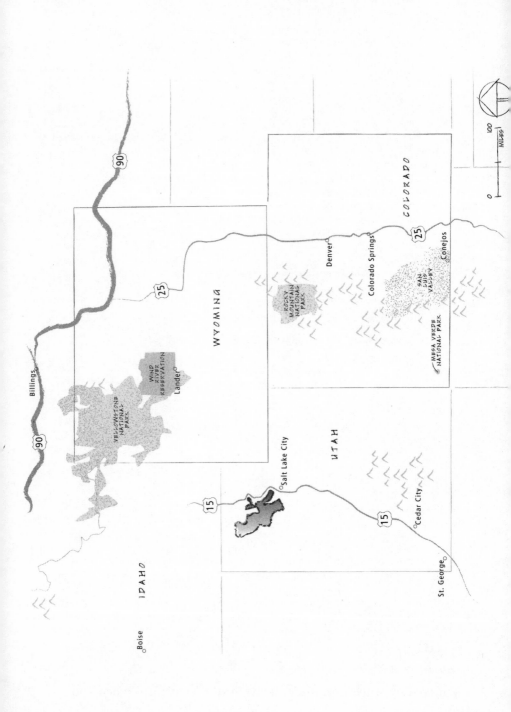

CHAPTER 2

WYOMING

I got home from climbing, it's just a normal day, get unpacked, feed the dog or whatever, then I start wondering, Where is she? Make some calls, drive around a little bit. It gets to be like eight p.m., nine p.m., ten p.m., that incredible anxiety builds up. You're just worried. I hope she didn't break her ankle, I hope she didn't run out of gas, those normal things where you're like, this sucks. But you're not going, "I hope my wife wasn't grabbed by some psychopathic serial killer."

—Steve Bechtel

ERWIN SCHRÖDINGER WAS an Austrian physicist who in 1935, in response to a quantum mechanics problem, stated simply that if you stick a cat in a sealed box—along with something that can kill the cat (in his case, a radioactive atom)—you won't know if the cat is alive or dead until you open the box. Before you open the box and look inside, the cat is both *alive* and *dead*. Until a person is found you don't know if they're dead, their remains entombed forever under a rockslide or hidden in a crevasse, scattered by wolves or, more likely, birds. What then, when you open Schrödinger's box, and there's no cat inside at all—what if it's empty?

Furthermore, you don't know for sure if a person is missing at all. While it's not likely, there's an outside chance they're alive and perhaps living in South America under a new identity (this happened recently, which I'll get to). A missing person is Schrödinger's cat.

I first stepped through the missing persons portal in July of 1997. Olympic marathon hopeful Amy Wroe Bechtel disappeared at age twenty-four while running on the Shoshone National Forest in the Wind River Mountains of Wyoming, 150 miles from where my soon-to-be-wife, Hilary, and I lived at the time. Her car was found up-country near midnight, along with her keys and wallet, but the woman had vanished without a clue. Law enforcement, family, and residents spent nearly two decades suspecting her husband had gotten rid of her, and some still do. I don't.

In 2017 I wrote a feature story for *Outside* magazine called "Leave No Trace" in which I was challenged by my editor to come up with a number representing just how many people are still missing out there, in the wild (magazine editors love figures). Neither the United States nor Canadian governments are keeping track. The Department of the Interior, which oversees the National Park Service, doesn't seem to know. Same with the Department of Agriculture and its U.S. Forest Service. And this isn't getting anywhere close to the Bureau of Indian Affairs—Indian reservations have an epidemic of people, especially women, gone missing. All to say, coming up with figures for people vanished in the wild is harder and far less exacting than Chinese algebra. And uncertainty, of course, leads to speculation and conspiracy theories and, in this case, cryptozoology.

Virginia Woolf wrote in *The Waves*, "On the outskirts of every agony sits some observant fellow who points." I felt like an empty-ambulance chaser with four-wheel drive. But I was getting paid to try.

My intrigue only grew. I tend toward insomnia and the analog, and each night in bed I listen with earbuds to Coast to Coast AM on a tiny radio. The program, which explores all sorts of mysteries of the paranormal, airs from one to five a.m. in my time zone. It's syndicated on more than six hundred stations and boasts nearly three million listeners each week. Most of the time, the white noise talk of space aliens and ghosts lulls me to sleep, but not when my favorite guest, David Paulides, is at the mic.

Paulides, an ex-cop from San Jose, California, is the founder of the North America Bigfoot Search (NABS), established in 2004. His obsession shifted from Sasquatch to missing persons when, he says, he was visited at his motel near an unnamed national park by two out-of-uniform rangers who claimed that something strange was going on with the number of people missing in America's national parks.

He wouldn't tell me the place or even the year "for fear the Park Service will try to put the pieces together and ID them." I wonder how actual those park rangers might be—it's curious that park employees would say, *let's go tell the bigfoot guy we have a missing persons problem*, but it makes good lore.

In 2011, Paulides launched the CanAm Missing Project, which catalogs cases of people who disappear—or are found—on wildlands across North America under what he calls mysterious circumstances. He has self-published six volumes in his popular Missing 411 series, most recently *Missing 411 Hunters: Unexplained Disappearances*. *Missing 411: The Movie*, a documentary codirected by his son, Ben, and featuring Survivorman Les Stroud, was released to mixed reviews in 2016. *Missing 411: The Hunted*, about hunters gone missing, came out in 2019.

Paulides makes his living off both Bigfoot and missing persons—selling self-published books that read like seed catalogs for the missing, making documentary movies with the tone and editing tricks of horror flicks, and speaking at events like Colorado's Mile High Mystery Conference—but he does his homework. Paulides's Missing 411 series of books aggregates hundreds of wildland missing persons cases in the U.S. and Canada. Paulides is coyly careful not to present theories as to what is behind all the disappearances, but the books fact-check out, even if he traffics in confirmation bias and foments tinfoil hat theories about space aliens, string theory portals, and cryptoids. He didn't come out and offer a number, so we played a sort of editorial numbers game. Paulides, who claims to have researched more than a thousand cases, agreed with me that 1,600 missing in the wild is not a stretch.

That number has been quoted many times since my article came out in 2017. It's a number that drives fact checkers and mathematicians nuts, a rounded guesstimation. It sounds wiser, more profound than it really is; in actuality, like most things involving missing persons, it's ham-handed at best and maybe even a little irresponsible in its inability to accurately quantify such an important phenomenon. But it would be impossible to come up with an exact number. In most states—Washington is one—after seven years a missing person is considered deceased, *dead in absentia*, so they're no longer *missing*. Before seven years, someone who wants you declared dead needs evidence you're not alive. After seven years they need evidence you're not dead.

I've had a couple years to live with the figure, and today I'll argue that 1,600 is *wildly* conservative. I'm surprised Paulides hadn't coined a number much larger long ago; he'd have gotten away with it. Consider Oregon's national parks and national forests alone. Just since 1997, 190 men and 51 women have vanished. Then there's all the non-public wildlands in Oregon. There's Portland, a city with a bad homeless urban-wildland interface camping problem. More Oregonians go missing every week, and by the time you read this, the math—cloudy to begin with—will be off.

It's not just Oregon that has strange topography on the charts. Most states' missing persons statistical figures climb irregularly upward; however, many of the missing on public wildlands aren't counted. Or they're not separated from the urban missing. In most states, no one even knows who should be counting. It seems a special mess considering the technological resources we have in our pockets. Sometimes the lost are found, but often not. The mountains are shrouded in fog.

Paulides has identified patterns of "unique factors of disappearances." He lists such recurring characteristics as dogs unable to track scents, the time (late afternoon is a popular window to vanish), and that many victims are found with clothing and footwear removed, even when hypothermia has been ruled out. Severe weather often coincides with the disappearance or the beginning of the search. Children—and remains—are occasionally found unlikely distances from the PLS—point last seen—in improbable terrain. Most mysterious to me are the bodies discovered in previously searched areas. This happens with odd frequency, sometimes right along the trail.

While many of the incidents are readily explained—swept down a roiling river, caught in an avalanche, dragged off and eaten by a mountain lion, hypothermia, suicide, etc.—I'm drawn to the stories that defy conventional logic. The proverbial *vanished without a trace* incidents, which happen a lot more (and a lot closer to your backyard) than almost anyone thinks. These are the missing whose situations are the hardest on loved ones left behind. The cases that are an embarrassment for park superintendents, rangers, and law enforcement charged with search and rescue. The ones that baffle the volunteers who comb the mountains, woods, and badlands.

The stories that should give you pause every time you venture outdoors.

That summer, 1997, I read about Amy Bechtel in the paper, listened on the statewide NPR affiliate (my preferred *daytime* listening), and talked to people who knew Amy and her husband, Steve, a professional rock climber, from the close-knit world of outdoor athletes in Wyoming. The disappearance split the family. Amy's brother Nels Wroe sparred in the media with Steve. Statistics show that most of the time it is indeed the husband. But in Wyoming—hell, all over this continent, all over the world—there are so many other possibilities for how someone goes missing.

Hilary and I attended a benefit run a month after Amy vanished. We wanted to help raise awareness and a little money for search efforts, but mostly we were curious. I wanted to trace the probable route that Amy had run the day she disappeared. I wanted to meet her husband and see if I could size him up. Also, we enjoyed weekend running events, and it would be good to get into those gorgeous mountains for some exercise with a purpose.

Informational flyers were included in our race packets. I can remember the race T-shirt for the Amy Bechtel Hill Climb vividly. A large color photograph of smiling, blond-haired Amy had been hastily screen-printed on the front of a basic white T-shirt, along with the words HAVE YOU SEEN AMY? and a phone number: 1-800-867-5AMY. Amy's photograph started to mute with the first wash. The shirt was one that got noticeably softer with each laundering, and I wore it often since it was so comfortable. It wasn't long until Amy faded to the white of the shirt, like a ghost, and all that remained was HAVE YOU SEEN AMY? and the phone number, which has long been disconnected.

I wish I'd saved that shirt, but I ripped it crawling under a barbed-wire fence, a bullet-sized hole in the back, and it took two runs in the 7,500-feet Wyoming sunshine that resulted in a painful sunburn on my back the size of a quarter before I tore it to rags to be used on my greasy bicycle chains. But even now, twenty years later and without a T-shirt to trigger my memory, I often think about Amy Bechtel and wonder what happened that summer day back in 1997, a time in my life when I was convinced I had more answers.

JULY 25, 1997, 1 A.M.

The car chugs around switchback after switchback, crunching gravel beneath its tires as it ascends the Loop Road through Sinks Canyon in mid-central Wyoming. Its headlamps cast twin beams of light that pierce the midnight blackness. Todd Skinner and Amy Whisler scan the edges of visibility for something—anything—that would hint at their neighbor Amy Wroe Bechtel's whereabouts. To their right lies the inky Frye Lake, which was to be the terminus of a 10K hill climb Amy was planning for the fall. They pass the lake, drive a few miles, round a bend—and then they see it. Directly ahead, a flash of white where the road forks.

Amy's white Toyota Tercel wagon is parked by the side of the road where the Loop Road splinters out to the smaller, pine-shrouded Burnt Gulch turnoff. There are puddles below the driver's door and behind the vehicle, but no footprints, no tire tracks in the mud. If she parked before it stormed that afternoon, she may have gotten caught in the rain, but where? There is no sign of Amy, though, so Todd pulls out his cell phone to call her husband, Steve.

From here, the calendar will hurtle forward days, months, years at a time. Meanwhile, Steve, authorities, Amy's family and friends— America—will rewind the clock on that single day, patching together hazy eyewitness accounts and scarce facts in hopes of uncovering what happened to the runner who never came home.

Amy Wroe Bechtel, twenty-four at the time of her disappearance, had been missing for nineteen years when *Runner's World* magazine sent me back to Wyoming to update the story that Wyoming—and much of the subculture of runners—never forgot. Nineteen years, with nary a shred of evidence other than what was found in her car in those early morning hours on the Burnt Gulch turnoff. There were her sunglasses, her car keys left on the driver's seat, and a to-do list—a small scrap of paper written in Amy's light, busy hand. Her last words to the world. She'd already contacted phone and electric companies to have services turned on at her and her husband's newly purchased home (check), dropped off the recyclables from the gym where she worked at the recycling center (check), been to the photo store (check). There were other things she hadn't yet done, or at least hadn't yet checked off the list. At the bottom: run.

It's heartbreakingly ironic that what would become such a disorganized investigation began with this tidy little window into Amy's plans for the day.

The cable television network Investigation Discovery took a crack at solving Amy's case in a 2013 episode of its *Disappeared* series; a flurry of local news stories followed suit. Behind the renewed interest in Amy's case: a new lead detective taking a fresh look at decades-old clues.

Wyomingites are fond of describing their state as America's biggest small town, and like nearly every other resident in 1997, Hilary and I followed Amy's disappearance in the *Casper Star-Tribune*—the paper of record in the state—and on KUWR, Wyoming Public Radio, day to day as it transitioned from a local to a national story that made Amy Wroe Bechtel a household name. The story was featured on *Unsolved Mysteries*, the *New York Times* covered it, and *Runner's World* went so far as to put Amy's photo on its cover in January 1998 for a story by John Brant. (The story generated more reader mail than any other in the magazine's history.) Most media accounts, driven by the hunches of the lead investigators, named but one suspect: Amy's husband, Steve Bechtel.

Nearly two decades later, however, it appears that there were hardly enough facts to merit such an intense focus on Steve. In the absence of hard evidence, what happened in the immediate aftermath of Amy's disappearance more closely resembled a work of fiction than the stories documented in *Serial* or *The Jinx*. In HBO's award-winning 2014 crime drama *True Detective*, Marty Hart, played by Woody Harrelson, tells his partner, "You attach an assumption to a piece of evidence, you start to bend the narrative to support it, prejudice yourself."

The "evidence" investigators had was Steve's journals. They contained poetry and lyrics that sometimes erred on the violent side and included troubling philosophies about male-gender dominance. To law enforcement, Steve was a cocky, wisecracking, superfit slam-dunk—he killed his new wife and hid her body somewhere remote. After all, it's almost always the husband.

Steve talks about being interviewed by the FBI. "What happened with these guys was that they decided what they wanted the answer to be and then tried to build the story around it."

A week and a half after Amy vanished, Steve sealed his public fate as the villain when he lawyered up and refused to take a polygraph test.

The narrative bent toward Steve. *Chauvinist. Coward. Wife killer.*

Meanwhile, potentially crucial evidence was rendered useless by shoddy crime-scene management. Meanwhile, a critical lead was ignored.

Meanwhile, a monster roamed free.

JULY 24, 1997, 10:30 P.M.

*"Uh, yeah, hey, I've got a person missing here, I
think, and I wondered if you had a spare around
anyplace?"*
—Steve Bechtel, in a phone call to Lander
(Wyoming) authorities to report his missing wife.

Amy and Steve had been married for a year and a month. After
they'd graduated from the University of Wyoming in Laramie
with degrees in exercise physiology, the couple moved to Lander,
population around 7,000, and lived at 9 Lucky Lane, a small white
house in a group of twelve utilitarian miners' houses the locals call
Climbers' Row. The Bechtels were tenants of the neighbors who
would eventually find Amy's abandoned car, Todd Skinner and
Amy Whisler. Skinner, who died in a tragic fall at Yosemite in
2006, was a world-renowned climber and Steve's frequent climbing
partner.

In 1997, Lander was on the cusp of becoming a destination
climbing town and, in that world, Skinner—and to a lesser extent,
Steve—were stars. Today, it has evolved into an outdoor enthusiast's mecca, hosting the monstrous climbers' playground of Sinks
Canyon in its backyard, the National Outdoor Leadership School
(NOLS), and an emergent road-racing and ultrarunning scene.
Now, just as then, cowhands sit on stools next to "rock rats" at the
historic Lander Bar, the prominent watering hole that happens to
be owned by a climber. But in 1997, to some, the climbers who now
in many ways give the town its identity were aliens, transients who
didn't appear to have real jobs. They were fraternal and secretive,
almost cultish.

Amy was a runner within this climbing clique. She had been a
standout distance runner at Wyoming—she ranked first in school

history in the indoor 3,000 meters (9:48) and second in the indoor 5,000 (18:07) in 1995—and, with a marathon Personal Record of 3:01, had aspirations of qualifying for the 2000 Olympic Marathon Trials. She and Steve both worked part-time at Wild Iris, the local climbing shop, and Amy also waited tables at the Sweetwater Grill and taught a youth weight lifting class at Wind River Fitness Center. The two had the appearance of happy young newlyweds. They had recently bought a house in the residential heart of Lander and were preparing to take the leap out of their "no need to knock, door's never locked" climbing-bum shanty on Lucky Lane.

When Amy vanished, Lander divided. The climbers and NOLS crowd rallied around Steve, insulating him when it was clear the authorities suspected him. That raised suspicions with many of the townies, fueled by frustrated questions in the newspapers posed by law enforcement and Amy's family. As Bryan Di Salvatore, a Montana-based writer who reported on the case for *Outside* magazine in 1998, puts it, "That town was freaked out. Scared and angry."

The fact that there was no body, no real sign of violence even, made Steve the go-to target in the fog of mystery. After all, he was familiar with many of the remote mountain areas in Wyoming. In the first few days after Amy vanished, however, Steve was hardly a suspect—he was helping lead the search. In fact, for the first few days, foul play wasn't even considered by investigators.

"Here's the whole problem," says Fremont County Patrol Sergeant John Zerga, who was assigned Amy's cold case file in 2010 and remains the lead detective today. "Nowadays, everything is viewed as a homicide. Back then it wasn't viewed that way. She was just a missing runner. For three days."

A stuffed wild turkey keeps watch from the corner of Zerga's small office in the Fremont County Sheriff's Office facility in Lander. A stout forty-eight-year-old with a close-cropped haircut and a cowboy's Fu Manchu mustache, Zerga is essentially the Lone

Ranger on Amy's case, and has the nigh impossible task of cleaning up a two-decades-old mess made by the first lead investigator on Amy's case, Dave King.

"We didn't close off any routes out of here," Zerga continues. "We didn't close off any vehicles. All we had was a bunch of people up here looking for a missing runner. We actually ruined it with the vehicle, because we allowed the Skinners to drive it home. [The investigation] was not good for at least the first three days. There was a lot of stuff that was lost."

"King rolled in a week late," says John Gookin, PhD, a search-and-rescue veteran who helped coordinate the mountain search for Amy. "He was off in the mountains on a horsepacking trip—so this guy who had just been promoted to detective from jailer was in charge of the search. The promoted jailer asked me, 'Well, what do I do?' The detective asking the volunteer running the search teams, 'What do I do?'"

The search began with just Steve and two dozen of his friends, but later that day there were ATVs, dogs, dirt bikes, and more than a hundred volunteers on the ground. The next day horses and helicopters joined in, and by the third day, the search area had been expanded to a thirty-mile radius—a big wheel of rough country. But it would take a full week after Amy's car was found for the area around it to be declared a crime scene.

On August 5, an FBI agent named Rick McCullough accused Steve of murdering Amy. Steve then retained the counsel of Kent Spence. By then, Steve had already been interviewed four times by investigators, and Spence advised him to refuse the FBI's request to take a polygraph test. Spence thought the situation had taken a turn to harassment.

Then, two months after Amy vanished, King relinquished the case to Detective Sergeant Roger Rizor and turned his focus on campaigning for Fremont County sheriff, a position he would be elected to in 1998. The campaign didn't stop King from discussing the case alongside Amy's sisters on *The Geraldo Rivera Show* in February 1998. Spence would later say that he believed King used Amy's case as a grandstand to help him get elected sheriff. King wouldn't hold that title long, though: On November 3, 2000, he resigned amid allegations of impropriety, and was later convicted of stealing cocaine from a law enforcement storage locker.

"Everybody that investigated this was focused on Steve," Zerga says. "And they had good reason. But there again, there was information coming in pointing in different directions."

One tip came from a man named Richard Eaton, who told investigators that his itinerant stumblebum of a brother, Dale Wayne Eaton, may have been involved. Rizor's team, dead-set on nailing Steve, was unconvinced, and may have missed its chance to close not just Amy's case, but at least nine cold-case murders. By not pursuing the lead, they may have allowed the notorious Great Basin Serial Killer to get away.

JULY 24, 1997, 4:30 P.M.

Steve arrives home after a day of scouting climbs with Sam Lightner Jr., a travel writer. Amy's not home, but he knows she had had a busy day planned.

Earlier in the day, he had rendezvoused with Lightner in Dubois— a town roughly equidistant from Steve's home in Lander and Lightner's in Jackson, eighty miles or so. The climbing partners had a history. They'd climbed throughout the west and in Asia, but just a year earlier, on a trip with Amy to Australia, the men were not getting along, and Lightner flew home early. But they always trusted each other on the rocks. From Dubois, the two climbers, accompanied by the Bechtels' yellow Lab, Jonz, had ridden north together into the Cartridge Creek area of Shoshone National Forest. They'd both carried guns, Lightner and Steve will later tell authorities, because "that's where they dump all the bad bears from Yellowstone." But the scout had been a letdown. The rock wasn't that great for climbing, had been a slog to get to, and wouldn't have been worth the effort. Thunderstorms had lurked nearby and had driven Steve and his friend back to Dubois, where they'd gone their separate ways.

A few hours pass. Amy's not home for dinner. Steve makes a few calls. Nobody's seen Amy, so he drives around town and rallies friends to help him find her. A few more hours pass.

Steve begins to panic.

"I actually got along with Amy better than I did with Steve in Australia," Lightner will say years later, reflecting on the constant skepticism he received from investigators. "I'm not gonna cover for somebody who might have murdered a friend of mine."

Lightner, and the trip to Dubois, will be Steve's alibi.

A trip to Dubois was the beginning of the end for Dale Wayne Eaton.

It's a wonder Eaton was a free man at all when police found him just outside the mountain town on July 30, 1998, nearly a year to the day after Amy's disappearance and, more specifically, just ten and a half months after he attempted to kidnap the Breeden family.

The botched kidnapping took place in an area called Patrick Draw, less than a three-hour drive from Lander. Shannon Breeden, her husband, Scott, and their five-month-old baby, Cody, were traveling the country when their van broke down at a pullout along Interstate 80. An overweight, disheveled fifty-two-year-old stopped his off-green '85 Dodge van and offered them assistance. The man—Dale Eaton—asked Shannon to drive. Eaton then pulled a rifle from the back of the van, kidnapped the family at gunpoint, and directed them south of the highway into the desert.

In a scene straight out of a B-grade seventies chase movie,

Shannon stepped on the gas and turned in a tight circle instead, which enabled Scott to jump out of the van with the baby and Shannon to get out the other side. Eaton grabbed her and would have plunged a knife into her ribs had Scott not grabbed Eaton's arm and gun and hit him over the head with the rifle butt. A struggle ensued in the dirt, and ended with Eaton stabbed with his own knife, beaten with his own rifle, and left in the dirt while the family sped for help in the van.

It wasn't long before Eaton was arrested, and he quickly confessed to the attempted kidnapping.

The incident got Eaton's brother, Richard, thinking. He knew that Dale had been camping in the Burnt Gulch area at the time of Amy Bechtel's disappearance. Burnt Gulch, average elevation 7,860 feet, is not far from where Amy was marking her 10K route, and was a favorite elk hunting and trout fishing spot of the Eaton brothers. But after Richard called Rizor with his suspicions, the detective dismissed the tip, choosing to believe instead the word of Eaton's niece, who said Dale was visiting her in Greeley, Colorado, on July 24. A $100,000 reward out for information leading to a resolution of Amy's case was enough to cast suspicion on Richard's motives.

Astonishingly, a plea deal for the attempted kidnapping meant Eaton would serve just ninety-nine days in jail, where samples of his DNA were taken, before being paroled to a halfway house in Casper due to prison overcrowding. He remained on strict probation—which included a curfew—but was allowed his Dodge van so that he could work welding and construction jobs.

Eaton, however, failed to report to work on June 16, 1998, and a warrant was put out for his arrest. Police finally spotted his van more than a month later on a short dead-end spur road near Dubois in the Bridger-Teton National Forest. He was arrested at gunpoint and told police he was about to commit suicide. A shotgun was found in his van, leading to his imprisonment on federal weapons charges.

Four years later, those DNA samples taken while Eaton was incarcerated would be linked to unspeakable horrors.

JULY 24, 1997, 2:30 P.M.

She walks into the portrait studio on the second floor of the Camera Connection in downtown Lander, dressed for running.

No, not like she's already gone for a run, Lonnie Slack, who worked part-time at the studio back then, remembers. She's not sweating. She looks like she's about to go for a run.

She drops off some pictures to get matted and framed. She's excited, talking about her forthcoming entries in the Sinks Canyon Photo Contest.

She's there fifteen minutes, maybe. Then she leaves out the back door.

Well, it was after lunch. Maybe it was two o'clock.

I wonder if Amy would have approved of the photo.

Hilary and I were living in Kemmerer at the time, two and a half hours southwest of Lander, and when the race was announced, we put it on our calendar: September 28, 1997.

Race morning was a sunny autumn day on the eastern shoulder of the Wind River Range, and 150 or so runners gathered for a bittersweet attempt to actualize the 10K course that Amy had been working on when she'd gone missing. The run was to be a steep, steady, warm, and dusty climb up the gravel switchbacks of the Loop Road that ended at Frye Lake, where divers had searched for a body. Most of the field had been involved in the search or were close to Amy through running or to Steve. There were NOLS employees and a posse of hard-core climbers who run to stay in shape but don't consider themselves runners. Amy's sister Jenny Newton was there. As was Steve, who by this time had come under intense scrutiny from investigators and a sizable segment of the Wyoming public as the number-one suspect in the case.

Steve was remarkably composed during a prerace talk. Amy had wanted to do this race for a couple of years, he said. She was told the only people who would show would be eight of her former track teammates. This brought cheers from the field. We're in this together. We know Amy is alive.

I remember trying to size up Steve Bechtel—is this a man who was capable of killing his wife and hiding the body? He didn't carry himself like my idea of a wife-killer. He had been, after all, the one manning the phones and computers at the recovery center in his and Amy's garage and kitchen, responding to leads that poured in from all over the country, none fruitful. But then how are you supposed to act when your wife disappears? A 10K seemed like the best thing for exorcising anxiety, in part for lack of knowing what else to do—and because it was what she had wanted to do—and it got a little media coverage that kept the search alive.

But after the local search fizzled out, Amy's mom, dad, brother, and two sisters returned to their respective homes and tried to carry on with lives that would never be the same again. Their concerns about Steve grew a few weeks later when they were presented with previously undisclosed information about the search findings and Steve's journal entries. Although each family member responded differently, their frustrations with Steve's lack of overall cooperation and engagement with the investigators lingered. Amy's father, Duane Wroe, told a news source years later, "I still feel angry, because if he's not guilty of anything, the son-of-a-bitch should take the lie-detector test and give us some peace." Her brother, Nels, was especially angry at Steve's reluctance to take the test and co-operate fully with investigators. When her sisters, Casey Lee and Jenny Newton, appeared on *The Geraldo Rivera Show* with detective

King, the host made a plea for Steve to be more cooperative with authorities.

A year passed, then two, then four. Steve followed a new girlfriend to Salt Lake City, but found he missed Lander, so he moved—with the girl—back to town two years later. He still refused to take the polygraph, and many people in town continued to believe he was responsible for Amy's disappearance. Steve's girlfriend ended up leaving. More years slipped by. Eventually, Steve had Amy declared legally dead, and in 2004 he married Ellen Sissman, with whom he now has two children.

All these years later, Nels Wroe has accepted that the family may never find closure, but remains frustrated with Steve's refusal to take the polygraph. "I will not shy away from that," Nels said to me when I visited him at a coffee shop near his home in Longmont, Colorado. "The one person who can help the most in possibly resolving what happened to Amy is the guy who for whatever reason—cowardice, selfishness, I don't know—refuses to engage.

"This stressed the family out. My father passed away a number of years ago. The whole situation with Steve not being cooperative, that really caused frustration for the family."

JULY 24, 1997, 10:30 A.M.

"Boy, if it were me, I'd be running down the mountain," Erle Osborne jokes out his window as he drives past the woman running up the Loop Road. The mechanic for the county slows down so as not to dust her, as he makes his way uphill to change the carburetor on an old fire truck that sat idle at a youth camp.

The woman, blond, blue-eyed, and wearing a light-colored singlet, black shorts, and a fanny pack, smiles and waves at Osborne.

Odd, he thinks, a runner on the third switchback of the Loop Road.

It would be years before this would become a common sight. And yet authorities will later confirm that another witness, a road surveyor, independently described seeing the same woman on the Loop Road at around the same time of day.

Osborne arrives at the fire truck and works with haste—he can feel a storm closing in. He gets back in his truck and rolls up the windows just in time for the rain and lightning to come down. A goose drowner. Raining so hard he can hardly see the road.

He remembers the woman running uphill. If he sees her on his way down, he'll offer a ride.

But Osborne doesn't see the runner again. He does, however, have to inch around an old blue-green vehicle—he'll later strain to recall that it may have been a van—stopped in the road.

It's possible, if highly unlikely, that the surveyor and Osborne saw a different runner who just happened to look like Amy. Petite, pretty—Amy looked like a lot of women, like a lot of women who also vanished without a trace from the Great Basin region of Nevada, Utah, Idaho, and Wyoming.

Amy's isn't even the most famous case. A series of other murders between 1983 and 1997 have been suspected to have come at the hands of one Great Basin Serial Killer, but the case of only one of them has been resolved: Lil Miss.

On March 25, 1988, eighteen-year-old Lisa Marie Kimmell was driving alone from Denver to visit a friend in Billings, Montana, in her black 1988 Honda CRX Si, which had a Montana vanity plate that read LIL MISS. She'd first planned to stop to see her boyfriend in Cody, Wyoming, but she never made it. Eight days later, two fishermen found her body tangled in the weeds along the North Platte River near Casper, and an autopsy showed that she had been repeatedly raped, bludgeoned, and methodically stabbed. After her family buried her, a strange note signed "Stringfellow Hawke" was found on Kimmell's grave.

Few answers emerged for the next fourteen years, until July 2002, when investigators researching cold cases examined the seminal DNA from her rape kit and found a match for an inmate incarcerated on weapons charges since 1998: Dale Wayne Eaton. Eaton was due to stand trial that fall on a manslaughter charge after killing his cellmate with a lethal punch to the man's vertebral artery—but he was never convicted. He wouldn't be so lucky this time.

A handwriting analysis from the note left on Kimmell's grave also matched Eaton. Then, following a tip from neighbors who recalled seeing Eaton digging in his desert-scrub yard, authorities found her car buried on his property in Moneta, just an hour-and-forty-five-minute drive east from Lander. The sewer line from his decrepit trailer house had been run into it—he'd been using his victim's car as a septic tank. A portion of the Montana vanity plate LIL MISS was found nearby. Inside his trailer, authorities also found women's clothing and purses, and newspaper reports about other murdered women.

In the ensuing investigation and trial, it was determined that Eaton had kidnapped Kimmell at a remote rest area in Waltman, then held her captive in a filthy converted school bus and repeatedly raped her before murdering her and tossing her body off a bridge. An FBI profiler who examined the case would note that this public display, the trophy-keeping of Kimmell's car, and the known kidnapping attempt of the Breedens all fit the profile of a serial killer.

In the Kimmell trial, Eaton was charged and found guilty of all counts, including first-degree murder, and sentenced to death by lethal injection in March 2004. Eaton's lawyers won him a stay of execution in December 2009, arguing among other things that he was mentally unfit to stand trial and that he'd previously been given ineffective counsel by the Wyoming Public Defender's Office. He remained Wyoming's lone death row inmate until November 2014, when a U.S. district judge overturned his death sentence on similar grounds—though Eaton will never be released from prison, where he is serving a life sentence plus fifty years.

No one believes Kimmell is Eaton's only kidnapping and murder victim. Sheila Kimmell, Lisa's mother, mentions Amy's case in her 2005 book *The Murder of Lil Miss,* and is very well versed in other disappearances and homicides connected with the Great Basin Murders. "The Utah Criminal Tracking Analysis Project suggested that the Great Basin murders stopped around 1997. That's about the same time Dale Eaton went to prison," Kimmell writes.

That's why, beyond closure for the Wroes and Bechtels, Amy's case still matters, why Richard Eaton's tip, delivered years before his brother was known to be a killer, still matters. A confession by Eaton may resolve not just Amy's case but numerous other cold-case mysteries swirling in the abyss of the Great Basin.

And yet, even after Eaton's conviction, Steve Bechtel remained the prime "person of interest" in Amy's disappearance. In July 2007, the ten-year anniversary of her disappearance, Roger Rizor, the detective who succeeded Dave King on the case, commented on the cold case to the *Billings Gazette.* "In my mind there is only one person that I want to talk to, only one person who has refused to talk to law enforcement," he said, "and that's her husband."

That thinking didn't begin to change until 2010, when Detective Sergeant Zerga's supervisor dropped Amy's cold-case file on his desk, asking him to see if something would jump out at him. That something was a note about Richard Eaton's tip. It was enough for Zerga to put other cases on hold in order to travel with an FBI agent to Colorado to try to interview a madman's brother, and to Wyoming's death row to interview the madman himself.

"Dale's brother and sister-in-law are absolutely convinced he was in the area at the time," Zerga says about his summer 2012 meeting with them. "I told his brother that's not a place to camp. The area is, like the name has it, a gulch—there are more picturesque camping spots close by." But Richard Eaton described in detail the beaver ponds and a fire wheel and other specific geographical details of the area. "To me, once Richard said Dale was there when she went missing—and he has those capabilities—immediately that went up on top."

But Dale refused to speak with Zerga. And with the death penalty no longer hanging over Eaton's head, Zerga doesn't have any bargaining leverage.

When I met with Nels Wroe, he brought up the subject before I could ask. "Are you familiar with Dale Eaton?" he asked me. "There are some things like that that have bubbled up. If it was to be a random occurrence, or some high-probability random occurrence that may have happened, Dale Eaton is one. But even though there's no real compelling evidence at all that he may have anything to do with it, the circumstances that surround him, where he was, the way he operated, it certainly raises him as a high level of interest, maybe. What hasn't changed, which drives me crazy, is Steve's lack of involvement, and lack of cooperation."

I asked JoAnne Wroe, Amy's mother, in an email, if the new focus on Eaton has affected her life. "Though I am constantly aware that he may be responsible for Amy's disappearance," she writes, "it's very difficult to allow my mind to dwell on this, knowing what he has done to his victims. Not knowing what has happened to Amy or who is responsible is constantly in my thoughts, which makes me very frustrated and angry. It has taken me a long time to learn to live with this and there are days when it overwhelms me."

Periodically, cadaver dogs have been brought in from as far away as Montana. The dogs are so deft they will run straight across wildlife carcasses; they're looking for human carcasses and know the difference. This happened a couple of years ago when they followed a scent down Burnt Gulch and stopped at a depression. "We were pretty stoked when we found that sunken bog," Zerga says. "We thought it was what we'd been looking for for a long time." They sifted through every ounce of dirt in the hole and found only a single bread tie.

Zerga hasn't officially ruled out Steve as a suspect. But he talks about Steve, who now runs a gym just a couple of blocks from Zerga's office, in tones that imply respect, as if he were talking about a friend. Still, there are elements in the case that puzzle the detective. The fact that they had no log showing that Steve phoned the hospital when he said he did. A youth camp minister's account of seeing a vehicle that matches the description of Steve's truck being parked by itself on July 24 in the spot where Amy's car was found.

"The thing with Steve, and the shape he was in," Zerga says, "is he could run a marathon in three and a half hours. He had that type of capability. He coulda run back to Lander." Though it has to be in a list of scenarios, Zerga doesn't buy it. "To me, why would he wait until she was running? It would be so much easier in the house.

"I would really like to rule Steve out," Zerga says. "My only way is to sit down with Steve. You know what, let's do the polygraph. You'll be able to choose who's gonna do the polygraph. You'll know the questions before they're asked. And they're not gonna be questions like, 'Did you kill your wife?' They'll be questions like, 'Is it true the last time you saw your wife, alive, was the morning you woke up and went to Dubois?'"

I point out there's not an attorney in the west who would advise a client to take the test, and Zerga agrees. "That's exactly what attorneys do—the first thing they do is say, 'Don't take the polygraph.' To me, I can understand it in a sense. But the way polygraphs are, if you really wanted to rule yourself out, you'd take one."

"This is a whole different generation," Steve, now forty-six, says. I meet him at Elemental Performance and Fitness, his Lander gym, where he jokes with clients and checks in with his wife, Ellen. Steve—rarely seen without a baseball cap—has short gray-blond hair and the modesty and forearms of Peter Parker. Now he's taking me for a tour of his world in '97. We drive to Lucky Lane—Climbers' Row—in his 2006 Toyota Tundra pickup; there are kids' car seats in the back. He shows me the garage where he and friends ran the recovery effort. "After the initial search shut down," he says, "as we started realizing we weren't just looking out in the woods for her, we moved to a nationwide search the best we could."

According to Detective Zerga, authorities had been to Lucky Lane with a search warrant within the last five years. "We've actually done luminol searches with the FBI in that building," Zerga told me. "We brought in cadaver dogs. And luminol picks up any type of blood splatter, whether they paint over it or whatever." The dogs found nothing, and the luminol tests came out negative. Zerga even followed up on a rumor that Steve had buried Amy below the driveway of their would-be new home at 965 McDougal Drive before the concrete had set; he found nothing there, either.

"I'm impressed with him," Steve says of Zerga, "because he's taking, for all intents and purposes, this cold case and he's really working on it. He got handed this really badly put-together case. Looking back on King now, he had drug problems, problems telling the truth. So what's really fascinating and really sad was they were so cycloptically focused on *'Let's see if we can nail the husband,'* that they missed a lot."

Steve estimates he hasn't talked to his attorney, Kent Spence, in ten years. Spence is the son of the buckskin-wearing Wyoming native Gerry Spence, who gained fame defending high-profile clients like whistleblower Karen Silkwood, Randy Weaver of Ruby Ridge standoff fame, and Earth First! eco-radical Dave Foreman. Many thought Kent Spence was suspiciously high-powered. "He pro-bonoed I don't even know how many hours to us," says Steve. "Just hiring those guys was controversial. But imagine having heart surgery and saying, 'Well, I'll just get a crappy doctor.'"

Steve drives at a contemplative mosey. "Living is so fascinating. I have these two little kids and more than anything in my life, those two are what I was born for, to raise those kids. It means everything to you. And the thing that's a really profound challenge emotionally for me is knowing that those two kids never would have existed if I would have been able to keep hold of Amy. You look through history, and these tragedies happened in order for wonderful things to happen."

There's a tendency to talk about Amy-the-victim rather than Amy-the-person, especially when you're badgered by law enforcement and writers, but it's clear Steve thinks about Amy often. "It breaks your heart," Steve says. "She was so cool, Jon. Her greatest fault was that she was so friendly she was always taken advantage of. 'I'll take your shift.' 'I'll watch your dog.' It just makes you so sad."

We drive up the canyon on the now-paved Loop Road. I haven't been here since the awareness race.

"You could take the strongest woman—a Division I athlete—and the average guy is gonna be able to overpower her," Steve continues. "And a man will be able to sprint faster and he's gonna have this capability of overpowering this woman. There's a fantasy of knowing self-defense moves or that an athletic woman, a runner especially, is going to be able to outrun a guy. In practice that doesn't occur, I don't think." This gender philosophy may fit with some of the poetry and lyrics that raised eyebrows with investigators and members of the Wroe family in the early weeks of the investigation. Steve tells me he still regrets bringing Jonz to Dubois with him the day Amy disappeared, since she most likely would have taken the dog on her run.

In 2002 Steve and his father, Tom, went to the sheriff's department in neighboring Natrona County when the Eaton theory wasn't taken seriously in Fremont County after news of the Lil Miss murder broke. They wanted to see if any evidence taken from Eaton's property belonged to Amy. "Maybe there's a watch or a shoe or something we might recognize," Steve says. But the Natrona officials wouldn't let them see anything, claiming that the Fremont County sheriff had already looked everything over.

The pavement ends, and we hit a mixture of frozen mud and snow. We soon come to a branch in the road. "Right here," he says. "Her car was parked right in there." Steve narrates the night she disappeared.

"It's one or so in the morning, find the car, get here. I brought sleeping bags and a cookstove and food—first-aid kit—we gotta find her. Todd and Amy had been driving and found the car. They called. We raced up here. You get here—this was a big error—we're looking for a missing runner. Everybody was crawling through that car. Knowing what we know now we should have cordoned the thing off—fingerprints. It's like the classic cluster of stupid crap."

I ask him if he'll take the polygraph to relieve Zerga of all doubt. "The polygraph is like one of those monkey traps," he says. "Anybody who needs me to take that test—I don't need them in my life." He holds the relaxed confidence of an athlete, even while talking about a painful past. "I don't need people to be looking at Eaton," he says. "I don't mind being a suspect, but to me everyone else is a suspect."

Lizard Head, the mountain, looms in the east as we head back toward Lander. "Running is this beautiful thing for people—it's the thing they get to do," Steve says. "You have all these things you have to do, then once a day you get to go running. You don't want that to be compromised." He seems to understand that people want answers because they can't accept that something as simple and pure as running could end in terrible tragedy. "I think that's the thing: You don't want to be afraid."

We pass underneath the hulking dolomite that lines Sinks Canyon. "My wife will go running alone," Steve says. "*My wife*. She knows as well as anybody the story of Amy."

JULY 24, 1997, MORNING

The day is filled with possibility. Steve is off from his part-time job at Wild Iris, and Amy has her shift at the fitness center before she is off, too. The morning sunshine tugs at both of them to get outdoors.

Steve's plan is to go scout some dolomite bands with Sam Lightner in the mountains above Dubois. It's grizzly country, so he's taking guns, bear spray—and Jonz.

Amy is going to take care of some errands, including scouting the course for her 10K in September—wow, it's only two months away. And she still needs to design the flyers, plan for the road closure, measure the course…

She sits down to make her list. The last thing she writes is "run." Amy would never check it off.

If Detective Zerga finds out why she never checked off "run" by way of an Eaton confession, we may also learn why Naomi Lee Kidder never came home. Why Belynda Mae Grantham never came home. Why Janelle Johnson never came home. Why perhaps at least nine other young women never came home. The question persists, obscured in a Great Basin haze.

Why didn't the runner come home?

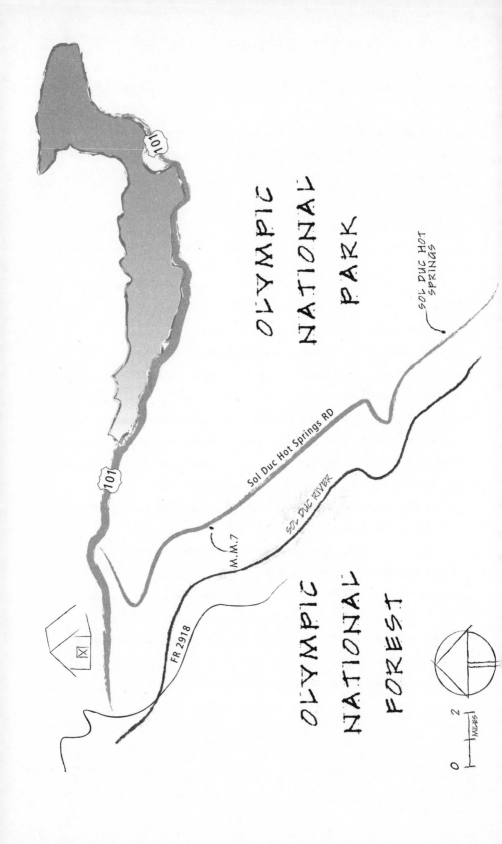

CHAPTER 3

THE SOL DUC RIVER

People don't take trips, trips take people.
— *Amelia Earhart*

A PERSON ISN'T *missing* until they're *reported* missing. Even then, if you're over eighteen years old, going missing isn't a crime or even an emergency. In this case no one reports Jacob missing at all— rangers don't have a missing person puzzle so much as they have a case of a found bicycle. Still, they need to find who it belongs to.

On the morning of Friday, April 7, Ranger Wray calls Mallory, whose number is one of several on the list found among the gear. Wray learns Mallory is the sister of Jacob Gray, native of Santa Cruz, California. For the park, this is progress—bikes don't have license plates or vehicle identification numbers like autos; they have serial numbers, but change hands without paperwork and are much harder to track, especially less-expensive models. Mallory Gray, who is a year older than Jacob, doesn't panic—her brother is an adventurous kid and prone to doing things his own way, on his own. But a call from a federal law enforcement officer is rarely good news, and she urges Wray to phone their parents in Santa Cruz right away.

Ranger Wray then calls Jacob's mother, Laura Gray, at 10:14 in the morning. He informs her they're going to do a search. Jesus, a *search*. Laura calls Randy, her ex-husband. The parents are, of course, concerned—a search is serious. But they too remind themselves that Jacob has taken off on mysterious pilgrimages before. He'll come back, drag-ass tired with wet gear and a bunch of new stories.

Rangers tell the family they don't have much to go on, other than the abandoned bicycle. POC stands for "probability of *containment*"—are they looking in the right place? Jacob's bike and trailer are functional—the tires are not flat, there's no evidence the rider (rangers don't even know for certain the gender of the cyclist at this point) had been hit by an automobile. Nothing appears malfeasant—enough gear to stock an REI store is there, and he probably has his wallet and phone in his pocket.

The Sol Duc Hot Springs Resort is checked out, but no one has seen him. A thousand feet above the bike is the snowline skirt of the Olympic Mountains' High Divide, source of the Sol Duc River. As the elevation rises, the snow quickly gets ass-high when you punch through it in hiking boots; the snowpack gets deeper foot-by-foot as you go up, and snowshoes are mandatory equipment. Rangers figure no one but Bigfoot would go up that early in the season.

It's not until Sunday afternoon, April 9, when Wray calls Laura again, this time to tell her they think Jacob fell into the river, that they panic. Wray also tells her the water is too high with rapids to do much, if anything, and that it might be summer before they know anything more.

Jesus.

In a wilderness bereft of clues, all theory leads into the Sol Duc— Quileute Indian for *sparkling waters*. Jacob needed water, he skipped to the river to filter into his CamelBak, he slipped. He fell in and got swept downriver. The current knocked him against boulders and deadfall and pinned him under. That's a plausible scenario. And that's what led Olympic National Park rangers to tell the family things like, *We think he fell into the river—we'll check the river in the summer*. And *he could be in the Pacific Ocean by now*.

After rangers photograph the bike, trailer, and gear like an accident—or crime—scene, they load everything up and lock it in a boathouse on Lake Crescent, where they take a detailed inventory. Rangers tell Laura they have a lot going on in their park. In a place that's 200,000 acres larger than Yosemite and sees almost four million visitors a year, they're wildly understaffed with nearly two-thirds of their law-enforcement personnel having been transferred to other parks and not replaced due to budget cuts. Within a week of Jacob's bike being found, there is also a plane crash. Another young man goes missing at the opposite end of the park.

Then there's the usual police work of booking drunk drivers, investigating visitors with dogs off-leash, illegal campsites, someone shooting a firearm, and parking violations that, in a park this huge, can eat up most of a single shift. On April 8, as Ranger Wray is headed to the vicinity of Jacob's disappearance, he gets a dispatch call to a "vehicle pointing a gun from his vehicle at another vehicle." This type of call is regular. Three big events at once along with all the pedestrian duties, and the tourist season is still three months away.

A park visitor reports hearing a whistle on the Sol Duc Falls trail, believing it to be a distress call. Rangers Wray and Bowie check it out. Wray's report would state: "Only whistle heard is that of a Thrush."

Laura calls Randy to inform him that rangers believe Jacob fell into the river and is headed to the Pacific Ocean. Randy, who when he isn't working is surfing, and vice versa, drops his hammer gun and throws his wetsuit into his white Ford work truck, picks up

Mallory, and speeds north, driving the thousand miles from Santa Cruz straight through.

"I drove all night," Randy says. "I got stopped going a hundred miles an hour in Oregon. I told him what was going on. He said, 'I'm not the last cop to not give you a ticket. Just be careful.' He walked back to his car, turned around, and drove off like nothing happened."

Time is, of course, vital in search-and-rescue events, and it's already Tuesday by the time Randy and Mallory reach the scene and—sleep deprived, amped up on adrenaline and caffeine—begin to get some semblance of bearings. Family members and friends fly into Seattle and drive to the park. Jacob's aunt and uncle, Dave and Elise Stokes, from Bellevue, ferry over. It's an unfortunate occasion for a reunion. The rain only stops intermittently, and fingertips and toes feel perennially pruned. They can't tell, but just a couple thousand feet above them it's snowing, atop mountains hidden above clouds and fog.

Jacob's bike was found fifty feet from the river. The river, running at between 3,000 and 4,000 cubic feet per second—brisk, but not extreme, especially for a surfer like Jacob—was less than fifty feet wide. On the other side is the Olympic National Forest, another jurisdiction, another federal department. The National Park Service is under the umbrella of the Department of the Interior, while the United States Forest Service answers to the Department of Agriculture. Unlike national parks, national forests operate under the county model, and the sheriff of Clallam County, Washington, is in charge of search and rescue there. While the sheriff has no authority in Olympic National Park, you could throw a rock across the Sol Duc River from the park and it would land in the Olympic National Forest, the Clallam County sheriff's charge.

But for now, Olympic National Park, overwhelmed with other events as they were, held onto jurisdiction and had invited no outside resources to the search. Absent were the man-trackers and dog teams, trained boots on the ground. A swiftwater rescue team. Drones, fixed-wings, helicopters. In the United States, national parks operate like sovereign countries; search-and-rescue personnel from outside the park must be requested by park officials in order to search. Otherwise, they risk being blackballed from future missions—the park sets the rules.

The U.S. Coast Guard, based in Port Angeles, is notified through channels that begin with Jacob's older brother Micah, who is an active-duty Coast Guardsman stationed on Lake Champlain in Vermont. Micah's father-in-law is a Coast Guard officer in Alaska. He makes some calls, but that's not enough, and their MH-65 Dolphin was never sent in the air over Olympic National Park, because ONP have not requested a flyover, even though the USCG sometimes perform aerial rescue training with ONP. Neither were aircraft from Naval Air Station Whidbey Island, which assists with some Olympic National Park searches. The weather was pea soup, and the forest overstory makes an aerial sighting difficult, though there are technologies such as FLIR—Forward-Looking Infrared Radar—that can locate heat sources, a warm body, from above.

Laura, Jacob's mother, and Dani Campbell, a cousin and ex-perienced surfer who worked construction for Randy and helped renovate the Gray family home, meet Randy and Mallory. The family sensed lethargy with park officials and was advised to shake the tree themselves. Elise Stokes, Laura's sister, with whom Jacob lived while he attended Bellevue College, tells Ranger Wray: "We as Jacob Gray's family demand an intense search." Facebook helps magnify the message; the hope is that Olympic National Park will be pressured into action in the way United Airlines or Chipotle have to respond to a frustrated customer on Twitter. Stokes is told by Wray, *Okay.*

Randy is never dry. He hedgehogs through doghair, sapling whips, and devil's club in the rain. When it's not raining, the trees still drip from when it had, so it's hard to tell it isn't raining. Randy doesn't have proper terrestrial gear and wears cotton under his PVC rain suit, and cotton socks inside his lightweight hiking shoes, so that by nightfall he's just as soaked on the inside as on the outside. The rainforest paradox. He soon suffers trench foot, a painful immersion syndrome coined in reference to soldiers slogging through sodden trenches in World War I, from the soaked socks. He never complains—Mallory and Dani Campbell attest to this; water is Randy's element.

The rangers are adamant that Jacob fell—or jumped—into the river. If he did, Randy thinks, then he climbed out. Maybe on the bike side, maybe on the other side. But Jacob grew up surfing the world-class breaks of Santa Cruz since he was a toddler. In high school he'd surf storm swells. He'd surf at night. He'd surf in trunks when everyone else was in mandatory wetsuits. He's been pounded by every kind of rogue wave in the book. "There's no way he didn't get out of that river," Randy says. "Not Jacob. For him that current was frickin' nothing." Randy proves it by swimming it himself, sometimes holding big rocks for weight, sometimes "roping off" with a line tied to a tree on shore so he can climb back out. "He's wet, he's cold, but he climbed out."

POD stands for *probability of detection*—would searchers recognize the target inside the search area? From where the bike was found, the Sol Duc runs seventy-eight miles to the Pacific Ocean. Swiftwater rescue authorities will tell you that if he fell or jumped into the water, it's nearly impossible that he went that far, and it's improbable he'd flow downstream more than a mile. It's thought Jacob could be wearing a wool coat and canvas Carhartt dungarees. This is not an outfit you want to fall into a river wearing, but they don't necessarily weigh you down like a lead belt. Besides, Jacob is as strong a swimmer as they come. In the water he knew when to relax and go with the current, and when to stroke like hell. There are logjams not far downstream from the bike, whereon he might have landed and picked his way ashore like an otter, river to tree to bank. A person who falls into a cold river and inhales water will sink. A body—limbs and fingertips—catches easier than you'd think, so it's not likely he'd travel very far downstream. Eventually in cold water—three weeks, a month or so—decomposition produces gases that will cause the body to bloat and often float to the surface.

Randy isn't about to wait around that long. "I didn't cuss before this," Randy says. "Before Jacob went missing. All this. Now I curse all the time. I'm thinking, where the hell is my boy?" Where the *fuck* is Jacob.

"Jacob told me he'd always go up," Randy says. "Dad, I'm goin' up." Rangers are doubtful. Randy follows trails up, toward the High Divide. He sees footprints, blurred and fossilized by midday thaws and night freezes—maybe they're Jacob's, but they could be anyone's. But they're *someone's*. Olympic National Park is comprised of 1,400 square miles; 95 percent of those miles are designated wilderness. When Randy gets high enough that snow and ice make finding the trail impossible, he sticks limbs and sticks in the snow like arrows so he can find his way back out.

What case histories have shown is that when it comes to a missing person inside national park boundaries, outside help is always an option, but not always requested. The Navy and Coast Guard, obviously, are federal agencies, as is the National Park Service. But unlike the NPS, the military branches are no strangers to partnering on missions. Most, if not all, of the other outside help the NPS has access to is volunteer-based search-and-rescue outfits staffed with highly dedicated veterans in locating the lost. Search-and-rescue personnel train for countless hours and metaphorically sit by the phone awaiting requests that don't often come.

*　　*　　*

Volunteer trackers from Olympic Mountain Rescue are finally approved by Olympic National Park's upper echelons. On the late afternoon of April 11, nearly six days after the bike was first discovered off the side of the road, a three-man ground team searches along the riverbanks, while a two-man team searches the immediate area around the bike. The two trackers find spoor—evidence—that someone had swapped hiking boots for running shoes, walked to the river's edge, slipped and fell in, leaving a "bun" mark on a mossy rock.

Thirty yards downstream there is spoor, evidence, that *something* clawed vegetation, indicating someone may have scrambled out. Or tried to. This was on the ONP side. On the west side—the side that borders Olympic National Forest, outside Olympic National Park—trackers find week-old footprints in the root ball of a tree that had fallen partially in the river. The prints are unlikely from a fisherman, who would have had to do some serious bushwhacking in slick, steep jungle conditions to get there. If Jacob had gone for a dunk and gotten out—on either side—someone would have found him sooner or later.

One technique for survival from hypothermia is to cover yourself with leaves and forest duff, an insulator. But Jacob would have been close enough to the road to jog back to his bike, change clothes or, worst-case scenario, make an illegal fire until a car came along, perhaps not until the next morning. At any rate, he'd survive that, or they'd find a body close by. Things in and along the river just don't make sense for Randy.

Tracking is not an exact science. And in this case the prognosticative nature of man-tracking makes it just slightly more useful than psychics in Jacob's case. (Psychics will get involved very soon.)

Two Washington State Fisheries biologists—not swiftwater-rescue divers—are counting salmon in the area and are assigned two logjams—strainers—to search for a body. Randy dives in after them to verify Jacob isn't there.

Weeks later Randy shows me the "bun" mark on the rock. "[Trackers] said there was evidence he slipped in," Randy says, pointing at what I suppose could be a slip mark—it also seems to my untrained eye that it could be just about anything else. "Okay, but then they say there was also evidence he climbed *out*. So where is he?"

Mallory had called a dog team while she and Randy were driving bats-out-of-hell north, but the team they coordinated with were not approved by the park, who wanted to use a different dog team; except, for several days, they didn't want to use any dog team at all. National parks are dog-shy. Pet dogs are not allowed in most areas of national parks so as not to affect the experience of visitors and disturb wildlife. The rationale wasn't squaring with Randy because these would be professionally trained SAR dogs, not pets, and there are hardly any visitors in the park in April.

Several pilots offer drones to the cause, but park rules disallow them, and ONP was sticking to it. Drones might be of limited use above the thick overstory of two-hundred-foot-tall Sitka spruce and Western hemlock, but they can fly river corridors and open alpine meadows and rocky sections. Another tool declined.

Randy and Mallory sleep in Randy's work truck, which is parked at the Sol Duc Hot Springs Campground—Mallory in the cab and Randy under the camper shell in the cold bed. The resort management, which contracts with the National Park Service, lets them use the hot showers for free and even comps them some meals. But the camper shell isn't insulated, leaks a little, and never does feel truly dry. They eat most of their meals—energy bars and Gatorade—standing in the rain and fog. Buzz of phones. The onslaught of family and friends is like a soggy montage of people met in dreams.

Dad and daughter bushwhack through the trailless brush on both sides of the river. If he'd gone into the Sol Duc, some sort of clue surely would have emerged. Nothing. It's possible he's somewhere else, somewhere not in the river.

Laura, Dani, Audrey Stokes—Laura's niece—and Jennifer, a family friend, hike the nearby Aurora Ridge Trail to Eagle Lake, which is under deep snow. They get about 2.5 miles up the trail. Laura sees footprints and photographs them, but they're fuzzy and inconclusive. Jacob's uncle Dave drives up and down Highway 101 looking for any type of clue. Trackers on the west side of the river—the national forest side—find Randy's tracks, but nothing that suggests Jacob had been there.

While the family is combing through the forest, along and in the water, Jacob sightings—some credible—are reported in Port Angeles and Forks, the two largest communities bracketing the north side of Olympic National Park. On the morning of Wednesday, April 12, Scott Jenson, a manager at a Port Angeles communications company, saw a young man who looks like Jacob near the County Fair grocery in town. Jenson reports that the kid had disheveled hair and a wild look in his eyes—"He looked lost." A woman in Forks reports seeing Jacob at the deli—police check, but the lead doesn't pan out.

At one p.m. Randy—in wet socks and underwear—is near the location of Jacob's bike, next to Sol Duc Road, and Mallory is along the river, where rangers believe Jacob fell in. Mallory sees—across the river, on the national forest side—two hikers wearing what look like Jacob's light blue jacket and camouflage backpack. She yells, "Hey! Hey! Who are you?" They don't appear to hear her above the rush and roar of the river. Or they're ignoring her on purpose.

She scrambles to the road, and she and Randy drive around—about a half-hour trip—and frantically try to find the strangers. An hour, two hours—no trace. What's odd is that few people would choose to hike in the devil's club and thick, wet ferns along the river—there's no trail there. And they didn't appear to be fishing.

Later that afternoon David Johnsen and Kevin Swem, trackers with Olympic Mountain Rescue, head to the west side of the Sol Duc, on the Olympic National Forest side. The GPS coordinates they use are not accurate, and they are dropped off in the wrong location. The trackers get lost. They ford the swollen river above the bike—which they say *wasn't that bad*. The trackers walk downriver along the road on the park side until they get to the location of the bike and start over. The search seemed to be an ouroborus, the ancient serpent that eats its own tail.

In late afternoon the trackers again go to the west side, this time with Randy and Dani. They find—opposite side of the river from the bike—what they believe to be a sneaker print in moss and mud, about a week old. The sneaker track appears to be coming out of the water.

The trackers recommend dogs.

Sorry all, but without official request from Park Service our Sheriff is not allowing us to deploy, wrote Dietrich Biemiller of Snohomish County Search and Rescue in an email. A cardinal rule among search-and-rescue volunteers is that you never, but never, self-deploy. *I wish you the best of luck in finding him!* Biemiller's message is typical of volunteers wanting to help but whose hands are tied with red tape.

Self-deploying will get a team or an organization blackballed. A mission number had been generated for Jacob's case with West Coast Search Dogs of Washington (Mission #17-201). The mission has to have been generated by park officials, but approval still needs to come from Olympic National Park higher-ups before dogs can deploy, boots and paws on the ground.

Ranger Steve Rice, who had been in communication with Dani, is deployed on the airplane crash and cannot work Jacob's case—he calls his supervisor, a district ranger, who phones Dani to tell her ONP never called West Coast Search Dogs and did not okay a mission number. In short, the mission number is a ghost number.

The district ranger tells Dani she should be communicating with the liaison, Kristin, indicating to her he has more important demands on his limited resources. Dani tells him the liaison did not return calls to her or Laura. The dysfunctional phone tag and bureaucratic ghosting goes on for several days before the district ranger informs Dani the search is turning into a passive search and they will not be dedicating any more resources to Jacob's case. Not even dogs.

"Not even though the trackers recommend dogs?" Dani says.

He tells her he'll check with his boss, Chief Ranger Jay Shields, but not until the next morning. Dani tells him she wants to start at 7:30 a.m. and is told there's no way they're gonna search at that time.

"West Coast Search Dogs is ready to deploy tomorrow," Dani says. "Based on your information, would you approve the use of a dog unit tomorrow morning?"

"No," the district ranger says. He doesn't think dogs will help.

"What are our options then?" Dani asks. There is no answer.

Dan Fox from West Coach Search Dogs of Washington tells Dani they have a team ready to jump on the ferry and get to ONP within hours. Fox is also nonplussed as to why ONP would have opened up a mission number if they didn't intend to request K9 help.

Communications with the park remains fuzzy at best. The district ranger is still sluggish to return calls, though his phone is blowing up. Randy calls dispatch at 9:35 a.m., Thursday, April 13, again trying to contact him. This time he calls back, requesting a meeting with Randy and Laura at Olympic National Park headquarters in Port Angeles, 10:30 a.m.

It takes a call from 6th District State Representative Derek Kilmer, coverage in the *Peninsula Daily News* and area television stations, and the recommendation from trackers Johnsen and Swem, but ONP officials give in and approve dogs a half hour before the meeting.

The district ranger wants to meet with just Randy and Laura, but Randy insists that Dave Stokes and Dani attend as well. Park officials tell them they had dogs lined up but coordination fell through; they take the number of West Coast Search Dogs from Dani.

A different dog team arrives, an air-scent dog and two handlers from Snohomish County, and begin searching at five p.m. It's now one week after Jacob's bike was spotted. By this time it's clear they're searching for a body and not a live cyclist. It's also clear rangers are convinced Jacob is either in the Sol Duc River, the Pacific Ocean, or he's hitchhiked out of the country altogether.

The dog team, Guy Mansfield and Suzanne Elshult from both Everett Mountain Rescue and Snohomish County Volunteer Search and Rescue, along with Elshult's trailing dog, a certified search-and-rescue K9 named Keb, search both sides of the river. "During our search K9 Keb showed no indications of detecting scent, and we did not see any signs of the subject," Mansfield wrote in his report.

The other missing person in the park that week, twenty-year-old backpacker Zach Krull, is reported missing on April 11, on the far opposite side of the immense park. Triage seems to put Krull's case above Jacob's—Rangers believe Krull could still be alive. It feels cartoonish to express this, but if Jacob had indeed fallen into the river and couldn't get out, he'd be dead. If he'd swum to the far bank and scrambled out, he would have quickly come to the Forest Service road used by loggers and recreators. Other than that, there just aren't enough clues in the Park Service's estimation to allocate more resources to Jacob's search.

"It's beyond finding a needle in a haystack," Chief Ranger Jay Shields told me. What about the spoor on the mossy rock, the scramble marks on the vegetation, the footprints in the root ball downstream. Shields, a tracker himself, puts the probability that the tracks are Jacob's at less than 5 percent—myriad things could have made those spoor: an otter, a beaver, a mountain lion.

Miraculously, the two people aboard the crashed jet survived. Keb is back in the kennel, and Jacob's search has again gone passive. Now the trail they can't find is colder than the snow on Mount Olympus. If there's a trail at all.

CHAPTER 4

OLYMPIC NATIONAL PARK & OLYMPIC NATIONAL FOREST

bewilder

vb (tr)

1. to confuse utterly; puzzle

2. *archaic* to cause to become lost

THURSDAY, APRIL 13. Chief Ranger Jay Shields tells Laura and Dani in another meeting at park headquarters in Port Angeles that the search inside the park will be shifting to a "limited continuous search." In attendance at the meeting is Acting Park Superintendent Lee Taylor and Chief Criminal Deputy Brian King of the Clallam County Sheriff's Department.

"Is that the same thing as a passive search?" Laura asks. Shields confirms it's the same thing. Essentially, the park will not be dedicating resources to a search for Jacob because they feel they don't have any *viable* clues.

"What is a viable clue?" Dani asks.

The rangers tell her it's different for every case. In Jacob's situation it means an article of clothing, gear, or a reliable sighting in the park.

What about the trackers: The sign of slippage on the rock. The sneaker print in the root ball on the other side of the river. The rangers tell the women no, those aren't viable clues.

Laura tells the rangers—and Lee Taylor, the boss—of her frustration at the miles of red tape and horrible communication. Taylor says she values the feedback, and it will be documented.

The upshot is that Deputy King informs Laura and Dani he will be taking over search efforts—which means, primarily, outside of the park, west, across the Sol Duc River from where Jacob's bicycle was found. In forty-eight states—exceptions being Alaska and New Mexico, where state police are in charge, and Hawaii, where the respective island police and fire departments have authority—the county sheriff is responsible for search-and-rescue operations. Further exceptions are military bases and national parks. Lyman Moores, a sergeant with the Clallam County Sheriff's Department who is in charge of coordinating Clallam County search-and-rescue missions, gets involved and intends to primarily work the west side of the river, on Olympic National Forest land—outside of the park's jurisdiction.

On Saturday, April 15, a larger, organized search—the first one in Jacob's case—is mustered inside the park. The family meets with Sergeant Moores in Port Angeles at 6:45 a.m. They drive to a base camp along Forest Road 2918, in the Olympic National Forest. The country's national forests—all 190 million acres of them—are not nearly as regulated as our national parks. In most national forests it's legal to shoot fireworks and firearms, let your dogs run free, and have campfires and camp just about anywhere you want. Mountain bike. Ride your horse. Hunt everything (in season, of course). Race your motorcycle and four-wheeler all over tarnation. Fly your drone. National forests are regulated by the U.S. Forest Service under the Department of Agriculture. Cattle graze our forests, wood is the major crop, mining happens. For a forest visitor, it'd be difficult to even know a search of any official capacity was going on.

Volunteers from various organizations sign waivers and get search assignments. Lyman organizes searchers into four teams. Team members carry whistles and wear bright safety vests. They bushwhack sixty feet apart. It's slow going. It's unlikely they'd miss a body, but possible—it's unsettling how often a subject is eventually discovered in "previously searched" territory. David Paulides lists this as one of his oddities, and it often is, but ask a friend wearing brown and green to go into a forest and lie down behind a rotting log or a tangle of multiflora rose—things are disturbingly easy to miss.

Searchers include a dog team from West Coast Search Dogs with two types of dogs—an air-scent K9 team and a cadaver K9. The ground walkers move out to allow for the dog team to operate with priority. After the air-scent dogs examined likely paths of human travel, the cadaver dog moves through. The dog team searches both sides of the river. At the sign the trackers pointed out on the rock that may have indicated Jacob fell into the river, the trail-scent dogs begin barking intensely and snapping at the water above and below the rock. This is the first development in the search since Jacob's bike was found along the road ten days prior.

The dog handler switches to the cadaver dog, and he behaves the same way at the rock, upstream and down. Trackers believe this validates the theory Jacob walked to the river and fell in. Or it's possible he walked to the river and returned to the bike and then to who the hell knows. The dogs don't indicate scent anywhere else.

The cadaver K9s—different from an air-scent trailing dog because they're smelling for scent molecules specific to the missing subject—hit on a logjam, a clue. It could mean a corpse—or piece of a corpse—is trapped underneath. It could also mean cadaver material washed by or in from the bank, and scent molecules collected on the log. The jam is certainly big enough to hide a body.

The official search ends at two in the afternoon. Sergeant Moores orders a dive team to check the river near the area the dogs indicated, but the divers won't be available until sometime early the next week. Randy won't wait that long—he and Dani drive back into Port Angeles and buy dive masks, snorkels, and neoprene gloves. They devise a plan to get into the water the next morning. An elderly couple has offered Randy, family, and friends a two-bedroom bed-and-breakfast studio in their home at no charge, so he no longer has to sleep in his truck. Randy's feet are blistered, and he doesn't sleep well.

Tomorrow is Easter Sunday.

In the morning two locals, a man named Graham Hawthorne and a woman named Brook, meet with the Gray family to point out places on the river Jacob could have become entangled or trapped. Graham and Brook seem to get a lot of information from paramilitary websites and don't belong to any official group; but Randy is grateful for anyone willing to help. Graham suggests Snider Creek, the bend at Klahowya Campground, and Gunderson Creek, features downstream from the bike.

Randy Hall, a private investigator and friend of Randy Gray, arrives after driving up from California. Micah, Jacob's older brother, arrives from Vermont to help search. Micah is a professional waterman, and with Randy and Dani and the local knowledge Graham and Brook bring, it appears there's an A-team of swiftwater skills on scene.

The team of family and friends enter Olympic National Park and park at a pullout just north—downriver—of where Jacob's bike and gear were found. Dani and Randy Gray suit up in 4-3 wetsuits, which means the neoprene foam of the body is four millimeters thick, and the arms are three millimeters thick. "Good for surfing," Randy says, "but a little cold for the river." He understates it—that water was snow a couple hours ago. "That suit leaked at the seams, too." A retired police officer named Candy, from Port Angeles, shows up with her son to give the searchers sandwiches and drinks.

No one says it out loud, but after what the trackers had suggested, there's a damn good chance Jacob is under the big logjam. After some scouting of the best way to approach the big tangle, Randy ties off with a rope, one end around his waist, the other around a Sitka spruce tree on shore. Micah works the rope, reading the current and giving Randy slack when he needs it and reeling in the slack when he doesn't. Randy can hold his breath for an impressive length of time, but the neoprene suit makes him buoyant, and he struggles to get deep into dark holes under the jam, so he grabs river rocks that take him to the bottom. He drops the rocks and comes up for air. Another rock, back under.

He works the width of the Sol Duc, sweeping back and forth. Dani gets in, and the pair scour the river for two hours. There's another logjam, and the current is sucking into it. Randy can't stand not checking it out. The suction takes him under, into the snarl, so it's like being pinned under a big wave, but with a fishtrap underneath. Instead of panicking, Randy relaxes, lets his body go with the hydraulics, pushes off, and pops out the other end. He got enough of a look under the jam to see that Jacob wasn't there.

The two climb out exhausted. They eat sandwiches while shivering and moving around to keep warm. After some Gatorade they jump back in and keep sweeping the river, working downstream. No sign of Jacob.

Late that afternoon Randy Gray and Randy Hall, Dani, Micah, Laura, and Audrey drive to the boathouse on Lake Crescent to pick up Jacob's bike, trailer, and gear. Ranger Brian Wray is there to meet them. He tells them about finding the bike and how busy that weekend had been—prisoner transport, the other lost hiker, drunk drivers, a plane crash. They talk about how a body in a river tends to behave and cases in the Colorado River. "The Sol Duc is nothing like the Colorado River," Dani says. "There's no comparison—not width, flow, velocity, depth, terrain…"

"I'm sorry for the situation," Wray says. "Get in touch with me if you need to."

Randy takes the bike and trailer apart so they'll fit in his truck. Micah flips through the bible found with Jacob's things and tries to divine a clue. "I feel like if he got out of Olympic National Park he may be moving east," he says. There is a sense that Jacob might be on a mission. That sense gives Randy and Micah hope that if he's not found where they'd been looking, he's in what search-and-rescue personnel call TROTW—the rest of the world. And if he's in TROTW, he may be alive. Laura doesn't understand why Jacob wouldn't call her, though he left his phone back in Port Townsend at his grandmother's house.

Flyers are tacked up on park kiosks and in gas stations in Port Angeles to the east and the logging town of Forks to the west. On his missing poster Jacob looks happy and handsome.

Dani and Audrey visit places in Port Angeles to see if they have security camera footage of a possible sighting downtown. No luck. Local media—especially Jesse Major, a reporter with the *Peninsula Daily News*—run near-daily updates about Jacob's vanish, which puts a hot spotlight on Olympic National Park.

Dave Stokes, Jacob's uncle, goes back to Wyoma's—his mother-in-law's—house in Port Townsend to check out the Internet search history on her computer. Jacob searched cycling routes from Port Townsend to Glacier National Park, Montana. Another search pulls up a map going south, toward Oregon. Wyoma tells Dave that Jacob mentioned going south, then east toward Vermont, because of some closed passes. He'd also searched sites pertaining to Badlands National Park in South Dakota. Then there were sites from Alberta, Canada. Jacob was in the process of applying for a passport, at least as far as obtaining the required form, but did not have a passport as of April 2017.

Randy—exhausted from searching in the swift current of the Sol Duc—will dream about tangles of logs in a roaring river. In the morning he'll need to go to urgent care because his trench foot has made it hard to walk. Laura leaves to head back to California. Dani, Micah, and Audrey will drive back to Seattle, leaving *MISSING Jacob Gray* posters along the way and asking gas stations if they have security footage they can view. Randy's niece, her husband, and their new baby arrive to help search. That's how these searches tend to go—family is spelled by other family, including babies. And without family putting pressure on bureaucrats and officials, there's often not much of a professional search at all.

Until there is more to go on, searchers—including Lyman Moores's county crews—have other obligations. Graham and his ragtag band of volunteers endeavor in and along the river at night. He uses the verb *deploy* myriad times and asks on his Facebook posts if anyone has a kayak, a raft, and some half-inch rope.

For anyone close to Jacob it seems as if the gears of bureaucracy are grinding at a snail's pace if they're moving at all. If Jacob had been alive and out there in the wilderness, he most certainly isn't anymore. If he is alive and has taken off voluntarily or otherwise, he isn't the park's problem anymore. Continuous Limited Mode is a nightmarish purgatory. Officially, that's how things go.

CHAPTER 5

WASHINGTON & SANTA CRUZ

The most effective way to do it, is to do it.
—Amelia Earhart

JACOB'S NOT *HERE,* so maybe he's not here. Randy spends nearly two weeks in the river, in his wetsuit, scouring every cubic foot of the Sol Duc for twelve miles. There's a fish hatchery just off Highway 101 between Beaver and Sappho with screens and check dams—it's highly unlikely a body would make it past there.

Perhaps Jacob walked uphill from the bike—upriver—before falling in. There's a large waterfall a mile or so upriver, Salmon Cascades. Randy again ties off to a tree, lowers his mask, and grabs a boulder the size of a baby. He leaps from the cliff into the pool behind the falls. No Jacob, but here's what he says when he emerges: "The salmon down there are huge!"

It's possible no twelve-mile section of mountain river has been searched more thoroughly than the Sol Duc where Jacob's gear was found. That includes tributaries. The North Fork of the Sol Duc is not wide and not deep, but there are holes and several caves that could hold a body. Randy grabs his wetsuit, takes a boogie board (he always has a boogie board in the bed of his work truck), hikes up the North Fork on aching feet. He sees a black bear (black bear are legion in Olympic National Park) and cusses the bear into the brush. At ten miles up he pulls into his wetsuit, then spends the next ten hours getting pinballed off every boulder in the river. When he reaches the Sol Duc he's so bruised and sore he can hardly get out of the water. He's also, ironically, dehydrated. Hockey players face less physical abuse.

The North Fork is an unlikely place for Jacob to be, but by now most places are unlikely. Randy doesn't eat, and he drinks only river water. He takes a board check against the rocks every couple of minutes. His feet still burn from the trench foot inside his neoprene booties. Sixty-three years old. It nearly kills him. But every day he doesn't find a body is a day of hope his son is still alive.

On Sunday, April 23, at first light, Randy hikes up Aurora Ridge Trail, headed to Eagle Lake. Jacob would have seen Eagle Lake on the map—it's a place he'd go, Randy thinks. *Eagle Lake*. That name alone would draw Jacob up. Randy reaches snow just a mile or so up the trail. When he gets out of the trees and the country opens up, he drives limbs into the snow so he can find his way back out. No sign of Jacob. If he's lost up here, was here the day after his bike was found, a helicopter could have spotted him in the open. A helicopter with heat-seeking FLIR technology would have sensed him in the foliage. A dog team could have tracked him up the Aurora Ridge Trail. The what-if tango will drive a searching father insane.

The good monkey on Randy's shoulder—the one that reminds him he's a Christian and a good father who taught Jacob courage and how to survive in the wild—tells him Jacob's out there. "He's on a walkabout," Randy says. "He's trying to figure things out."

Meanwhile, a woman thinks she sees Jacob getting into a black Saturn in Port Angeles. Someone on Facebook sees Jacob walking east along Kitchen-Dick Road in Sequim. Jacob is spotted at the Chevron station in Port Angeles. Jacob is seen on the bus that runs from Port Townsend to Forks, across the top of the Olympic Peninsula. Every day there's another sighting; every account, while mostly well intended, is elusive.

Mark Curry of Texas EquuSearch (TES), a Houston-based all-volunteer search-and-recover nonprofit that works with local law enforcement and the FBI, but originated as a horse-mounted field team, talked with Jacob's aunt, Elise. "You wouldn't believe how many missing persons they find in jail," he says. They discuss the possibility that Jacob has been picked up by law enforcement somewhere and won't give his name, or he's a John Doe in a hospital or mental ward. Curry's advice includes contacting all hospitals and morgues they can; his advice also includes stopping the search on the ground in and around Olympic National Park now, before someone gets hurt or killed. He tells Elise they've done all they can for now. Though, of course, things will change when—if—something else, a clue, turns up.

Randy doesn't buy it, the not-searching, but after it becomes very apparent Jacob won't be found quickly or easily, he drives back to Santa Cruz to close on selling the family home and begin shuttering his successful contracting business. The plan is to buy a camping rig of some sort, a slide-in pickup camper maybe, and live on the road, in the forest, along the beach, moving every few days or so, until he finds Jacob.

For someone close to someone missing, the world is reduced to this binary: *missing* and *searching*. Two awful gerunds. Most people left to search don't know what to do, don't know where to look. Wildlands can be overwhelming in their scope and scale. Or they're physically incapable of doing much footwork in rough terrain. And they need to get back to their day jobs, to support their families and keep the plates in the air that we all have to juggle. Randy Gray will liquidate his world in order to find his son. Or die trying. Living on the open road in a self-contained camper, changing parks, forests, and cold Pacific beaches on a whim—that's every rich man's dream. Except that Randy Gray has lost a kid.

Randy and Laura get along out here—Olympic National Park— because they have to, it's Jacob's best shot, but I can tell it's not easy for Randy, who feels Laura pulled the living room rug out from under him.

"Randy is *go-do*," Laura says. "Randy is driven. There's no middle gear, and reverse is broken." She says this admiringly. "Jacob is me—he's mini-me. We were in the mountains together all the time. He called me the day he left."

Laura plays the tape in her mind once again. *Jacob told Mom he was heading out and left sometime in the night. He promised her he'd check in from time to time.* Laura believes him. "I just think he would have honored that," she says. "I don't know if his head was in a different place. If he had a moment of clarity he would have called me. *Jacob would call me.* We talked about everything. I can't say he's gone, either. Not without proof."

Four years earlier, domestic life at the once idyllic Gray house became something of a shambles. Randy and Laura split—Jacob took the divorce hard. Laura and Jacob had gone for a long walk on Christmas, while Jacob was back, living at home in Santa Cruz for a month. "Things were a little off at Christmas," she says. "Curling in depression on the couch." This was not typical behavior for Jacob, who would ordinarily be out surfing with his surfing buddies, the other dogs of winter. Most alarming is that Jacob sold his favorite surfboard.

But then things looked up again. Jacob had recently repaired his relationship with Mallory, which had ruptured during the divorce. The two took to walking in the hills that shoulder the redwood-camouflaged University of California, Santa Cruz campus. "We would walk it out all the time," Mallory says. But Jacob was showing signs of mental instability that Mallory hadn't noticed before. On one walk he asked her to promise not to ever read his mind. He insisted they shake on it. "Mallory, do you know what a handshake means? Do you know what it *means*?" Another time he made her swear, literally, on his bible.

Jacob was in the prime position wherein schizophrenia can surface. Divorce is a common trigger. Laura took to the Internet and consulted with healthcare professional friends and calls his behavior "almost textbook schizophrenia."

Laura quotes something Jacob said at Christmas verbatim: "You know, Mom, I'm just really sad. I just wanted to have children."

It's the past tense that unsettled Laura the most. "He was talking about a life past at the age of twenty-two," she says. "I said, 'What's going on, Jacob?'

"'Nothing.'

"He just kinda shook himself off," Laura recalls. "I sensed it— *something's going wrong with Jacob*. I was worried he was suicidal."

"He took off on foot for the Golden Gate Bridge," she says. "Anthony, Mallory's husband, drove by on his way to work and saw him." Jacob had already seen the famous bridge dozens of times, so it worried her that he might have intended to jump off it this time.

A few months before he disappeared for the long haul, Jacob borrowed Randy's old dinged-up brown Mazda sedan without asking and lit out for a road trip that took him through northern California, Oregon, Idaho, and Nevada, where he got a speeding ticket. Jacob ended up at their rental house in the Sierras, near Sonora Pass and Yosemite, where Randy found a note: TELL MOM TO KEEP THE HOUSE SO WE HAVE A PLACE TO MEET. Randy did not sell it, but he did have to rent out the place. Jacob returned to Santa Cruz, but the sortie only served to fuel Randy and Laura's concern.

They thought a change of scenery might do him good and made arrangements for him to move to Bellevue, Washington, to live near family, attend community college, find a job, and transition into adulthood. Jacob moved near his aunt Elise and uncle Dave and went to community college. He had a roommate, Hudson, and kept his gear in Dave and Elise's garage. "He was really happy up there," Laura says, but she was worried he wasn't making friends. "He told me, 'I don't need friends, Mom—I've got my family.'" Jacob gave school the ol' college try, but it didn't take. He got a job working in the kitchen of a nursing home. He liked the residents there, loved them, but the constant death got to him, and he quit to work in a climbing gym.

Dave walked in on Jacob in the garage one day to find Jacob with his hands on his head. "I just can't figure it out," he said. "I just can't figure it out." His behavior began to worry his aunt and uncle and parents back in Santa Cruz. He was smoking a little pot, which isn't unusual, but it tended to make Jacob paranoid. He talked of demons. He'd try to get people to swear oaths on the bible. He'd see the color red everywhere and ask his uncle, "Why is everything colored red? Don't you see it?"

Jacob left Bellevue on his bicycle, caught the Kingston Ferry across Puget Sound, and pedaled the rest of the way to his grandmother's house, Wyoma Clair's, in Port Townsend, just over sixty miles away.

Jacob befriended Bob Chung, owner of Port Townsend Cyclery. The shop is one of those local bike shops that smells like bicycle tires, chain lube, coffee, and chili sauce. Port Townsenders spend more time than money in the place, and Jacob—who didn't like crowds or scenes—felt at home there. Jacob and Bob talked bikes and camping and maps in the way that cycling tourers do, which is nothing if not optimistic. Jacob had a girlfriend, Makenzie, who lived next door to Wyoma, but it didn't seem especially serious, and his family didn't think much about it when things seemed to have cooled on that front.

Jacob was in Port Townsend for a couple months planning for the journey across the country. Chung, an experienced tourer and local cycling historian who trades in classic used bikes, looked at Jacob's setup and told him it was heavy and the frame too small, but adventure is about making do with what you have.

Randy told me that Jacob had started listening to Alex Jones's Infowars and other conspiracy theory outlets. "He was thoroughly engaging in biblical talk and the End Times. What I was really upset about was this was not my son, he was not my kid."

"It wasn't my normal Jacob," Laura says. "We flew up." Randy and Laura met Jacob at Wyoma's house in an attempt to get him some professional help. Randy wanted his son to see Dr. Daniel Amen, founder of the chain of Amen Clinics in California. Amen is a celebrity psychiatrist, brain disorder specialist, and bestselling author of such books as *Change Your Brain, Change Your Life*. His website offers supplements purported to aid in brain health. Randy is a fan of his Brain on Joy energy bars. Jacob feared the family meeting in Port Townsend was an attempt to have him institutionalized.

Jacob grew up in a devout Christian, surfing household. Randy was a Santa Cruz surfing "Jesus freak" who explored denominations; at church he'd meet celebrities like Carlos Santana and members of the Doobie Brothers. But in Santa Cruz celebs are just residents. Besides, Randy would rather go surfing than hobnob. But he practiced what he preached; for a decade he ran a sort of unofficial halfway house and helped to get many men back on their feet after life and addiction had knocked them down. It was a money-loser for Randy but he didn't care. Good at making money, Randy doesn't seem very motivated by it. Randy has always been—and still is—a doer. Active. Envision something and go make it happen, whether it was a design on a house or a big wave.

Randy questions the trappings and apparatus surrounding religion, but the bible has always been at the core of his worldview. The same is true for Jacob, but he seemed to be taking it to an extreme. Now, the bible had become a rune to Jacob, and his planchette was a bicycle.

Talk switched to the rangers, Olympic National Park. "They were like, 'Well, we'll just do a quick search.'" Olympic Peninsula locals were furious at the lack of response from ONP. "They didn't act like he'd gone missing," Laura says. "No dogs, no drones. When trackers found what they said were footprints on the other side [Olympic National Forest land, outside of the national park] they were thrilled to pass me off to the sheriff." Those footprints may have been Jacob's. Or they may have been anyone else's. The area across the river is popular with forest visitors who like to shoot, make fires, ride all-terrain vehicles, and camp wherever they want. "It was becoming a real shitstorm. If I was visiting a park I would not be offended if I heard a [search] dog barking."

It wouldn't be full-on tourist season for another couple months. To say he'd drowned and to say those footprints were Jacob's is hypocritical. They could not be both. "Cadavers don't walk out of the water," Laura says.

A footprint was found at Eagle Lake, away from the river. Laura saw a picture of it. "This looks exactly like my son's step," Laura says. But a footprint is so inconclusive. She sighs, and her mind jumps again. "There are cults—we've got them here. You just don't know. Every little thing that could happen you scramble for. I really think he would have called me." Her sister, a psychiatric nurse, told her, "They always check in, eventually."

In Santa Cruz, the drugged-out homeless culture wasn't his scene. "It drove him nuts," she says. "We drove all over Olympia—

everybody looks just like him. He wouldn't choose a town. Jacob goes up. He'd always choose the high point." Micah, who studies lost person behavior in the Coast Guard, told her, "That's what young men in their twenties do—they go up."

"He loved his family. But who knows," Laura says. "You just can't keep waiting and waiting. It's Dante's *Inferno* for crying out loud."

I recall Randy's new habit of cursing. "I buy cigarettes now," Laura says. "Just so I have a pacifier at night."

IF YOU HAVE INFORMATION CALL
SANTA CRUZ CA PD (831) 420-5820
CASE NUMBER: 17S-01626

The phone number on the *MISSING Jacob Gray* poster is for the Santa Cruz, California, Police Department, because the missing persons case remains open. The search for Jacob broadens to include other possibilities. "We live in a really big, strange, creepy world," Mallory says. For a year, as a teenager, she left home and lived a version of on-the-street, except it was in a tent in the redwoods near the University of California, Santa Cruz. She told me Jacob—an introverted kid who struggled with the transition to adulthood—envied that move in a way. "Jacob was really lost. He didn't know what he wanted to do in life, where he wanted to go, what he wanted to be. The state of the world had gotten him down. He sought answers in the bible." Found with Jacob's things from the bike was a bible with Isaiah 34:14 circled: *And an abode of ostriches. And the desert creatures shall meet with the wolves, The hairy goat also shall cry to its kind; Yes, the night monster shall settle there.*

Mallory talked with Randy about the possibility of human trafficking. Jacob is a handsome man who had gotten headshots done and did some modeling around Santa Cruz—including a couple auditions for commercials. It was enough to know he didn't like modeling and didn't want to pursue it. It's unlikely, though possible, someone feigned needing help along the Sol Duc Road and tazed him.

Another thing they didn't rule out was cults. Randy drove to Forks, just twenty-five miles west of the Sol Duc. Forks is the setting of the *Twilight* series. "I mean, I was driving around in the full moon, looking for devil worshippers," Randy said. "I never thought I'd be doing anything like that."

Randy walked around downtown Port Angeles at two a.m., talking to dope addicts and street people of every stripe. There were reported sightings, but nothing proved out.

Mallory thinks Jacob left his bike and took a set of throwing knives she'd given him. And a pair of crampons for alpine climbing. A warm jacket and a backpack.

In the winter of 2017 Jacob walked from Santa Cruz to San Francisco because he felt like walking. Jacob had called her during the walk and said he was hungry, Mallory told me. She took him some supplies partway there. Randy and Mallory believe it is possible Jacob is on a Chris McCandless–style escape. Twenty-four-year-old McCandless ventured into wild Alaska and lived in a remote school bus along the Sushana River and starved to death there in August of 1992. His body was discovered in September of that year and his life documented in Jon Krakauer's 1996 book, *Into the Wild*.

Considering what was not at his grandmother's house, and not with his gear at the bike, Mallory figures Jacob had everything he needed for a long walk, a hegira, what Randy calls a *walkabout*. What no one knows is whether Jacob would be on a walk away from something or a walk *toward* something. Mallory wishes he'd call now.

"Anything is possible at this point," Mallory says. But she doesn't think self-harm is likely. "He couldn't kill a spider, let alone kill himself."

Laura had talked with Jacob a couple nights before he left Port Townsend. She understood that Jacob was geared up for a long tour to Vermont to see his older brother, Micah. Jacob told her he figured he might take two years to make the trip. He could do odd jobs along the way, maybe wash dishes and get a little seasonal work as a transient organic farmhand. "He was going to *Vermont*," Laura says. "Why did he go *west*? It does *not* make sense." She describes him as a very smart, capable young man. "He was sharp." The past tense of *was* hangs in the air like a smoke ring. "He was paranoid. The country is going to hell. Going to war, declaring war—I don't know what to read into it."

Bob Chung had given Jacob some gloves and tuned his bike and told him a shakedown test ride would be a good idea. The next he heard was that Jacob's bike and gear were found up the Sol Duc.

"He took off in a storm," Randy says. He's a little perplexed, but also a little impressed. He elongates storm—*stooooorm*. "If he was determined to do something, he'd go do it," Randy says. "Big waves in a storm, whatever it was."

Ranger Brian Wray wrote in his general report regarding the discovery of the bicycle and subsequent search efforts:

Laura told me that Jacob had smoked some cannabis in the past, but that she didn't think he was doing any drugs now. Laura also told me that Jacob had recently quit school and was experiencing trouble becoming an adult. Laura said that Jacob had experienced trauma from the divorce between her and Randy Gray (father), and that he had suffered a "schizophrenic" break from reality. Laura based this conclusion on Internet research and an aunt's

knowledge who works as a psychiatric nurse. Laura stated that
Jacob's behavior recently left her feeling like he was a different
person than the one that she knew in the past. However, because the
family was unable to articulate that Jacob was a danger to himself
or others, they were unable to force him to get help. Laura stated
that Jacob refused to seek help on his own because he didn't think
he needed it. Laura stated that his "episodes" manifested as Jacob
becoming paranoid and taking off without letting anyone know
what he was doing. Laura told me that Jacob had been to Olympic
National Park in the past... Laura stated that Jacob was paranoid
and told her he would be back when he worked through his
difficulties. Laura told me he left his phone at Wyoma's house.

Jacob's family was rightfully concerned for him. He wasn't as
disciplined as older brother Micah, who gravitated toward the
structure of the Coast Guard. But Jacob had not been formally
diagnosed by anyone, and the preparation for an epic bicycle tour
across the country seemed just what the doctor would order. A
self-propelled ride across the continent was a chance for growth
and change. A good goal. Major bike tours are all-consuming in the
planning alone, and it can be harder for your mind to turn in on
itself when you're making grocery and gear lists and studying maps
and weather forecasts.

The three biggest puzzles that remain unsolved are, first, that he
went west. Second, after all the time he put into prepping for a bike
journey, that he would abandon his bike. Third, that, though he left
his phone at his grandmother's house, he hasn't called his family—
his mom or his sister—like he did on the walk to San Francisco.

"He's my little brother; we've been through everything together,"
Mallory says. "Every day I'm like, Goddamit, Jacob, just come back.
Let's get tacos."

*　　*　　*

A strange phone call puzzles Randy. Less than a month after Jacob vanished, Jacob's aunt Judy, Randy's sister Judy Baldwin, got a phone call at the Santa Cruz pharmacy where she works. A male called and asked for Judy Baldwin. Another employee answered the phone.

The caller said, "I need to speak to Judy Baldwin about her nephew, Jacob Gray."

I'll page her. May I ask who's calling?

"Did you know her nephew is missing? We know he's not dead."

By the time Judy picked up the line the caller was gone, and efforts to trace the call were unsuccessful.

Later, in the early winter of 2017, a park service employee stationed at Olympic National Park got drunk and blurted to a friend, "I took the call—it's not what everybody thinks—he's not dead." He refused to expound.

Prank calls. Drunken boasting, maybe. No one can be sure at this point. But it's curious. And for Randy it's motivating.

Was it Jacob calling Judy? Randy wonders. Perhaps he was trying to get the message through that he's okay, he just needs to figure things out. Few people outside of family would know Judy Baldwin is related to Jacob Gray. Of course a handful of people in Santa Cruz know, but the call seemed too anemic to be a prank. Randy put it in his pocket, another small beach stone of hope.

CHAPTER 6

PORT ANGELES

Everyone who dies out there dies of confusion.
—*Laurence Gonzales,* Deep Survival

JESSE MAJOR, THE reporter for the *Peninsula Daily News* who followed Jacob's story from the beginning, wrote a story that ran on Sunday, May 7, 2017, a month after Jacob's bike was found in the park: "Olympic National Park lacks search protocols."

"Olympic National Park does not have park-specific written guidelines or policy related missing persons so uses the National Park Service policy," Olympic National Park Acting Superintendent Lee Taylor wrote to Major after he submitted a Freedom of Information Act request to the park. Major points out in the story that the eighty-two-page *National Park Service Search and Rescue Reference Manual* requires that "every park unit with a SAR Program will prepare a park SAR Plan approved by the superintendent."

One could conclude that Olympic National Park is actually a Potemkin village, or Potemkin park. The place is certainly grand and beautiful and dangerous, but perhaps rangers in Smokey hats and "pickle suits" driving SUVs with light bars give the place a false sense of a professional SAR response in the case of an emergency. "It's shocking that such a big place doesn't have protocol to do search and rescue," Randy Gray told Major for the story. "I don't want anybody else to go through what we're going through right now."

Zach Krull, the twenty-year-old Evergreen State College student, was reported missing on the other side—the southeast corner—of the park, near Lake Cushman in an area referred to as the Staircase, on April 10. The next day, April 11, a search lead by the Mason County Sheriff's Office deployed more than seventy searchers and helicopters from Naval Air Station Whidbey Island and King County. That Friday, Olympic Mountain Rescue had dogs on the ground. The cooperative search encompassed the southeast corner of Olympic National Park and surrounding Olympic National Forest land. The Krull search—which also included SAR teams from Thurston and Pierce Counties—appeared to be an extreme opposite of the early attempt by rangers to find Jacob Gray.

The Krull search ended five days after it began when aircraft located human footprints leading into a large avalanche debris field. Personnel were stopped due to "severe" avalanche danger. The official verbiage was that the search was "suspended."

In January of 1992 Stefan Bissert, a twenty-three-year-old German exchange student and Fulbright scholar at Oregon State University, separated from his hiking partner on the Sol Duc Trail, near where Jacob's bike was found. Bissert tried to hike twenty-three miles to the Hoh River trailhead via the connecting Hoh River trail. He was not prepared for the weather and hiked into a brutal weeklong storm. Searchers, including dogs and helicopters, searched for five days before calling it off. Bissert has never been found.

In the summer of 2006, former Army paratrooper Gilbert Gilman, age forty-seven, of Olympia, Washington, disappeared in the Staircase area, near where Krull went missing.

Seventy-one-year-old Bryan Lee Johnston, a Port Angeles

resident, vanished from the Ozette Trail. His pickup was found at the trailhead, near the Pacific Coast in the northwest corner of the park, in 2013. Johnston is still missing in Olympic National Park.

Because the federal government doesn't keep track of missing persons on public land, and because there are likely missing persons that no one knows are in the park, there could be more—maybe significantly more—people missing in Olympic National Park.

In August of 1939, a thirty-three-year-old Chicago botanist named Marion Frances Steffens vanished from the Mount Olympus area of the park. A search crew of fourteen rangers and wildland firefighters, as well as Coast Guard aircraft, searched the west side of the mountain. Near the end of the Hoh River Trail, rangers found some of Steffens's gear and food. The area was rife with deep glacial crevasses. That fall searches would include more overflights and bloodhounds. Steffens has never been found.

The first helicopter used in a National Park Service SAR operation was deployed at Olympic National Park. The rescue heli ended up needing the rescue. It was October of 1948, and the search for a seventeen-year-old Eagle Scout, Robert Thorson, had turned into a recovery—Thorson had fallen to his death while descending Brothers Mountain—necessitating an airlift of the remains. The Army Air Rescue Service Bell H-13 Sioux (the kind you see on *M*A*S*H*) helicopter took off from McChord Field; over the mountains the engine quit and the pilot attempted to land in a small meadow near Upper Lena Lake. A gust of wind swept the chopper into the lake, where it landed upside down forty feet from shore. The three-man crew survived and the rescuers were rescued the next day by rangers and Coast Guard personnel.

Military aircraft have crashed in the park from time to time, including in 1956 when two F-89H Scorpion jet fighters collided south of Mount Olympus. First Lieutenant Robert Canup perished when he failed to eject from his aircraft. Two more airmen "punched out"; one was rescued from a peak after an aircraft spotted him, while another walked more than thirty miles to a road. First Lieutenant Eugene A. Hamby parachuted safely to the ground and drew from the *Air Force Survival Manual*, which instructed that he spread out his parachute and wait for rescue.

John Devine, age seventy-three, a Sequim resident, disappeared from the steep Maynard Burn Trail south of Port Angeles in 1997. A Bell 205A-1 helicopter crashed during the search for Devine, killing three people—including the pilot and a dog handler—and injuring five aboard.

On Sunday, April 2, 2017, near the time Jacob Gray and Zach Krull went missing, a single-engine Cirrus SR-22 crashed into the side of a mountain near Mount Jupiter. The two people aboard sent out an emergency call, which was picked up by a Delta commercial jet. An MH-60S Knighthawk helicopter from Naval Air Station Whidbey Island sling-plucked the survivors off the steep mountain grade. Aerial rescue is dangerous work, but there's a long history of helicopters being deployed in Olympic National Park.

In order to recognize current and future needs, Olympic National Park, like every national park, is required to conduct an SAR Needs Assessment every five years. The needs assessments are useful in detailing visitation numbers, visitor activities, and SAR staffing levels.

Most helpful, perhaps, is that the needs assessments also aggregate the numbers of varying types of SAR incidents each year and evaluate successful missions and what can be learned in order to improve future SAR missions.

Following the SAR Needs Assessment, each park is required to draw up a proprietary SAR Plan. That's what was missing at Olympic National Park. Rangers assess situations on the ground and make case-by-case decisions—it's not certain an SAR Plan specialized to ONP would have made a difference in a mission to find Jacob Gray. It's also not certain it would not have helped.

Randy is too busy bushwhacking through the forest and diving the river to give the bureaucracy much thought.

For the Gray family it's a melancholic Independence Day. On July 5, 2017, an Associated Press article with this headline ran all across the region:

3 Bodies Found and Recovered in Different Areas of Olympic National Park

None of them was Jacob Gray.

It was a busy holiday weekend for rangers. They recovered the body of a sixty-year-old man—William "Dave" Woodson, an entomologist and solo hiker. He was found in a boulder field near the Norwegian Memorial, on the Pacific Coast section of the park, north of La Push.

Also discovered and recovered was a woman from a minivan found in the popular Hurricane Ridge on the north side of the park. Fifty-seven-year-old Kathryn Kennedy's body was extracted from two hundred feet down an embankment along Obstruction Point Road.

On July 1 a hiker found a body near Flapjack Lake in the Staircase region of ONP; gear found with the dead man led the Mason County coroner to believe the body was that of Zach Krull. An examination confirmed it.

Krull's body spent nearly three months in the park. Stewart Krull, Zach's father, first called the Mason County Sheriff's Office

(MCSO) on Monday, April 10, when Zach failed to return to his dorm room at Evergreen State College in Olympia. A deputy returned Stewart's call "immediately."

"Although Zach wasn't officially a missing person yet, the deputy was incredibly proactive," Krull says. "He took down all the details we knew at the point, informed us about possible next steps should a search become necessary, and even reached out to security officials and Zach's friends at the Evergreen State College. That same night, of his own accord, the deputy drove out to the Staircase campgrounds, Skokomish campgrounds, and the Big Creek Trailhead camping area to see if there were any signs of Zach." The deputy, according to Krull, spoke with Olympic National Park maintenance workers at the camping sites. "The next morning, a U.S. Forest Service ranger participated in a visit to Staircase with MCSO to scout the campsite. I also believe an ONP ranger was part of that initial reconnaissance."

The official search got underway the next morning, Tuesday, April 11. MCSO controlled the incident command, essentially meaning they were in control of the search for Zach. "I don't recall," Stewart says, "whether this was due to concurrent investigations (including the search for Jacob Gray) taxing ONP's resources, or to the fact that the investigation had originated with Mason County."

ONP rangers found Zach's tent in the Staircase area on Friday, April 14. Stewart tells me Zach had pitched his tent in a secluded spot on April 8 because the campground wasn't officially open for the season. Dogs from Olympic Mountain Rescue were brought in.

Helicopters and fixed-wing aircraft were greenlit, but searchers faced terrible weather that week, which made consistent aerial searching impossible.

The Krulls had a different experience than the Gray family. "At no point during the initial search-and-rescue operation, or during the many weeks that constituted the search-and-recovery operation, did we ever feel either underserved or under-resourced. On the contrary, we were repeatedly impressed by the humanity and professionalism of all involved."

Zach was snowshoeing. I asked Stewart if he feels that the search for his son was called off too early, when aircraft spotted tracks leading into the avalanche debris field. "No," he says. "I don't feel the search was called off too early. During that impossible week when hope was still alive, everyone from MCSO to OMR to ONP was incredibly responsive and detailed in their explanations for every action taken (or not taken)."

On April 15, after the tent was found, eighty people searched on foot. OMR deployed backcountry ski teams in order to vector around avalanche terrain. Aircraft flew on the sixteenth, Easter Sunday. Two days later, teams even dragged the area rivers.

When the hiker found Zach, they also found his gear and clothing strewn about in a curlicue pattern, a classic sign that he succumbed to hypothermia.

CHAPTER 7

NOVA SCOTIA

I am tired, very tired of being a "stranger."
—world cyclist Frank Lenz in a dispatch from
Persia in Outing *magazine, 1894*

HIKERS GO MISSING with frequency; it stands to reason, there are many of them out there. Runners too. Berry pickers and mushroom hunters. David Paulides is obsessed with disappeared game hunters. Children, of course, get lost in the woods. Skiers occasionally go missing but are usually found when the snow melts. But cyclists, not so much. Mountain bikers and touring riders vanish about as frequently as golfers.

Long-term mysterious vanishings of touring cyclists with as few clues as Jacob Gray's are so rare that Robert Koester, aka Professor Rescue, the foremost academic on SAR statistics, lists only "lost mountain biker" in his seminal 2008 book *Lost Person Behavior*. Koester is certified as a Type 1 SAR incident commander and holds a PhD in search theory from the University of Portsmouth. "All cases of mountain bikes were resolved out of 189 incidents," he told me. But mountain bikers did—do—go missing, as opposed to missing touring cyclists, who don't even get a category.

But of course it happens. Our Amelia Earhart is a cyclist named Frank Lenz, who in 1892, at the age of twenty-four, lit out from Pittsburgh to circumnavigate the globe on his Victory Safety Bicycle. He wouldn't be the first to do it, but *Outing* magazine sponsored his trip so he could chronicle the adventure while demonstrating the high-tech wonders of the newfangled "safety" bicycle. Two years into the trip, Lenz fell off the edge of the earth somewhere in the Ottoman Empire. You can imagine how slowly no-news traveled then. When his family expressed concern, *Outing* sent another famous cyclist, William Sachtleben, to Turkey to find him. He didn't, but came back with the information that his probable fate was Lenz pissed off a Kurdish chief, and the warlord had him killed. At the time Sachtleben's rescue attempt was considered on par with the famous hunt for David Livingstone: *Dr. Livingstone, I presume*.

Koester's statistics missed a 2014 Canadian vanish that is as confounding as any I've heard of. It's easy to miss the Canadian missing—the country is huge and quiet. They like to take care of their own and not broadcast their troubles. I only learned about the case because his identical twin brother Marcel contacted me after he read the article I'd written for *Outside* magazine that focused on a missing runner, Joe Keller. Marty Leger, from Halifax, Nova Scotia, was thirty years old when he went for a routine ride at a popular trail network at Spider Lake. There isn't anything extremely remote about the area—the trailhead is even in a residential area. But it's the Canadian Maritimes, so wildlands are never not close.

May 29. Marty was riding a new black Santa Cruz Heckler. He planned to ride singletrack for a couple of hours and return home around four in the afternoon. He didn't. First his family went looking for him. Then the Royal Canadian Mounted Police—RCMP—mounted a search that included nearly five hundred people. Volunteers, dogs, and helicopters searched a search zone that was eighty square kilometers. The search for Marty Leger was one of the largest in Canadian history. Not a granola bar wrapper was found, let alone a fat-tire bicycle.

"With a bike, you can cover more ground…so you can likely get yourself out," Marcel says. "Also you tend to have to stick to the trails when biking." Marty almost certainly went off-trail, perhaps in an attempt to take a shortcut. "I am not surprised they didn't find his bike because if they would have found it they would have found him. I cannot imagine him leaving his new bike; it was maybe his third ride on it." All cyclists will understand that; what's harder to understand is not finding a mountain biker.

"A body ended up being discovered roughly a year after he went missing," Marcel says. "It was someone else who had gone missing before Marty. He was found within the search area, so clearly it would have been very possible for them to simply not see Marty or his bike. They had a lot of people searching, but it only takes one person to miss him and then cross off that area. Everyone who searched for him tried so hard day after day but they had a radius they needed to look at based on age/weight/time of day/weather and how long since he's been reported missing. And there's a good chance Marty was out of that radius when the search started."

What's your theory about what happened? I asked him. "My best guess is that he got off trail and got lost. Once he realized he was lost, he found the nearest dirt road and tried to follow that until he hit a highway or a neighborhood. He likely went as far as he could and tried to sleep the night off and go back at it in the morning." This happens a surprising amount in Canada, where logging roads and ATV trails web and spiral and sometimes go for hundreds of kilometers. "My guess is that he tried hard to get out and covered a lot of ground but unfortunately that likely put him out of the radius they were searching. It was cold that night and he was wearing shorts and a T-shirt. So I'm thinking he went to bed and hypothermia set in and he simply didn't wake up."

Trying to apply logic to a case like this one is painful.

According to Marcel it's possible the trail got too technical for Marty, and he fell hard and succumbed to injuries. That's certainly possible, but if he'd fallen so hard that he was badly injured, it doesn't make sense he'd have stumbled or crawled far from the trail; at least the bike would have been located. "I have a hard time believing he got hurt badly—he rode very conservatively, never did jumps or crazy lines he could not handle," Marcel says.

Marty had only ridden the area one time previously, and it's not believed he intended to ride very far. He brought a map, but it was found in the car, so perhaps he was comfortable enough with his intended route without it. The area is bordered on one side with a highway but all other directions are dense wooded areas. The Army was eventually called in and, Marcel told me, even the soldiers had a hard time bushwhacking through some of it.

"I keep telling myself it would be easier if it was a heart attack or car accident—at least we could be angry at something," he says. "Not knowing if or how much he suffered at the end is what haunts me. It might have been a quick ending, but the thought of him being really hurt and yelling for help will stay with me for a while. I try not to focus too much on the fact that he disappeared and more so just think of him as *gone*." The family likely will never know what happened. "There is no getting past it or moving on," Marcel says. "No being okay with it or getting over it. Closure isn't an option, unfortunately."

His is a case of double-negative indemnity. "The fact that we are identical twins makes it a bit more complicated. Not only do I see him every time I look in the mirror, but I'm also a constant reminder to my friends and family that he is gone. Whenever they see me they most likely see both of us." In 2018 their father took his own life. "He just could not make sense of Marty simply disappearing," Marcel says. "He really needed closure. My dad was not a depressed man before this."

What people don't think of are the social pressures for the family after a loved one disappears. "For the first few years we all lived in fear of leaving the house," Marcel says. "We all knew we would at some point run into someone we know and they would ask, *How's it going? Any news? Did they find anything? How did he get lost on a bike ride?*"

It occurs to me that I asked Marcel those same questions. "There's also small things people would likely not think about that much. I have a hard time answering the phone. I never liked the phone much before, but when you get two phone calls—Marty and for my dad—and on the other end is panic and news that will crush you and change your life forever, it's not easy to answer the phone comfortably anymore. Also being in the woods alone is almost impossible now unless I'm very familiar with the trails or with other people. I also overpack now to be sure I'm okay if anything happens."

CHAPTER 8

OLYMPIC PENINSULA

Jacob,

The rangers have your bike and gear down at the boathouse. I've got your money from selling your car. Call me if you get this.

Love, Dad

> *—note Randy left at the spot where Jacob's
> bike and trailer were found*

ANOTHER OFFICIAL SEARCH coordinated by Sergeant Lyman Moores of the Clallam County Sheriff's Office takes place on the last Saturday in July—nearly four months after Jacob's abandoned bike was discovered. This is a search-and-recovery operation, a search for answers—no one expects to find Jacob alive in the park, but it's helpful to cross sections and hotspots off the map, having been searched and re-searched: *Okay, we don't know where Jacob is, but we know where he isn't.*

A week prior to the new official search, and three weeks after Zach Krull's remains were recovered, a textbook survival story took place in the Olympics. On her seventy-first birthday, Port Angeles resident Sajean Geer and her Chihuahua-terrier mix Yoda went hiking toward Obstruction Point, in northern Olympic National Park, with the mission of spreading the ashes of her husband of thirty-four years, Jack. She got disoriented, and even though she climbed to a high point to survey the area, she couldn't find Obstruction Point Road. She and Yoda were prepared for a short hike. "I was just going to go in for a short walk and find a nice place with flowers to scatter his ashes," she told Jesse Major of the *Peninsula Daily News*. "I scattered his ashes and everything went fine, but I couldn't find my way back to the road." They would spend almost a week in the wild. For two nights they slept under a rotting log.

On the third day she built a shelter by piling branches onto two fallen logs and plugging gaps with moss. Geer ate pine needles, and both she and Yoda munched on insects and drank from a creek. She was dressed only in a Hawaiian shirt and capri pants with nothing to start a fire. At night temperatures dipped into the forties; she spooned Yoda for warmth.

Jack Eng, her brother, became concerned when he didn't hear from Geer and alerted the Clallam County Sheriff's Department, who were unable to locate her; two days later a missing persons alert was issued. A ranger discovered her Ford Explorer along a remote road in the park—he recognized it from the missing persons alert. A hasty search was conducted near the vehicle. On July 23 a helicopter from Northwest Helicopters in Olympia was requested by the park to fly the area—Geer was spotted in a clearing as she walked to a creek for water at 4:20 in the afternoon. The crew dropped Geer a note that said to stay put while the Port Angeles–based Coast Guard MH-65 Dolphin equipped with a hoist was en route to extract her and Yoda.

Nineteen searchers from Olympic National Park, Clallam

County Search and Rescue, and Kitsap County Search and Rescue, not including the Coast Guard, assisted on the search. The SAR team that extracted Geer also found and recovered the urn used to carry her husband's ashes—she'd dropped it, and it had rolled down a steep slope.

This time the search for Jacob got some special help. "If you're gonna murder somebody, do it in Olympic National Park because no one's gonna find you," Tanya Barba says. "It's harder than a needle in a haystack." She should know—the former Multnomah County parole and probation officer and private investigator has hiked hundreds of miles of it, many of those in search of Jacob. Barba lives in Portland. After she read about Jacob's case on a Facebook page called Missing Persons she was transfixed and commuted the nine-hour round trip every weekend for months.

Less than a mile west from where Highway 101 intersects with the Sol Duc Road, there's a red barn in a small meadow tucked against the mountains on the north side of the highway. The Olympic Discovery Trail, a bicycle route running 140 miles from Port Townsend to the Pacific Ocean at La Push, flanks the property. It's thought that Jacob may have ridden sections of the ODT on his journey to the Sol Duc.

The property was perfect for an RV park, which an owner had intended. But it was bought by a Bigfoot aficionado named Wally Hersom because there were several rumored sightings of a Bigfoot crossing Highway 101 through the property. Hersom offered the use of the facility to Bigfoot researcher Derek Randles. It's possible you've seen Randles on television—he's a frequent guest on Sasquatch-seeking reality shows and speaks at Bigfoot conventions. Randles co-founded the Olympic Project, which is one of the most renowned Sasquatch investigators' organizations in the world.

In 2017, in response to Jacob's disappearance and the difficulties surrounding early search efforts, Randles, along with James Million, an Olympic Project field researcher, hunting guide, and gear tester, and Tanya Barba, put their knowledge of the region together in a group called Olympic Mountain Response Team, with the idea of responding to missing persons in the mountains. The trio collectively knows the Olympic Mountain Range better than perhaps anyone, including ONP rangers. All three are exceedingly fit because they do their reconnaissance work in the mountains on foot. In short, Randy could not have stumbled across a better group to help find Jacob.

No one says Sasquatch has anything to do with Jacob's vanish; no one says Sasquatch doesn't have anything to do with it, either. Tanya told me she believes that Bigfoot does have to do with the cases of toddlers who go missing in bad weather and/or remote places and are found safe and healthy days later.

The OMRT gave Randy total access to what has been endearingly called the Bigfoot Barn, as well as all the gear and tools inside. The barn has a galley, a bathroom with a shower, beds, couches, and a bar stocked with good whiskey. The bar is decorated with Sasquatch paraphernalia: plaster castings of really big feet, a full-size papier-mâché Bigfoot that towers over the bar, and a signed photo from James "Bobo" Fay from the show *Finding Bigfoot*. Trail cameras. Rifles. Near the bar there's a small library with a copy of David Paulides's *The Hoopa Project: Bigfoot Encounters in California*. There are maps on the bar, maps on the walls, maps on the folding tables standing in the bay. The barn smells of concrete, mouse poison, and Irish Spring soap.

The team searches for evidence of Bigfoot through scientific methods. Randles believes Bigfoot exists in DNA evidence and the fossil record. One night when there were a half dozen of us at the barn, he told the story of his first encounter with Sasquatch, in 1985 in Olympic National Park, when he was a teenager. He was with friends, backpacking. A pair of Bigfoot shadowed them, then lobbed coconut-sized rocks into their camp. The boys vamoosed, Bigfoot throwing rocks at them all the way out to the trailhead.

The Bigfoot Barn is the closest outside-the-park private property to the Sol Duc Road and where they found Jacob's bike. When Jacob vanished less than ten miles away, the team turned their energies away from Bigfoot and onto the search for Jacob. They also took Randy in as family. Access to the barn allows Randy to live where his son vanished. As time goes on the search for Jacob becomes no less mysterious than the search for Sasquatch.

I ask Tanya if she sees the irony in the locations, that Jacob vanished in Sasquatch Ground Zero. "None of this happened by coincidence," she says. "It's not Bigfoot, but it's Jacob."

"Jacob woulda loved this," Randy says to me one night. "Bigfoot searchers! Come ooooon!"

Port-a-pots are trucked in, and the Bigfoot Barn serves as home base for the search where searchers have parked their RVs or pitched tents. Besides personnel from Clallam County and Olympic National Park, teams from Jefferson, Kitsap, Mason, Pierce, and Snohomish Counties joined the search. Inmate crews from Clallam Bay and Olympic corrections centers combed the forest. Olympic Mountain Rescue and Northwest Search Dogs, who were on the ground in April, volunteered. They comprise over a hundred people from the Pacific Northwest who show for the daylong search.

Just up the Sol Duc Road and past the park entrance gate there's a gravel pit that is the staging area and central command. After some heated discussion with the Saturday search's operations section chief, Guy Mansfield, Barba, Randles, and Million are assigned the role of making sure Randy and Laura stay safe.

Mansfield has divided the search into eight zones. The dogs are charged with canvassing both sides of the Sol Duc. Randy, Laura, and the Olympic Mountain Response Team bust their asses bush-whacking and wading where they can. Volunteers from a local ATV club zoom up and down Forest Road 2918. Searchers on foot bushwhack along the river, picking through ferns and checking under rotting logs. There is a swiftwater rescue team. Three cadaver dogs join the search. Meanwhile, it's backpacking season, and the backcountry is getting visited by thousands of backpackers from all over the world—surely, if Jacob is up high and died up there, someone will find some gear, clothing, or a body.

But the three cadaver dogs *indicate* in three places on the river. Two indications are deep holes. One of the areas is a logjam, a snarl of imposing Sitka spruce and red cedar pick-up-sticks with a deep, dark depression underneath. It's the logjam that haunts Randy—Moores doesn't want him going near there, where a rope could get tangled in a branch and the current could pin him underwater. The river is still high and running hard—the swiftwater team gets cameras near, but it's too dangerous to perform a thorough enough search under the logjam. They plan to come back in mid-August when the river should be significantly lower.

Ground teams find two dozen items, including bones. A University of Washington anthropologist quickly identifies them as animal bones. Several clothing items are found—sweatpants, mismatched socks, a bandanna, and a pair of shorts in Jacob's size. The apparel could be summer tourist detritus or it could hold solid clues.

Moores says that because it was early April when he vanished it's unlikely Jacob would have been wearing shorts. But sometimes a cyclist will wear tights under shorts. And Jacob does not mind the cold, whether it's air or water. And they fit the description of a pair of shorts his brother-in-law Anthony, Mallory's husband, gave him for Christmas: Bermuda plaid with the brand name Burnside. The shorts are found at a popular swimming hole a mile downstream from the bike. Moores sends them to the Washington State Patrol

Crime Lab in Seattle just in case. These tests can take months, and even then the exposure to the elements and river often make obtaining conclusive information impossible.

"Jacob would wear mismatched socks," Randy says. "Socks." Randy repeats a thing, a verb or a noun. "Socks." This way he can watch the word and regard it from a slightly different angle. A new vantage. Sometimes it's to release a thing, get it out of his mind forever; sometimes it's to keep it close, so he can work with it in his mind. He lets go of the socks.

The logjam fills Randy's dreams, and he'll wake up thinking about it at four a.m. The dog handlers explain to him that it's unlikely the dogs *indicated* on a dead animal—they're trained for human cadavers. They could be sensing clothing from a cadaver. Tissue from a cadaver may have washed against a log. A dislodged body part may be trapped under there. Or it could be a whole cadaver.

What they don't emphasize is that it could be none of the above. Dogs are dogs, and sometimes, it seems, about as useful as psychics; they want to help, but sometimes their help just gets in the way. Randy is torn. Three cadaver dogs keying in on a logjam focuses all the energy on the logjam. It's more than possible there's nothing to the logjam, that Jacob's not in the river at all. But there's a tendency to want to believe the dogs. There's a tendency to want to believe the Bigfoot people and the psychics, too.

There's a drought and a heatwave in the Pacific Northwest, and a big wildfire is raging in British Columbia so that the Olympic Peninsula is shrouded in smoke and the sun is gauzed. Randy is living in the Bigfoot Barn when I drive over from the Bainbridge Island Ferry to meet him. I open the door and call, "Randy?" "You made it, grom!" he says. He's icing his knee on a couch but gets up and hops toward me. We'd talked on the phone at length, and it's like we've known each other for years. He's six feet tall and lanky with longish gray hair that suits him. He looks like he could be a Carradine brother with a touch of Iggy Pop thrown in. He punches me in the arm. "Good to see ya." Randy's ringtone is "Dear Mr. Fantasy" by Traffic, and his phone rings often, filling the barn with psychedelic sixties rock. He offers me an organic prune—he eats a lot of prunes.

We jump into his Dodge Ram diesel dually—the one he's gonna slide the camper onto when he buys it—and he takes me up the Sol Duc Road. Blind Faith's "Can't Find My Way Home" plays on the Sirius XM. He stops at the little Olympic National Park entrance station to show the attendant his lifetime senior pass. He jokes with her. I notice the *MISSING Jacob Gray* eight-and-a-half by eleven poster is taped next to the window, where everyone entering up the Sol Duc can see.

I try to imagine April 6 and Jacob turning left, south. He passes through the open but unattended gate and pedals uphill. It gets steep enough he has to go to granny gear and—with all that weight—stand on the pedals. Two, maybe three miles an hour. At the blind top—he won't realize this until he gets there—it flattens, then rolls gently downhill before it's back on the pedals and pumping uphill again. Rivers don't flow uphill, after all. He passes the trailhead for the Aurora Ridge Trail.

Randy hiked up the Aurora Ridge Trail back in April, when the snowpack started at just 2,700 feet and he sank up to his crotch in places. He stuck sticks in the snow like arrows so he could bread-crumb his way back out. The next month, May 2017, he hiked it again to see if he could have missed anything. "A bear growled at me!" he says. That started his obsession with avoiding bears. While hiking the North Fork Trail with Dani he saw another bear. "It was fat," he says. "We yelled at the sucker and it took off."

I think about how Jacob and his gear are soaked—probably some rain found its way inside his loaded-for-bear trailer. Wet wool gets heavy. Wet sleeping bags suck. He rolls slowly across the bridge over the North Fork; this is an easy place to access clean drinking water, fill his hydration bladder, but then Jacob has never been drawn by the easy way. But where they found Jacob's bike, it made no sense for him to get water here. It makes no sense to leave the bike here for any reason.

The handwritten note Randy left for Jacob is still there. He had attached a Ziploc to a small steel utility box a few yards up from where the bike was found. What's striking about it is the matter-of-fact tone. When Randy wrote it, he was confident Jacob would stride up to investigate what happened to his stuff, rip open the Ziploc bag, unfold the note, and think *Right, I better give Dad a ring*. It was important to Randy that Jacob knew he had the cash for the Volkswagen sedan he sold to Joey Thomas, a renowned Santa Cruz surfboard shaper and Randy's close longtime friend.

Randy illustrates what the trackers showed him four months ago, the trail to the river, the ass-mark on the boulder. "No problem for Jacob," Randy says. "No *proooooblem*. I know my kid, this river is nothing for him. *Noooooothing*. No problem."

The vegetation has been flattened by searchers so that there's a faint trail down to the embankment and to the river's edge. There are still wooden orange pencil-sized sticks the trackers placed in the ground at footprints and evidence that plants had been disturbed. The sticks were placed with confidence, but the trackers' conclusion is just so inconclusive. Creative nonfiction at best, fiction at worst. Trackers need to be confident. Psychics need to be confident. Tracking dogs need to be confident.

Uphill, just upriver from the bike, are Salmon Cascades. Nine miles up from the bike are Sol Duc Falls. There are waterfalls all over Olympic National Park. A psychic from Oregon named

Laurie McQuary and four other people, including Marcus, Randy's four-year-old grandson, dreamed they saw Jacob behind a waterfall. "You listen to a lot of people, you notice patterns," Randy says. "Several people have the same thought."

So naturally, Randy took on the charge of checking every waterfall in the Pacific Northwest. He roped off, grabbed a big rock, and sank to the bottom of a fifteen-foot-deep hole behind the falls. He'll do it again and again at all the falls—Sisyphus at SeaWorld. What a great time this would be if he and Jacob were able to do this together. "Jacob would *looooove* this," Randy says.

Now Randy hops from rock to rock, bad knee be damned. It's all I can do to keep up with this guy who is older than me by nearly a decade and a half—if he hadn't had a sore knee I'd have to stay in the truck. "It's just so pretty, gosh," he says of the stretch of river that may have taken his son. "I just love running on the rocks."

Randy is related to Francis Scott Key, he's told me a couple times; his great grandmother on his mom's side is a Key. He's a former Santa Cruz Assembly of God deacon—that's how he met and befriended Carlos Santana. Now Randy's denomination is the church of the ocean, the redwoods, and now the great spruce forests and snowcapped mountains of the Olympic Peninsula.

On the drive back downriver "Jack Straw" by the Grateful Dead plays on the satellite. At times, talking with Randy, it seems he's delusional, that this far hereafter he's still gonna find Jacob alive. But most often people around Randy get swept up in his optimism and want to believe they could channel some of that surfer spirit if they found themselves in his booties. "We can give back, help look for other missing people together." It takes a moment to realize when he says *we* he means himself and Jacob. The father believes Jacob is on a quest, and now Randy is, too. The wildfire smoke makes the full moon red.

CHAPTER 9

MICHIGAN'S UPPER PENINSULA & NORTH CAROLINA

You never climb the same mountain twice, not even in memory. Memory rebuilds the mountain, changes the weather, retells the jokes, remakes all the moves.

—*alpinist Lito Tejada-Flores*

THE U.P. IS ANALOG, as is going missing and most of search and rescue. When I moved here in 2013 there was a message on the marquee at a local gas station that read WE NOW HAVE PAY AT PUMP. I saw the missing persons flyer fall semester 2016, on the bulletin board outside my office at Northern Michigan University, where I work. I'm convinced no one—least of all students—pauses or looks up from their phones in order to study the bulletin boards, but I'm comforted that they exist. I figured missing persons flyers had gone the way of milk carton kids. But they haven't.

The flyer said her name is Malvika Bala Deshmukh, twenty-seven years old. Her car was found in September. Her credit cards had not been used in over a week. If she was indeed in the forest, this was most likely a recovery search, as compared to a rescue.

Malvi, to her friends, had an old Honda that was found by hunters. The car was apparently driven down an unused trace until it got hung up in a snarl of maple whips. The license plate had been removed. That could be a clue to a crime, or a sign of mental illness, which authorities and searchers were considering.

If you Google "missing person" and the name of your nearest national park or national forest, you will find clusters of the disappeared. In the Upper Peninsula of Michigan, there are at least six people reported missing on forest land within a hundred miles of my house. That's a lot, considering fewer than 300,000 people live in the entire U.P. The poster of Malvi outside my office made her case more real to me, less statistical.

An extended study into missing persons makes you believe less in coincidence, but coincidentally, North America's foremost backcountry search-and-rescue veteran lives in my county. Michael Neiger was leading the search for Malvi. He's a retired Michigan state police detective and now a backcountry—"bush," he says— search-and-recovery specialist—though he does work active search-and-rescue cases when he's requested. Neiger is exceedingly fit and treks into country where few others are willing to venture. I had contacted him through his website about the Malvi search, and he told me where and when to show up.

So here we were on a drizzly autumn weekend in 2016, on a search for spoor—the license plate that had been removed from the car, keys, a purse, a sock—or a body. There wasn't any calling her name, anything like that, just slow gridded walks through the leaves.

Malvi's friends had driven up from lower Michigan to help. They were all organic farmers and good company when we'd chat on breaks. They brought deer apples and homemade hummus to share. There were ten of us, plus a border collie named Sonofa who lives at nearby Rock River Farm and had already been over every inch of where we planned to search and then some. We conducted a grid search, twenty feet apart. At the end of a row—which reminded me of walking bean fields with a hoe, weeding—Malvi's friends would do a little yoga, salutations, tree pose, and whatnot. On breaks we'd talk about Malvi. I learned that she was a forager and would often return from the woods with a basket of things, cook them, and experiment with eating them. "Maybe she ate a bad mushroom," said a man named Rick.

In the terrain we were in—maple woods mostly—a grid search would give us at least a 90 percent probability of detection, meaning the chances that she was where we'd been were less than 10 percent when we'd finished.

If Malvi wasn't there, we were doing what search-and-rescue people call a *bastard search*—the subject isn't in the search area at all. That's what we wished for, that she ran away on purpose in the hope of making a new, anonymous life.

Malvi was found a week later, accidentally, by surveyors working to move a section of the North Country Trail on the border of the Rock River Wilderness. She was leaning against a maple tree less than a mile from where we'd searched. Bodies don't hold up well in the damp boreal climate of the U.P. Her skin was ashen, her nose missing. I talked with one of the people who found her—she said Malvi had a peaceful expression on her face. Malvi was a wandering spirit, and it appears she went into the woods and tried to disappear on purpose.

Her discovery fit a pattern that is strange and fuels the Paulidean paranormal fringe who follow these stories: The area where she was found had already been searched shortly after her car was discovered.

In July of 2017, Kara Moore went missing in Pictured Rocks National Lakeshore, along Lake Superior, near Munising, Michigan. The fifty-five-year-old woman had been on a casual hike on a beautiful summer day with her family. In the early afternoon the family turned to head for their car, and Kara couldn't be found. She'd stopped to put some things in her daypack and vanished.

As far as searches go, the effort to find Kara Moore was a clinic in how to conduct operations the right way. Within the hour National Park Service rangers arrived and executed a hasty search, just as they had with the area around Jacob's bike and gear. They quickly covered established trails in the area of the Little Beaver Campground, Moore's LKP—last known position. A Park Service patrol boat was dispatched to the search in case she'd gone into Lake Superior or stumbled out to the beach or shoreline, which extends for forty-two rugged miles of the park. When she wasn't located with the hasty search, a half dozen other law-enforcement agencies were called in to help. This is one of the main differences, since the National Park Service is not known to frequently ask for outside help.

But Pictured Rocks did everything right—not only by the book, but additionally, not worrying about ego or, more commonly, budgets. They spared no expense in the effort to find Kara Moore. In short, the morning after she was reported missing there were dozens of searchers on the ground, including trained SAR dogs, and a helicopter in the air.

Still, as twenty-four hours turned into forty-eight, then seventy-two, things did not look good for Kara Moore. But why couldn't that many trained, experienced personnel—and canines—find a middle-aged woman? Moore suffered from a short-term memory disability, which may have made the search for her more difficult. But the lack of success was as mysterious as it was frustrating for searchers.

Now it was nearly a week since she'd been seen. Statistics were not at all in her favor. That didn't keep the search from going full-steam into day six. By then the family had all but lost hope when a miracle happened—Moore walked out of the wild on the same trail she'd disappeared from. A couple of hikers asked her name. Kara. "A lot of people are looking for you," they said.

Kara Moore found herself. Dozens of searchers with canines and technology covering more than 73,000 acres, and six days later the missing person appears at the place she disappeared. There are myriad incidents where bodies are found in areas that had been previously searched, but rarely does a subject who wants to be found unintentionally evade an all-out search. It's as if she ventured inside a quantum physics problem of her own; perhaps stepped through a portal to another dimension, then hiked back through.

Not even Kara Moore herself can say. Because of her previous brain injury, Moore reported only vague memories of drinking from a pond and sleeping by a log. She didn't know how she got lost or how she found her way back. But she was fine.

Pictured Rocks typically sees between five and ten missing hikers a year—nearly all of them are found within twenty-four hours.

In January 2019, a young man who attends Northern Michigan University, Guiancarlo Estupigan, a twenty-five-year-old fish and wildlife major, went missing in the wild somewhere near the Yellow Dog River, about thirty miles from my house. Carlo, as he's affectionately called, was a keen wildlife photographer and spent hours in harsh conditions.

A winter storm advisory was in effect for Thursday after-noon, and I watched the system move in on my phone. It wasn't weather to be under on purpose, but Carlo was an outdoorsman who'd spent thousands of hours outside fishing and photographing wildlife—he'd been in those conditions before. Furthermore, he had a handrail—a geographical feature that simplifies navigation and makes getting lost less likely—the Yellow Dog, which flows into Lake Superior. He also had County Road 510, along which he'd parked his Subaru.

Carlo didn't return to his home in Marquette that night—on

Friday, after the storm broke, his roommates went looking for him and found his car. They called law enforcement and the Marquette County Sheriff's Department dispatched their search-and-rescue team—a highly trained, dedicated group with an outstanding success rate in finding lost persons. Unfortunately, the snowstorm was followed by several days of intense cold, with high temperatures not reaching zero.

The actual temperature (as opposed to the "real feel") is minus five Fahrenheit. The Yellow Dog is partially frozen and looks like a postcard. The day before, a police helicopter flew the area just above tree level. Now a dozen or so emergency vehicles lined the road near the bridge that crosses the Yellow Dog on Marquette County 510. His family was there, underdressed for the painful cold. Search-and-rescue members in yellow vests zipped up and down logging roads on snowmobiles. I asked a Michigan State Police K9 officer who was warming and getting something to eat before heading back out with his dog for an update. "It's cold—about it." I asked him if I could get some friends together and help search. Not yet, he said. "Right now, if you go out there, the dogs would just find you."

Nearly three days since he failed to return home, Carlo was found by a searcher. He'd succumbed to hypothermia—the telltale sign was that he'd shed clothes. Hypothermia victims feel hot when nearing death. It's mysterious why he wasn't able to find his way back to his car—his body was found just three hundred feet from the road. Carlo's camera—his prized possession—was found protected from the elements; the last several photos taken illustrate his cognitive decline as he froze to death.

The day Carlo went missing, three-year-old Casey Hathaway had been missing for nearly three days near his great-grandmother's rural Craven County, North Carolina, home. The weather was miserable—deadly—for a three-year-old not geared up properly; temperatures dropped to below freezing and rain blew in sideways, making swamps of the surrounding forest. Under three feet tall, Casey wasn't dressed for cold, wet nights. He had no food or water. At one point more than five hundred volunteers aided in the search for Casey. Foot searchers worked a grid through the woods, starting at the boy's last known point—his great-grandmother's yard—and walking line-of-sight so that chances of missing a clue were minimal. Crack canine teams were quickly brought in, and a heat-seeking FLIR-equipped helicopter flew almost constantly in the search for Casey. None of those resources proved effective.

On the evening of January 24, a woman walking her dog heard a cry in the brush. Shane Grier, an EMS coordinator, and his team walked through waist-deep water to where they found the little boy wet but alive, entangled in briars and whimpering for his mother. He checked out fine at the hospital, and within a couple of hours he was eating Cheetos and watching cartoons. The spot where he was pulled from the brambles was a quarter mile from his great-grandmother's house.

I'd been following the Casey Hathaway story with keen interest. If anything, I'd learned just enough through my research regarding missing persons in the wild that it was unlikely the outcome in his case would be good. How Casey managed to avoid deadly hypo-thermia is a miracle—similar weather has killed scores of adults. Casey's story gained international media attention when he told his grandmother that while he was missing he'd been kept company and taken care of by a bear.

Tanya Barba of OMRT told me this regarding Casey: "I am one hundred percent certain that these children are picked up by Bigfoot," she says. "How does a child travel four thousand feet in elevation in his bare feet in two days? Or, in Casey's case, travel through waist-deep swamp water?"

I think about whether it's any less likely that Casey had kept company with Bigfoot than that hundreds of searchers, dogs, and helicopters couldn't locate him a quarter mile from the LKP, forty yards from a road.

I'm most obsessed by the cold vanishings—and improbable *findings*—that don't make sense. There are a lot of them. And while my intent has never been to catalog these disappearances, David Paulides does a good job of that, although, prolific as he is, it's impossible to keep entirely up to date.

A couple years ago I would have smirked at Tanya's assessment and probably made a stupid joke, but I told her I wasn't about to argue with her. I'd studied too many cases with outcomes so strange as to be unexplainable. Or with no outcome at all and the person is still missing. Maybe Casey was befriended by a bear; maybe the bear was actually a Bigfoot. Maybe something else just as strange happened, and we'll never know about it. But these cases happen frequently enough that it can be misleading to simply dismiss the circumstances through conventional wisdom. I'd seen firsthand the kind of passion and intelligence OMRT exhibit in the response to Jacob's vanish, and it equals their passionate and intelligent quest for more knowledge regarding Bigfoot.

There are two cases that can't be overlooked when discussing missing kids in the wild. One is Dennis Lloyd Martin, a six-year-old from Knoxville, Tennessee, who vanished while playing hide-and-seek with family on an afternoon in 1969 in Great Smoky Mountains National Park. A downpour flooded the area shortly after the boy disappeared. Fourteen hundred searchers scoured a search area of over fifty square miles, which remains the largest search in the park's history. Searchers found a sock and a shoe as well as a child's barefoot prints in the mud. A tourist named Harold Key, who was about five miles away from where Martin was last seen, reported hearing "an enormous, sickening scream" and seeing a man covered in hair carrying something red on his shoulder. Martin was last seen wearing a red shirt.

The other infamous case involving a missing child is that of Jaryd Atadero, from Littleton, Colorado. On October 2, 1999, a group of eleven adults from the Christian Singles Network was staying at a lodge near Poudre River Canyon operated by Allyn Atadero, Jaryd's father. They offered to take Jaryd, age three, and his sister Josallyn, who was six, hiking with them on the Big South Trail, twenty miles away, in the Roosevelt National Forest north of Rocky Mountain National Park. The group was playing hide-and-seek along the trail and Jaryd vanished. A panicked search came up empty. A group of fishermen reported a small boy asking them if there were any bears in the area. A Huey UH-1 helicopter from Francis E. Warren Air Force Base in Cheyenne, Wyoming, crashed during the search, injuring five people. Nighttime temperatures dipped into the twenties. Nothing was found.

In June of 2003, two hikers found clothing that was confirmed belonged to Jaryd. Soon a single tooth and a piece of the top of his skull were found. The items were discovered five hundred feet above the trail where Jaryd went missing.

"When they took me to where they found the clothing, it was tough for *me* to get up there," Allyn, a teacher, told me at his home on the Front Range. "It was so rugged, I don't know how Jaryd could have gotten up there." He showed me Jaryd's shoes—white sneakers—alongside an identical pair still in the box he had bought for comparison. Jaryd's shoes had been exposed to the elements for four years but looked nearly as good as the boxed pair. Another odd thing, Allyn showed me, was that when they found Jaryd's sweatpants they were turned inside out. Hairs were found on the clothing, but lab tests were reported to be inconclusive.

Allyn and his brother Arlyn document the story in their book,

Missing: When the Son Sets: The Jaryd Atadero Story. Charges of negligent homicide were considered against the Christian Singles Network group—whom Allyn considered friends—but not pursued. Larimer County sheriff's officials consulted with Wyoming mountain lion experts who believe it's likely Jaryd was victim of a lion attack, but Allyn isn't convinced.

CHAPTER 10

OLYMPIC NATIONAL PARK

*Blessed be God in his Angels and in His Saints.
O Holy St. Anthony, gentlest of Saints, your love
for God and Charity for His creatures, made
you worthy, when on earth, to possess miraculous
powers. Encouraged by this thought, I implore you
to obtain for me (request). O gentle and loving
St. Anthony, whose heart was ever full of human
sympathy, whisper my petition into the ears of the
sweet infant Jesus, who loved to be folded in your
arms; and the gratitude of my heart will ever be
yours. Amen.*

—prayer to St. Anthony, patron saint of the lost

THERE'S A RENDEZVOUS with the Grays and OMRT. Laura. Tanya Barba. Tanya's mom, Elaine Bock. Randy. Derek. James.

We talk of Bigfoot, though nobody here floats Bigfoot as a connection to Jacob's disappearance. Derek takes a drink of good bourbon from the open bar, and, again, Sasquatch is the elephant in the room. He's always the elephant in this room.

Derek's been researching the creatures for thirty years and in 2000 was one of three cryptozoologists to make the famous Skookum cast in the Gifford Pinchot National Forest between Mount St. Helens and Mount Adams. The Skookum cast may show where a Sasquatch lay on its side in the mud. Hair and seventeen-inch humanlike footprints were also found in the area. Whether you subscribe to Bigfoot's existence or not, Derek is a fascinating guy to have in your camp.

Randy's a believer. Or at least he doesn't have enough evidence to the contrary so as not to believe. Randy listens intently and laughs with everyone. Tanya tells stories of trying to keep up with Derek in the mountains. Derek is known for his trademark hiking shorts and high wool socks that he wears hiking all year, even in winter. Randy laughs often—it would be hard for an outsider to guess he's shouldering the weight of not knowing where Jacob is. Randy doesn't drink, but he doesn't let that keep him from enjoying the company of interesting people. Laura drinks wine and laughs, and it's clear she's glad to have the company of Tanya and her mother. Randy plugs in walkie-talkies to charge and checks his pack and looks at maps with Tanya and Derek. If this were a real bar, it'd be a good one.

The plan is to head out early, so I say good night to sleep in my tent outside. Everyone else is sleeping on bunks inside, but I like staring at the sky through the bug screen and listening to birds and the jets descending into Vancouver and Sea-Tac. I'm nearly asleep when I hear semi-automatic rifle fire, close. The next thing I hear is Derek, who has shoved open the door of the barn. "Everybody stay inside!" he yells. I can hear him chamber a round into his pistol.

The vehicle drives off, but it's unsettling. The shooter shot into the air, but they had the entire Olympic Peninsula in which to do it and they chose the Bigfoot Barn; an idiot could just drive into the forest a hundred yards away if you want to just squeeze off some buzzed rounds. Maybe they were just some drunk locals who didn't know there were people at the barn. Or maybe it was someone sending a message. Tanya and Derek have an idea, one of the searchers who may have been involved in the drug trade, but tonight there's no way to prove anything.

People have tried breaking into the barn before. Whoever it was is messing with the wrong crew—they'd be better off tangling with Sasquatch himself. At any rate, the excitement dies down, and everyone goes back to their bunks. I sleep in that Lapland of dream and thought, Bigfoot and Jacob.

Hell's Angels. Aliens from space. Russian mafia. Portals to other dimensions. Sex traffickers. Moonies. Body-part merchants. Aliens from the hollow earth. String theory. Satanic cults. They're as unlikely as Sasquatch, yet they're all Randy's "possible impossibilities." "I've looked from basic to extreme," he says. "I knew the stepdaughter of Jim Jones. She didn't go to Africa." We talk about David Koresh and the draw of cults. They don't seem like Jacob's scene, unless, Randy believes, he found the right one.

Anton LaVey, founder of the Church of Satan, had his Black Lodge compound in the sixties in Santa Cruz. It's on Randy's mind. "These people are so frickin' twisted."

Those things—motorcycle gangs, syndicates, and cults—are probably more likely in a wild vanish than being attacked by a black bear or a mountain lion, and less likely than stepping off-trail to go to the bathroom and getting lost. Or a widowmaker tree falling on you. And far less likely than slipping off a slick rock and falling off a cliff or into a river.

If a person crawled out of ice-cold water, a known survival technique is to bury yourself in a blanket of pine needles and forest duff, where you could succumb to hypothermia and be hidden from searchers. A rotten log is enough to hide a body. The forests of Olympic National Park and Olympic National Forest are a giant's hair shirt of downed trees.

Another thing in the cascade of possibilities of what happened to Jacob is another half theory Paulides raises, concerning a rash of men found drowned with levels of GHB—gamma-hydroxybutyrate—in their bloodstreams. GHB is a depressant pushed toward body-builders and partyers as a strength enhancer, aphrodisiac, and one of several substances listed under the heading "date rape" drugs. That bodies are pulled out of water with GHB—and usually alcohol, too—in their system is obviously concerning, but Paulides seems to be ambulance chasing and giving oxygen to a new conspiracy before he races along to the next one.

This is the kind of thing Randy thinks about most of the time. I can tell when he gets to forget. Little wedges of relief when he talks about tides and surf breaks, the turnbuckle suspension he designed into a remodel job he'd done recently, flipping a renovation he's got his eye on, the advantages of hard-back insulation versus fiberglass and recycled decking over wood. And breakfast—thinking about bacon is one of his preoccupations.

"You go out and talk to people about it and when I come home I'm so tired," Randy says. He far prefers the physical fatigue of long drives, hikes off-trail, and scrambles in the river to the mental and emotional variety of listening to psychics and well-meaning people with theories. "I'm numb to it. I've heard all the possibilities. I've heard it all. I process it, but when I'm alone I may have my issues. I just want to fall asleep. It's exhausting."

The psychic named Lauren swears in her vision that Jacob had been followed, that he was abducted. Randy Hall, Randy's PI friend, believes Jacob's vanish looks like "an abduction-type thing."

"It's all information," Randy Gray says. "Good or bad, it's infor-mation. I want to know all of it so I can filter through it." Bigfoot, UFOs, suicide, portals, cults—it's a lot to suffer. "I just want to find my boy, and we're gonna do things together. Good things. Just let him know I love him, that's it. Hang out with him."

*　　*　　*

This may be one of Randy's last pushes of the summer, and the only thing left now is more improbable bush. It takes everything I have to keep up with him as he crawls up riverbanks and squirrels over downed Sitka spruce logs flicked through the forest like overlarge pick-up sticks. We walk through fresh bear scat and over the beds where they'd just slept. We're clawed again and again by the ubiquitous and noxious devil's club. The root of the shrub is traditionally used for medicine to treat ailments from arthritis to diabetes, but the stems are covered in nettle-like spines that scratch through gloves and sleeves.

He'll say he's looking for clues. An item that Jacob carried. A wrapper from a candy bar Jacob likes. Initials carved into a tree. But I can tell it's an exhausting relief when he walks for hours and hours and doesn't find anything at all. It's a relief when he doesn't find his son's body. Randy entertains his mind with speculating about all the things Jacob might be doing right now.

Psychics—Laurie McQuary and perhaps others, their visions run together—see Jacob behind a waterfall.

We come to a thick meadow that was especially difficult to scan for bears, and Randy pulls out a Raid-can–sized compressed air horn and honks—if a bear is in the bush, the idea is it'll poke its head up. Hopefully it'll take off in the opposite direction. "I'm a bear!" Randy roars, daring another to stop him. Soon we come to a big downed Sitka spruce. One of the tallest living things on the planet, they can get to be three hundred feet tall, fifteen feet in diameter, and this one is close to that. It's angled along a ravine so that when Randy skips up it, he's gaining height above the ground. I watch him, and he doesn't look down, rather ahead. Higher, higher. It's natural to him that you go where your eyes go—he doesn't want to fall so he doesn't look down. It takes me three times as long to worry my way slowly up the log.

Randy has been doing these twelve- to fourteen-hour days for four months. We take a water break, and Randy talks about how his divorce with Laura four years ago was especially hard on Jacob.

We're sitting on a big Sitka spruce log. Randy nibbles at an energy bar and pokes at a bag of prunes, but taking a breather doesn't come naturally to him, and I have the feeling he's doing it for my sake. Randy prefers moving, because if he stops to rest he'll start thinking too much. "I didn't plan any of this," Randy says. "Jacob's my buddy. You think I want to be out here searching for my son?" It's like surfing, you have to be fluid and reflexive—if you overthink, you're in trouble. When you're moving, flowing, you're not thinking, you're sensing. I get the feeling that Randy sometimes thinks he should be *thinking* more, that the limitations of his mind are why he hasn't found his son.

The not-knowing. That's the mental and emotional cancer, the thing Randy can't see, can't control. Jacob Gray could be in TROTW—anywhere else but Olympic National Park or the Olympic Peninsula or Washington State. Or he could be pinned in some freak hydraulic in the Sol Duc River or under a log off one of hundreds of miles of trail. The not-knowing is mad-making.

In the world of the lost-in-the-wild, people soon find out that the circle is small. Randy has been consulting with the family of Zach Krull, the backpacker who went missing in the park just three days after Jacob's bike and gear were found. Zach's body was found by a hiker in July, and Randy has studied that case to see if any behavioral patterns can be applied to Jacob's disappearance. The left-behind are Randy's tribe now.

People hang on. Randy Gray's arms are shaking, but he is hanging on. I'm reminded of the Rolling Stones' song "Emotional Rescue," which is the kind of SAR the Gray family needs right now, in order to stave off the probability that Jacob's case will require a *recovery*.

Researcher and family therapist Pauline Boss, author of *Ambiguous Loss*, coined the term *frozen grief*. A pain that's like radiation, a slow cook at your nerves that might take many years to kill you. Boss claims that a family member missing to the unknown is the hardest thing a human being ever has to face.

Her book places Alzheimer's disease in the second category of *ambiguous loss*, opposite of a missing person in the wild, whereby a person is physically present but *psychologically* missing. My dad suffered Alzheimer's, and it was difficult, but his personality was still evident. He'd get lost in his own house and his tastes changed— he switched from beer to Dr Pepper, Tabasco to ketchup. But he still loved animals and old westerns on television. His sense of humor held almost up until he died. He was there. We could talk with him and enjoy his presence in the room, even as he slept. He was *there*. Mostly. Alzheimer's disease is hard on everyone, my mom especially, but I don't think it can come close to a child being physically vanished when it's unclear whether or not that child is dead or alive.

Laura Gray speaks of Jacob in mixed tense—sometimes present, sometimes past—as if he inhabits two worlds. Randy talks about Jacob in the present tense. He plans to motor down and up the coast, stopping to surf and sleep, then move on. He's gonna spend a couple of weeks at La Push, at the northwest corner of the Olympic Peninsula, where the Sol Duc River enters the Pacific Ocean (swiftwater specialists claim the chances of a body making it that far—nearly seventy miles—in the river are practically zero). Then he'll drive east, toward Jacob's original destination, Vermont, where Jacob's brother Micah serves in the U.S. Coast Guard.

We walk a dry creekbed that in high water drains into the Sol Duc River. Randy is smelling the air, which is shrouded by wildfire smoke, though he's trying to see if he can smell a corpse through it so he can cross the creekbed off his map. Randy Gray has overturned every boulder in the Sol Duc River. The creekbed ties into the river at a logjam, another that searchers felt was a "high probability area." Randy has already been here, swimming in and around it, several times, but the water level was higher, so this is new country. "When I'm not up here is the hard part," he says. "I'm a basket case. I'm not hunting for my son." Today is hot, which amplifies the smoke from the Canadian fires, and a swim is in order. He's excited to get back in the water, though I can tell he's a little sad to be leaving this place tomorrow.

"Jacob planned to go to Glacier National Park," Randy says. This is based on his Internet searches and things he'd said and written. "So I'm gonna go there and do some backpacking. Then he wanted to go to Badlands National Park." I tell him that's near where I'm originally from. "Are there big rivers there?" he asks. Yes, but not like Washington, I tell him. "Then I'll hike," he says.

Then Randy walks high up the log and gives me the universal surfer's *hang loose* sign of quivering thumb up, pinkie down. "Shockaaaa!" he calls. It's a sign of good energy, positive vibes, and gratitude. Hope. And with a transition from tree to water like Tarzan, he dives in, underwater fish-flash of skin and blue trunks. He stays down there, so comfortable underwater. It's cold and clear and he can see—he can see again that Jacob isn't there.

BEAUFORT
SEA

Fairbanks

Nome

BERING
SEA

Anchorage

GULF
OF
ALASKA

0   300
MILES

CHAPTER 11

NORTH AMERICA

Out of the kiva come
masked dancers or
plain men.
plain men go into the ground.
        —Gary Snyder, "Through the Smoke Hole"

JACOB GRAY HAS joined the foggy stratum of the hundreds or maybe thousands of people who've gone missing on our federal public lands. He's far from alone. How many people are missing in our wild places, the roughly 640 million acres of federal lands—including national parks, national forests, and Bureau of Land Management property? I have laptop folders full of wild vanishings—they pop up in my Internet alerts every day. There are cases, besides Amy Bechtel and Jacob Gray, that I quite literally think about several times a day—or I wake up semi-dreaming about them at night. Cases like fifty-one-year-old Mitchell Dale Stehling, who, in 2013, vanished from a short petroglyph-viewing trail near the gift shop at Colorado's Mesa Verde National Park. Morgan Heimer, a twenty-two-year-old rafting guide, who was wearing a professional-grade personal flotation device when he disappeared in 2015 in Grand Canyon National Park during a hike while his group took a break. Kris Fowler, the Ohioan who vanished from the Pacific Crest Trail in the fall of 2016. Don't forget Samantha Sayers, the tough twenty-seven-year-old who vanished August 1, 2018, on a solo hike on Vesper Peak in the northern Cascades of Washington. There are scores more stories like this.

The National Institute of Justice, the research arm of the Department of Justice, calls missing persons (and unidentified remains) "the nation's silent mass disaster." They estimate that on any given day there are between 80,000 and 90,000 people actively listed with law enforcement as missing. The majority of those, of course, disappear in populated areas.

Those figures are big and lumpy and far from exacting. If fewer people vanish in the wild, it stands to reason there would be a better accounting of them. But the government does not actively aggregate such statistics. The Department of the Interior knows how many wolves and grizzly bears roam its wilds, but has a hard time keeping track of visitors who disappear. The Department of Justice keeps a database, the National Missing and Unidentified Persons System, NamUs, but reporting missing persons is voluntary in all but ten states, and law enforcement and coroner participation is voluntary as well. So a lot of the missing are also missing from the database.

According to NamUs, more than 600,000 persons go missing in the United States each year; thankfully, many of these are quickly found alive. Sixty percent of the missing are male, 40 percent are female. The average age for a missing person is thirty-four. California—a huge, wild state with a mammoth population—has the most missing persons: 2,133. In contrast and not surprisingly, Rhode Island has the fewest with twenty.

Of course, not all of the missing vanish into the wild. But consider that the state with the most missing persons per capita is Alaska, with a staggering 41.8 people missing for every 100,000. Outside of Anchorage and Fairbanks, Alaska is pretty much *all* wild. You could say there are only 309 missing persons there, but when you consider its total population is only three quarters of a million people, that's an unsettling number.

Arizona is a wild state and is number two in terms of the missing per capita. No one professes to know for sure how many people are missing in the Grand Canyon because the government doesn't keep those records—or, like UFO research, they're hiding them. Oregon is third on the list. Washington, Jacob's PLS, is fourth on the list.

For some reason the state with the least number of missing persons per 100,000 is Massachusetts, even though neighboring Vermont is fifth on the list, right after Washington. The top ten round out with Maine, Wyoming, Hawaii, New Mexico, and Montana.

After the September 11 attacks, the Department of the Interior tried to build its own database to track law-enforcement actions across lands managed by the National Park Service, Bureau of Land Management, U.S. Fish and Wildlife Service, and Bureau of Indian Affairs. (The Forest Service is under the Department of Agriculture.) The result, the Incident Management Analysis and Reporting System, is a $50 million Database to Nowhere—in 2016, only 14 percent of the several hundred reportable incidents were entered into it. The system is so flawed that Fish and Wildlife has said no thanks and refuses to use it. That leaves the mathematical prognosticating to civilians and conspiracy theorists. People like David Paulides.

While on my way to research a missing runner in southern Colorado in May 2016, I reached out to missing persons activist Heidi Streetman, who lives on the Front Range not far from Denver. Heidi was working as an affiliate faculty member at Denver's Regis University, teaching research methods, and has done a good deal of research into missing persons in Colorado and also lack of awareness and advocacy in Colorado's government.

The grisly murder of ten-year-old Jessica Ridgeway in 2012 was the case that set Streetman on the trail of advocating for missing persons. Ridgeway was kidnapped in Westminster, Colorado; an Amber Alert was issued and her remains were found in a park in Arvada five days later. Streetman read Paulides's *Missing 411* books and became frustrated that there was no searchable database for families of the disappeared.

She approached Paulides about it, suggesting he lobby the government about a database—Paulides suggested she do it. In 2014, she floated a petition titled "Make the Department of the Interior Accountable for Persons Missing in Our National Parks and Forests." The verbiage with the petition exposes the issue that there does not exist a centralized registry or database of persons who have gone missing in our federal public lands. Records regarding circumstances surrounding a disappearance are only required if a missing person is found. "When remains of the missing are found, again, no records are required to be maintained," Streetman says. "Often, attempts to acquire information regarding the missing are blocked by bureaucratic red tape and/or demands for exorbitant fees."

I think of the grieving family member searching the Internet at two a.m. because they can't sleep. "The families have holes in their lives," Streetman says. "They have no answers, they should be able to log on any day of the year and see, hey, there was a search last week." She's also concerned that families become out of sight, out of mind for law enforcement. Few families are able to quit jobs and relocate, dedicate themselves to full-time searching—for them a database would be a powerful tool. To families it can seem like missing persons remain largely a law enforcement secret, but what's more likely is that they're in the dark, too. "Police officers could use it. The park could use it to identify problem areas." Streetman also points out that it could help when there's overlap between, say, Bureau of Land Management land and Tribal Land.

She's aware of other databases, like the Charley Project, which lists cold missing person cases, and NamUs, but they're incomplete. "I would look at the different databases online, but they're all incomplete. Someone might take interest for a while, then lose steam."

Information is power, even when the world of missing persons seems so bereft of it. "We need information so we can make decisions about our own safety before we decide to go camping in an area." It seems like a sophomore in computer science could build one before midterm. She thinks such a database would encourage public awareness regarding outdoor safety, more law enforcement investigations into cluster zones of missing persons, more information and updates for families of the missing, and, perhaps most important, continued search efforts for missing persons.

The petition has been closed after exceeding signature goals and has been delivered to Colorado Senator Michael Bennet's office. "His office generally ignores me," she says. "They don't respond to emails. He's busy running for president. But they had verified signatures and talked with the Department of the Interior [which oversees the National Park Service], so it sounds like we may not get a database, but they're looking at accountability on the parks, so it looks like they are taking it seriously."

In May 2016 Heidi Streetman and I met Paulides at a pizza joint in downtown Golden, just west of Denver. Golden is perhaps most famous as the home of the Coors Brewing Company, and the air smells of warm wort. The athletic Paulides, who moved from California to Colorado in part for the skiing, is right out of central casting for a detective film. His good haircut and Mephistophelean goatee are suspiciously dark for a man in his sixties. He's a former youth hockey coach and his son Ben played college hockey as a defenseman at Miami University in Oxford, Ohio. David has just come from a workout and can really put away the pizza.

Paulides is congenial, but it's hard not to feel like he's selling me an Escalade. "I don't put any theories in the books—I just connect facts," he says. I mention Bigfoot, and he discourages me from conflating Sasquatch and missing persons, but his website does that very thing—canammissing.com is part museum of disturbing missing-persons cases, including the gift shop, and part calendar of upcoming appearances at UFO conventions. It's tempting to dismiss Paulides as a crypto-kook—and some search-and-rescue professionals do—but his books are extensively researched. On a large map of North America that has become iconic in the missing-persons-in-the-wild underworld, Paulides has identified fifty-nine clusters of people missing on federal wildlands in the U.S. and southern Canada. "I used pins and maps as a policeman," he says. "Take a bank robbery—it's helpful to visualize patterns." You can order a copy of the map for $16.99. The link to purchase the map gets you to the Bigfoot Store, where you can also purchase a Bigfoot map, hats, and stickers.

To qualify as a cluster, there must be at least four cases; according to his pins, you want to watch your step in Yosemite, Crater Lake, Yellowstone, Grand Canyon, Mount Rainier, Rocky Mountain, and Olympic National Parks. But then, it would seem you want to watch your step everywhere in the outdoors. The map looks like a game of pin the tail on the donkey at an amphetamine-fueled birthday party.

Paulides has spent hundreds of hours writing letters and Freedom of Information Act requests in an attempt to break through National Park Service red tape. He believes the Park Service in particular knows exactly how many people are missing but won't release the information for fear that the sheer numbers—and the ways in which people vanished—would shock the public so badly that visitor numbers would fall off a cliff.

Paulides routinely complains about Freedom of Information Act requests whereby he's blocked by outlandish fees, and he's right. There are some FOIA requests that I've been waiting on for this book that were filed over a year ago.

We left Paulides and headed out for Mesa Verde National Park near Cortez and the Four Corners region with our cars full of camping gear. We stopped in Durango for food and checked into our campground in the park in the dark. Our campsite was at about 7,000 feet and we could see the galaxy and feel the ghosts of the cliff dwellers who vanished from here seven hundred years ago.

I was sent out west by *Outside* to cover the disappearance of the runner in the San Luis Valley, several hours south and a little west of there. Streetman, a spirited fifty-something who spent her childhood camping all over Colorado, was game to go along—she'd been following the case in the *Denver Post*. But she is beset with the cold vanish of Mitchell Dale Stehling, the case that pushed her over the top from a reader of Paulides's Missing 411 series to a legislature-hounding activist.

Stehling was a fifty-one-year-old Texan who vanished on Mesa Verde's Petroglyph Point Trail on a hundred-degree Sunday afternoon in June 2013. The Stehling case is one of the strangest I've heard, so on our way to the San Luis Valley it seemed appropriate to make a big swing west to the Four Corners region—where you can put a limb in Colorado, Arizona, Utah, and New Mexico at the same time—and check out the Stehling case on the ground.

It was late in the afternoon, and the Stehlings, from Goliad, Texas, were on a day trip with Dale's parents. Dale wasn't geared up for anything more than a stroll through the gift shop, but that didn't keep him from wanting to check out Spruce Tree House, which Dale, his wife, Denean, and mother could clearly see from the parking lot. The trail from the interpretive center to Spruce Tree House is more of a sidewalk—it's wheelchair accessible for the less than a quarter mile, where visitors can view the dwellings from the shade of the overhanging cliff. From the parking lot, Spruce Tree House looks exactly like the memory I have of Mesa Verde from my third grade textbook. Though it's high, at 8,000 feet at its highest point, the park itself is not huge as national parks go, at a little over 50,000 acres, and it has the feel of a living diorama. Most visitors who are reported missing are found—or find their own way back—within a couple hours. No park visitor has stayed missing since the park's inception in 1906.

Things would have remained normal if he'd just checked out Spruce Tree House then gone back to meet his wife and mother. But Denean describes her husband as curious, and despite a bad back it didn't surprise her that he wanted to venture on to see the petroglyphs, another mile away on a more strenuous, rugged trail. The Petroglyph Point Trail is rated moderate, but it was hot and Stehling didn't have water. But then, Dale was a Texan and, if not the elevation, used to the heat. The trail is a gradual rise that hugs the east wall of Spruce Canyon. There are some boulders and sandstone stairsteps, but nothing small children and the active elderly don't do every day. But on this afternoon most people relegated themselves to shady Spruce Tree House or the air-conditioned museum.

At the petroglyphs, where Dale was last seen, there is an intersection with an old access trail. It's been arrowed off, and it's pretty apparent it doesn't get regular use, but Denean believes he may have left the main trail. "If there was a way to get lost, Dale would find it," she says.

But even if Stehling had taken the wrong, overgrown path, he surely would have realized his mistake and backtracked. He had a cell phone with him, and rangers traced a partial ping, but subsequent calls to Stehling's phone went straight to voice mail. Maybe he collapsed in the heat. But rangers searched that area extensively on foot, with dogs, on horseback, and in helicopters with firefighting crews. They sent climbers rappelling down cliffy areas and collected a footlocker's worth of knapsacks, cameras, purses, wallets, water bottles, and binoculars—none of them Stehling's. Not one physical clue regarding to Stehling turned up during the search.

Missing persons tourism isn't a thing the National Park Service promotes, and it feels a little macabre to be in Mesa Verde to badger employees about the Dale Stehling head-scratcher. At 7:30 a.m. on Memorial Day weekend I ambushed Mesa Verde superintendent Cliff Spencer on his way into the office. Paulides had stormed in with a video camera team recently, and Spencer was understandably media shy regarding the disappearance of Stehling. No one wants to be infamous for overseeing the one cold vanish in the hundred-plus-year existence of a national park. "Do you have an appointment?" he asked. He knew I didn't.

"No," I said. Government administrators like to hide behind appointments, but there was no one else around and I must have seemed relatively harmless with just a pen and notebook. He exhaled, his hands on his hips, then waved me into his office. Pictures of his family surround the fifty-six-year-old Spencer's desk. I can tell from his expression that Dale's disappearance still pains the thirty-two-year Park Service veteran. "It's an occupational hazard," he said. "Never fails—I can't go to a cocktail party without someone coming up to me to ask about Dale. *How did he just disappear?* they'll say. I don't know what to tell them."

Mesa Verde, the largest archeological preserve in the country, is more museum-like than most western national parks, but there's also a palpable energy there, to the point that I could believe one of the theories that Stehling stepped through a portal to join the ancients, which is what some believe must have happened. The Ancestral Puebloans, who in 1200 AD numbered around 30,000, had mysteriously vacated the Mesa Verde area by 1280. The dwellings of Mesa Verde remained hidden for seven hundred years, when cowboys looking for lost cattle stumbled across it in the 1880s. The area is sacred to the Ute tribe, who, long after the first Anasazi inhabitants vanished, would not venture there. Visiting Mesa Verde does feel like trespassing.

Hundreds of years before the cliff dwellings were built, between 500 and 1100 AD, residents lived on top of the 8,000-foot-high mesa in pit houses, or kivas. They were hunters and farmers, growing, among other things, corn. In the floor of the kivas is found a *sipapu*, or hole that symbolized the portal through which ancient ancestors first entered the world from inner-earth, changing from lizard-like beings to human form.

Wildfires periodically uncover new archeological sites in the park. In 1996 a wildfire uncovered as many as four hundred new sites previously hidden in the pinyon juniper and scrub oak. Spencer showed me search maps and heli photos that they've painstakingly studied. Spencer still holds search-and-rescue training exercises in the area, just in case they come across a clue. "The thing that gets me," he said, "is in all my years with the Park Service, I don't recall five cases like this."

The day after Stehling went missing, Jodi Peterson, a writer for the *High Country News*, based in Paonia, Colorado, was in Mesa Verde researching a story on diversity in the national parks and profiling African-American superintendent Spencer. The temperature that afternoon was 102 degrees—she went for a hike anyway. Peterson was hiking the Petroglyph Point Trail when, just past the petroglyphs, she heard a man's "gravelly, weary" voice call out, "I need some help." It was difficult to ascertain where the voice came from; she figured whoever it was was talking to fellow hikers, and she kept moving down the trail. Later, ten minutes down the trail, Peterson put it all together—she hadn't seen any other hikers on the trail, and a man had gone missing yesterday. Her phone had no signal. She finished the loop and reported the voice to rangers, who immediately went to check it out. Nothing.

One of the rangers told Peterson there'd been reports of a man calling for help the day before. Perhaps it was Dale Stehling. Or the ghost of Dale Stehling.

I recently emailed Jodi Peterson to ask if she'd heard anything, or given Dale's vanish more thought.

Hi Jon, I check for updates on Stehling's disappearance once or twice a year. No trace of him has ever been found, as you know, and the case definitely does haunt me. My hunch is that he tried to take a shortcut downhill from the Petroglyph Panel where he was last spotted, and fell into a crevice in the cliffy terrain where he couldn't be seen. —Jodi

Peterson's take is the best there is. If that's true, a man wouldn't last long with no water in hundred-plus-degree heat. And Stehling would have been camouflaged in the tan-and-brown clothing he was dressed in. While it's doubtful Stehling slipped headlong into a sipapu to the primordial underworld, I am confident searchers looked in just about every crack and cranny on the east wall of Spruce Canyon.

Streetman and I hiked the same path Dale Stehling took the afternoon he disappeared. Near the end we came across an interpretive ranger and asked him about the disappearance and the search and if there's any new news. "I hadn't heard about that case," he said. "I've only been here for two years."

"That's another reason for a database," Streetman says. "When the new batch of seasonal employees comes in, they're not telling them someone's missing."

It's not likely that legislation would help the Stehling family, but an amendment to an existing law recently made it easier for volunteer search-and-rescue outfits to access federal wildlands with less red tape. The issue of permit approval is largely one of liability insurance, but the Good Samaritan Search and Recovery Act of 2013 expedited access for qualified volunteers to national parks and forests, and now they can search within forty-eight hours of filing the paperwork. More such laws would make things easier for searchers. Michael Neiger lauds Streetman's database and wants to take it further. He'd like to see a searchable resource that gives volunteers like himself the same information that government officials have—including case profiles, topo maps, dog tracks, and weather.

Streetman and I headed east, along the thirty-seventh parallel, to the San Luis Valley. The thirty-seventh parallel is known as America's Paranormal Highway and runs through the UFO hotspot of the country. There are many documented cases of people vanishing here. I was there to look into the vanishing of Joe Keller.

July 23, 2015, was the eve of Joseph Lloyd Keller's nineteenth birthday. The Cleveland, Tennessee, native had been spending the summer between his freshman and sophomore years at Cleveland State Community College on a western road trip with buddies Collin Gwaltney and Christian Fetzner in Gwaltney's old Subaru. The boys had seen Las Vegas, San Francisco, and the Grand Canyon before heading to Joe's aunt and uncle's dude ranch, the Rainbow Trout Ranch, in the San Juan Mountains in southwestern Colorado.

The ranch is in Conejos County, which is bigger than Rhode Island, with 8,000 residents and no stoplights. Sheep graze in the sunshine; potatoes and barley are grown here and trucked north to Denver. Three new marijuana dispensaries in the tiny town of Antonito lure New Mexicans across the nearby state line.

Conejos—Spanish for "rabbits"—is one of the poorest counties in Colorado. It's also a helluva place to get lost. While its eastern plains stretch across the agricultural San Luis Valley, its western third rises into the 1.8-million-acre Rio Grande National Forest, which sprawls over parts of nine counties. Go missing out here and your fate relies, in no small part, on which of those nine counties you were in when you disappeared.

Joe, a competitive runner, open-water swimmer, and obstacle-course racer, and Collin, a member of the varsity cross-country team at Division I Tennessee Tech, had been running together often during their trip. Neither was totally acclimatized to the altitude—the ranch sits just below 9,000 feet. Joe was a bit slower than his friend. He had suffered from asthma as a three-year-old but had kicked it by age twelve. The workout would be routine: an hourlong run, likely along Forest Road 250, which bisects the ranch and continues into the national forest, following the Conejos River upstream.

Joe left his phone and wallet at the ranch house. He wore only red running shorts, blue trail shoes, and an Ironman watch. Shirtless, with blond anime hair and ripped muscles, he looked more like a California lifeguard than a Tennessee farm kid.

Four thirty p.m. The friends started out together. Neither runner knew the area, but old-timers will tell you that even a blind man could find his way out of Conejos Canyon: On the south side, runner's left, cattle graze in open meadows along the river. On the north side, ponderosa pines birthday-candle the steep tuff until they hit sheer basalt cliffs, a prodigious canyon wall rising 2,000 feet above the gravel road toward 11,210-foot Black Mountain.

As the two young men jogged by the corral, one of the female wranglers yelled, "Pick it up!" They smiled, and Joe sprinted up the road before the two settled into their respective paces, with Collin surging ahead.

The GPS track on Collin's watch shows him turning right off Forest Road 250 onto the ranch drive and snaking up behind the lodge, trying to check out three geologic outcroppings—Faith, Hope, and Charity—that loom over the ranch. But the run became a scramble, so he cut back down toward the road and headed up-river. A fly-fisherman says he saw Collin 2.5 miles up the road but not Joe. Collin never encountered his friend; he timed out his run at a pace that led to puking due to the altitude.

No Joe. Collin moseyed back to the ranch house and waited. An hour later, he started to worry. When Joe didn't show up to get ready for dinner, Collin and Christian drove up the road, honking and waiting for Joe to come limping toward the road like a lost steer. At 7:30, a small patrol of ranch hands hiked up the rocks toward Faith, the closest formation. By 9:30 there were thirty-five people out looking. "If he was hurt, he would have heard us," re-called Joe's uncle, David Van Berkum. "He was either not conscious or not there."

"The first twenty-four hours are key," says Robert Koester. Koester was consulted on the Keller case and noted that, like most missing runners, Joe wasn't dressed for a night outside. Plus, he says, it wouldn't have been unusual for a young athlete like Joe to switch from run to scramble mode. "Heading for higher ground is a known strategy for a lost person," he says. "Maybe you can get a better vista. And based on his age, it might just have been a fun thing to do."

Around ten p.m., the Van Berkums called the Conejos County Sheriff's Department, and Sheriff Howard Galvez and two depu-ties showed up around midnight. It was now Joe's birthday. At this point, the effort was still what pros call a hasty search—quick and dirty, focusing on the most logical areas.

It was a warm night, and everyone still expected Joe to find his way back at daybreak, wild story in tow. That morning, as ranch employees and guests continued the search, Jane Van Berkum alerted Joe's parents—Zoe and Neal. Zoe and Jane are sisters, originally from Kenya; their family, British expats, left the country in the 1970s. It took the Kellers and their seventeen-year-old daughter, Hannah, less than twenty-four hours to get to the ranch from Tennessee, flying into Albuquerque, New Mexico, and renting a car for the three-and-a-half-hour drive north.

The family arrived at two a.m. In the morning, at six a.m., the professional search began: starting at the point last seen, the ranch's big ponderosa pine gate, a deputy fire chief from La Plata County named Roy Vreeland and his Belgian Malinois scent dog, Cayenne, picked up a direction of travel, which pointed up Forest Road 250. More dogs arrived from Albuquerque—and identified different directions of travel or none at all. Additional firefighters drove over from La Plata County. Everyone on the ground—as is largely the case with search and rescue—were volunteers.

There was nothing to go on. In that first week, the search engaged about fifteen dogs and two hundred people on foot, horseback, and ATV. An infrared-equipped airplane from the Colorado Division of Fire Prevention and Control flew over the area. Collin's brother Tanner set up a GoFundMe site that paid for a helicopter to search for five hours, and a volunteer flew his fixed-wing aircraft in the canyon multiple times. A guy with a drone buzzed the steep embankments along Highway 17, the closest paved road, and the rock formation Faith, which has a cross on top. A $10,000 reward was posted for information. How far could a shirtless kid in running shoes get?

But after several days, volunteers began going home, pulled by other obligations. The few who remained did interviews, followed up on leads, and worked teams and dogs. But the search was already winding down. "We had a very limited number of people," one volunteer told me. "That's fairly typical in Colorado. You put out calls and people say, 'Well, if he hasn't been found in that time, I have to go to work.'"

The absence of clues left a vacuum that quickly filled with anger, resentment, false hopes, and conspiracy theories. A tourist with a time-stamped receipt from a little gift shop in nearby Horca swore she saw two men on the road but later changed her story. A psychic reached out on Facebook to report a vision that Joe was west of Sedona, Arizona. There was even a theory that he'd been kidnapped in order to have his organs harvested and sold on the black market. "We feel like he's not in that area, he's been taken from there," Neal Keller would tell me months later.

"I'm a scientist," Koester says. "I'm fond of Occam's razor." That's the principle that the simplest explanation usually holds true. "You could have a band of terrorists tie him to a tree and interrogate him. Is it possible? Yes. Is it likely? No."

Two weeks after Joe's cold vanish, Alamosa County undersheriff Shawn Woods, who had been called in to assist by the Colorado Bureau of Investigation, told Neal Keller about a tracker he knew named Alan Duffy. Duffy, a surgical assistant, became interested in bloodhounds when his twenty-one-year-old brother, David, disappeared in the San Gabriel Mountains in 1978; he was found dead of gunshot wounds six weeks later. Duffy has since taken his dogs to search JonBenét Ramsey's neighborhood and to track stolen horses in Wyoming. Calling in Duffy was a wild card, as are so many things in a case like this.

On August 15, Duffy loaded three-year-old R. C.—named after Royal Crown Cola, on account of his black-and-tan coat—into his Jeep and drove three hundred miles from Broomfield, Colorado, to the Rainbow Trout Ranch. A deputy gave him a scent item, one of Joe's used sock liners. "That's as good as underwear," Duffy said.

Duffy will tell you that bloodhounds are out of fashion. "They fart and they drool," he said. They're susceptible to disease, they die young, and you can't let them off a lead under any circumstances.

"Everybody wants a shepherd," he says. But going old-school has its advantages. "Who's gonna find you? It's not a shepherd. It's not a Mexican Chihuahua. It's not a pig. You know how they say a great white shark can smell a drop of blood in water five miles away? That's a bloodhound."

R. C.'s trigger word to sniff for a living person, as opposed to human remains, is *find*. For search-and-rescue assignments, R. C. wears his orange harness, with Duffy holding the lead. After four hours of searching, Duffy switched R. C.'s harness to his black collar and told him, "We're gonna go gizmo," the dog's cue for cadaver mode.

Four and a half miles up Forest Road 250, at Spectacle Lake— a murky pond, really—R. C. circled, tugged at vegetation on the bank, bit at the water, then jumped in and sat in the shallows. "He wouldn't leave," Duffy said.

Duffy wasn't convinced, necessarily, that a body was in the lake, and he explained that scent is drawn toward water and believed that there was a corpse somewhere nearby. Rain or critters could have deposited cadaver material in the lake, enough to set off alarms in R. C.'s snout. But at four and a half miles from Joe's point last seen, the lake was at the far end of the ground game's probabilities. Duffy offered up a few more scenarios, some of which upset the Van Berkums—such as when he told them that R. C. had picked up human-remains scents under buildings on the ranch. But with few other sources of help, desperation had led to Duffy. "At least he was trying," Joe's mom, Zoe, told me. "He could have been right."

Continued searches in August turned up nothing. Neal Keller was commuting back and forth between Tennessee and Conejos County, searching every moment he could. In October 2015, when he and the sheriff were no longer on speaking terms, he urged the county commissioners to provide more help, including a dive team to search Spectacle Lake. "I, as the father of a missing boy—my only son, actually—would like to have as much resources as could possibly be made available," he told the officials.

Keller was feeling the stress. He lost fifteen pounds from hiking and scrambling in the altitude. Just before Thanksgiving, he, David Van Berkum, and a small posse spent two days searching the snow-covered scree west of the ranch. It was the area that seemed most logical, but it's mean terrain. "We went in there because that area was likely the least searched," he told me. No Joe. Keller would have to spend the long Colorado winter still not knowing.

The canyon now belonged to the snowmobilers and coyotes. Next season's fly-fishers and ranch guests wouldn't show up in any numbers until the snow melted in spring.

On February 4, 2016, Keller went to Denver to attend a ceremony for the inaugural Colorado Missing Persons Day. With families of the missing gathered around them, legislators passed resolutions creating the annual event. Keller stood in the capitol, listening as his son's name was read aloud. It was one of three hundred.

In April of that year, two Antonito men had been reported over-due from a camping trip to Duck Lake, less than three miles southwest of the Rainbow Trout Ranch, during a spring storm that dumped two feet of wet snow. Teams were called in from Mineral and Archuleta Counties, along with the Wolf Creek Ski Area ski patrol, based a hundred miles west on Highway 17. One of the men managed to struggle back to Horca; the ski patrol eventually found the frozen remains of the other.

The search had also resumed for Joe. Earlier in May, more than thirty volunteers, including Keller, Collin, and eleven dogs from the nonprofit Colorado Forensic Canines, had spent about a week crisscrossing Conejos Canyon. The mission was to either find a needle in a haystack or to significantly reduce the probability that the youth was in a 2.9-mile radius of the point last seen.

The May search for Joe Keller was organized by the Jon Francis Foundation, a Minnesota nonprofit that helps families with loved ones missing on public land. This search for Joe turned up no sign. But bushwacking off the Duck Lake Trail, about three and a half miles southwest of the ranch, Keller and Gwaltney came upon a sleeping bag, a cook pot, a tarp, and some bug spray—the gear of the lost campers.

Streetman and I camped in a campground along the Conejos River operated by the Rio Grande National Forest. The campground is across the road from Spectacle Lake, which is really a pond, where Duffy told me R. C. hit hard, indicating that Joe Keller was in there, or at least molecules of him were. The woman who was the volunteer campground host reminded me no fewer than four times that she kept a loaded Glock 9mm in her trailer.

Around the campfire Streetman told me about the two encounters that made her a believer in Bigfoot. "I really wonder if some of these disappearances are due to cryptoids," she said. The first interface happened in January of 1983, at the Keystone ski area, when bears would be deep into hibernation. It was nighttime, cold, and she and her friend Laura had just finished ice skating on the pond near the shuttle area. They walked down toward a creek and saw a man on all fours, either puking into or drinking from the creek. "We called to him, 'Hey, are you okay?'" The man stood up, groaned, and walked toward them. "He was about a foot taller than us," she said. "Barrel shaped. We could see he had hairy legs." She realized it wasn't a hairy man in short pants—it wasn't a man at all. "It was whitish gray color. I said to Laura, 'I don't think this is a person.'" Lights from the shuttle area illuminated the creature. "No ski jacket, no pants. No protuberance like a bear's face. 'Run!' I yelled. I had to drag Laura to get her feet going."

The creature had walked along the creek in deep snow where there was no path, no trail. "I went back the next day to look for footprints. The snow was disturbed, but no footprints. It wasn't a person, it wasn't a bear. It wasn't brown or black like you always hear about."

At that time, the eighties, Bigfoot was limited to the Pacific Northwest. Now, of course, there are reported sightings all over North America, but Heidi swears she saw a cryptoid before cryptoids were a Colorado thing.

Her second encounter happened in Redmond, Washington's Marymoor Park, the largest park in King County, in 2007. She was walking her dogs along the Sammamish River on a March afternoon when she heard a nightmarish scream. She never saw the source of the scream, but says it was a loud, nasalized roar. Her dogs were terrified. The creature screamed again and knocked on wood, moved through the brush and knocked again and again. Streetman could hear large teeth clacking together, and the creature threw pebbles at them. She believes there may have been a group of them, and they were studying her and the dogs. "I reported the incident to BFRO [Bigfoot Field Researchers Organization]," she said, "but I never heard back from them."

The next day we drove and hiked and tried to get a sense of the scope and scale of Joe's situation. Then I said goodbye to Streetman, who went back to the Front Range to continue her petition and teaching work. I was now the lone stranger in the red rental car, parking on the side of the road to run the same gravel Joe Keller did the evening he disappeared, trying to observe a similar something as Joe.

My main duty that trip seemed to be to try and catch Sheriff Howard Galvez and convince him to talk with me. Several times I dropped by his office, which is connected to the Conejos County

Jail. I became almost friends with the jailers, who were skilled at shielding their boss from nosy media like me. One sunny afternoon I went looking for Sheriff Galvez and found him outside the Conejos County Jail, on the north side of Antonito, directing inmates in orange jumpsuits as they planted flowers. He wore jeans and a gray canvas shirt, with a pistol on his belt and reading glasses propped on thick salt-and-pepper hair. It was clear that he'd rather orchestrate landscaping details than talk with the press, and I can't blame him. His department has taken a beating on Facebook, Websleuths.com, *Dateline*, and in the *Chattanooga Times Free Press*.

"Are you a good reporter or a bad one?" he said.

"I'm not a reporter," I said. "I'm a writer."

He looked as me like I was slippery, took a breath. "It's been a rough year and a half," he told me. After the Keller search and the hunt for the Duck Lake campers, he said, "I don't agree that I should be in charge of search and rescue on federal lands. I'm thinking of going to the state senators and saying I'd like to be backed out of that, because I don't have a ninety-million-dollar budget." The starting salary for his five deputies is $27,000. "It'd be more effective, I think," he said. "We're a small department, a small community. I hear stuff like, 'I can't go, my equipment broke down.'"

Frustration between Galvez and Keller had continued to roil. "We had dogs, hikers, aircraft," the sheriff said. "Horseback, drones, scent dogs, cadaver dogs. We had so many resources, it was unreal. When searchers took a break, he criticized all the resources. Cut everybody down.

"This is an ongoing investigation for a missing person," he continued. "We have no evidence—he's just missing. It looks more like that than anything else. Over eighteen, you can run away all you want. If Joe was to call us, show me some proof he's okay, I'd close it up."

It matters tremendously where you happen to disappear. If you vanish in a municipality, the local police department is likely to look for you. The police can obtain assistance from the county sheriff or, in other cases, state police, tribal police, or even university law enforcement. If foul play is suspected, your state's bureau of investigation can be requested to get involved. Atop that is the FBI. With the exception of the sheriff, however, these organizations don't tend to go rifling through the woods unless your case turns into a criminal one.

But all those bets are off when you disappear in the wild. While big national parks like Yosemite operate almost as sovereign states, with their own crack search-and-rescue teams, go missing in most western states and, with the exception of New Mexico, Alaska, and Hawaii, statutes that date back to the Old West stipulate that you're now the responsibility of the county sheriff. And it matters a great deal where inside those states you fall off the map.

"There are no federal standards for terrestrial search and rescue," search-and-rescue researcher Robert Koester says. "Very few states have standards. A missing person is a local problem. It's a historical institution from when the sheriff was the only organized govern-ment." And when it comes to the locals riding to your rescue, Koester says, "There's a vast spectrum of capability."

Take Rio Grande National Forest: It has just one full-time law-enforcement officer, who wasn't given clearance to talk to me, which was odd because I could wave to him from across the parking lot.

Ranger Andrea Jones of the 377,314-acre Conejos Peak district, where Joe disappeared, did lament to me that sometimes she discovers cases in the weekly newspaper. "On occasions when we initially learn about a search and rescue in the forest from the local media," she explained, "it's difficult for us to properly engage, communicate, and offer available knowledge or resources." Imagine a system so analog, so trapped in time, that they use the weekly newspaper as communiqué. Smoke signals would be more effective.

On August 4, 2015, after Joe had been missing for thirteen days, Sheriff Galvez pulled the plug on the official search. What had begun as a barnyard musical was now a ghost story. The river—already dropping quickly—had been searched and ruled out. Dog teams had scratched up nothing. Abandoned cabins had been searched and searched again. "I mean, we checked the pit toilets at the campgrounds—we did everything," Galvez said. "We even collected bear crap. We still have it in the evidence freezer."

Galvez had been elected sheriff only nine months earlier, and while he had years of law-enforcement experience, he had no background leading search-and-rescue operations. One responder told me that by the time he arrived on the second day of searching, tension was already rising between Keller and Sheriff Galvez. Keller felt that Galvez wasn't doing enough; Galvez felt that Keller was in the way, barking orders and criticizing his crew.

A set of remains had been found on the Rio Grande National Forest, a hundred miles north, in Saguache County. I wanted to see if the findings had anything to do with the Joe Keller disappearance. I'd been following the case of missing mountain bike legend Mike Rust, who was fifty-five when he went missing from his off-the-grid Saguache County home under suspicious circumstances in 2009. Bones found on the forest in January 2016 caused some to wonder if they belonged to Joe Keller. But a distinguished chainring belt buckle found with the remains made the discovery most likely to be Rust, which DNA later confirmed. Saguache County sheriff Dan Warwick, who is bearded, bald, bespectacled, tattooed, and quick with a laugh, told me he was close to closing the Rust case. Indeed, in June of 2016, Saguache County resident Charles Gonzales, already in prison in Canon City for unrelated weapons and eluding-authorities charges, was collared with Rust's first-degree murder as well as other charges, including tampering with a corpse.

"You're like 'what the hell—everyone's dead up here!'" says Warwick. Bodies do seem to go missing and appear with odd regularity in the San Luis Valley. Over in Costilla County, on Wild Horse Mesa, Mike Walczak, who was sixty-two, left the cabin stove on and vanished. His truck, wallet, and dog were found untouched. On Valentine's Day in 2007, twenty-five-year-old Casey Berry vanished in the same county, near Blanca. Same with retired pastor Jack Gordon, age seventy-seven, who seemed to have been raptured in 2008. In 2011, Angelica Sandoval disappeared from Alamosa County. Custer County currently has three active cases in the wild. There are more.

Cindy Howard, director of the Custer County Office of Emergency Management, over the mountain from Saguache, says that it matters in her territory which cell phone tower gets pinged, even if the victim is in Custer County but hits a tower in Saguache County. Some counties will operate under a memorandum of understanding—MOU—with neighboring counties and federal land managers, which means they'll respond with appropriate resources with the best efficiency, even if they're not in the same county jurisdiction. Then again, some counties don't. SAR is a county responsibility, and the sheriff approaches it as he sees fit. That said, many if not most of the county SAR teams—volunteers—are professional in every sense of the word except payday.

Volunteer coordinators are quick to point out that searchers need to be on worker's comp insurance too, a big factor—authorities are in danger of lawsuits if they encourage uninsured volunteers to search. On December 14, 2019, Tim Staples, a thirty-two-year-old English teacher and nine-year volunteer with the San Bernardino County Sheriff's Department West Valley Search and Rescue Team, died when he fell on an ice chute on Mount Baldy while searching for a lost Irvine man, fifty-two-year-old Sreenivas "Sree" Mokkapati, who had vanished on December 8 after becoming separated from a group of hikers.

When the dogs and volunteers start to go back to their lives and the aircraft return to the hangar, a missing-persons search can look eerily quiet. "For a lost person, the response is limited to five days on average," Neal Keller, Joe's father, told me. "There needs to be a plan for applying resources for a little bit longer."

The Keller family hired two private investigators, who turned up nothing. Zoe Keller told me that it was a waste of eight hundred dollars a day; one of the investigators told me he'd never had a case with less to go on. The reward was raised from $10,000 to $25,000 and then to $50,000, but as David Van Berkum said, "There just isn't a sniff of anything."

But wherever you are, once a search goes from rescue to recovery, most of those resources dry up. Like Randy Gray, Neal Keller was left to search for his son—and pay for it—nearly alone.

Before I left Conejos County, I took another run up Forest Road 250. I parked at a turnout in front of a ponderosa pine with Joe's missing-person poster stapled to it, then jogged down to the point last seen and tried to retrace his run. Based on the varying sniffer-dog evidence, some figure that he ran up the road a ways, rounded the first or second bend, then got into trouble. I slowly shuffled upriver. A truck or SUV passed every three minutes or so. Locals told me that in July, the traffic on Forest Road 250 is even heavier. Someone would have recalled seeing Joe if he'd stayed on the road—the friendly kid from Tennessee would have waved at a driver. After my run, I rinsed my face in Spectacle Lake; according to Duffy, R. C. could tell him I'd been here.

On Wednesday, July 6, almost a year after Joe Keller disappeared, John Rienstra, a search-and-rescue hobbyist and endurance runner—and a former offensive lineman for the Pittsburgh Steelers—discovered Joe's body in a boulder field below the cliff band.

"I heard there had been a lot of searching for two and a half miles," Rienstra said. "I started looking for rapids, caves—cliffs, of course—and right at two and a half miles, there is a place to pull off the road, and there were cliffs close by. It took me about an hour to get up there to the base of the cliff, and I went left until I ran out of room. Then I turned around and went back toward the ranch on the base of the cliffs and found him." The area was too rugged for horses or dog teams. When the Colorado Bureau of Investigations came to retrieve the remains, they packed horses in as far as they could, then had to reach Keller on foot.

Joe's body was 1.7 miles as the crow flies from the ranch. Searchers had been close. In November 2015, Keller and David Van Berkum had come within several hundred yards. "I regret not searching there on the twenty-fifth of July," Keller told me. "That's where I wish I'd started. What part of here would take a life? It's not the meadow on top; it's the cliff."

"Hindsight is always twenty-twenty," Jane Van Berkum wrote me recently. "But since there was a blanket of snow, I am not sure they would have found him even if they had chosen to go higher. But it is painful to think that they were that close." Every day, she said, she and her husband had searched for Joe as part of their ranch activities. "I have sat on the cliffs many times since he went missing and scanned below over and over, and I never saw him," she said. "That tortures me."

The preliminary cause of death was blunt force trauma to the head. Jane told me he also suffered a broken ankle. It appears that Joe scrambled up and then fell—perhaps the lost-person behavior laid out by Professor Rescue, Robert Koester. Occam's razor wasn't as dull as it had seemed for most of a year.

Still, Joe's death remains a mystery to his mother. "The events do not fit for a one-hour run before dinner," Zoe says, "after they had just driven twenty-four hours straight to get to Rainbow Trout Ranch." The boys hadn't slept in over a day. Joe had just split wood with his uncle David's father, Doug Van Berkum. She can't see her son running up to the canyon rim—she insists that he did not like heights and was not a climber. "There is something we still do not know about what happened, is how I feel about it."

CHAPTER 12

SANTA CRUZ & THE OLYMPIC PENINSULA

...because the loss is confusing, people are baffled and immobilized. They don't know how to make sense of the situation. They can't problem-solve because they do not yet know whether the problem (the loss) is final or temporary.

—Pauline Boss

A HUMAN BODY weighs slightly more than fresh water. While a fatter body will float slightly better, all bodies will sink in fresh water; Jacob Gray carried very little fat on his body. I had assumed his wool coat would have been an anchor in the water, but that's not necessarily true, especially for a strong swimmer like Jacob. "A three-pound wool coat is not the same as three pounds of lead," explains Tate Thompson, an Escanaba, Michigan–based swiftwater-rescue veteran. The bigger issue, he says, is hypothermia. "In water, your temperature loss is twenty-five-times faster than in air. In moving water, [the loss] it's two-hundred times—the moving water washes the heat away."

But let's macabrely assume Jacob hit his head on a rock and succumbed to hypothermia and drowned. Thompson says that a body in that river is unlikely to make it a mile downstream, and even if Jacob swam and struggled for some distance, it's highly unlikely he'd float two miles before sinking and staying on the bottom until anaerobic bacteria in the digestive system bloated the body enough to float to the surface. Even if a body was trapped under a rock or a logjam, *something* would, before long, appear on the surface. But then, Thompson says, nylon will pull apart, while natural fibers—wool—will stay intact.

The DNA tests from the pair of plaid Burnside brand Bermuda shorts in Jacob's size found by volunteer searchers about a mile downstream of where the bike and gear was found came back inconclusive—the shorts had been in the water too long and any DNA material on them had been compromised by exposure to the elements. The shorts could have belonged to Jacob. Mallory says they're a style that Jacob would have worn; furthermore, Mallory's husband, Anthony, thinks they're like the shorts he gave Jacob for Christmas. Wyoma, Jacob's grandmother, says he did have those shorts; she remembers seeing similar shorts in her bathroom. The shorts also could have belonged to almost anyone else; they were sold at Kohl's department stores and found near a popular swimming hole. Even if they are Jacob's, their presence alone isn't much to go on without other evidence or clues: Jacob wasn't in them when they were found.

Surface current is very different from current at depths. Even if the surface of the Sol Duc was boiling with current, there would have been almost no current on the bottom. This means Jacob's body likely would have reappeared on the surface very close to where he went under. If a body does travel some distance downriver, it's usually after it surfaces due to the stomach gases bloating the person into a human buoy. That would have been nearly a week after Jacob's gear was discovered, and by that time the Sol Duc was being searched with intent by myriad eyeballs.

Randy is confident he's searched under every rock in the river for at least twelve miles downstream. Having seen him search, I'm confident he has, too. Then there are the scores of fishers and kayakers and swimmers and picnickers who are drawn to such a photogenic river in a popular national park. "I think I'm over the possibility he's in the river," Randy tells me. He's still supportive—and grateful—of people who want to continue to focus their energies there, but he's looking panoramically elsewhere. Which is an infinitely harder search. The river gave the search focus. Parameters. Limits. Now the search will go from a tiny line on a map of Olympic National Park to the entire map of North America.

"One," Laura tells me, "he would have been exhausted when he got there." She's talking about where he may have climbed back out of the river, downriver from where the bike and trailer were found. "Two, he probably would have been hypothermic." The science agrees with this. "Three, Jacob would bury himself."

I'm puzzled with this, the macabre image of a missing person burying himself. I asked Michael Neiger, who has become a friend whom I can call on a whim and pick his brain. Neiger is something of a bearded Wikipedia of missing persons and search and rescue. "That's a known technique for survival," Neiger says. But volunteers and dogs would have found his body, searching both banks between the water and the two roads—they would have stepped on him.

"One thing still missing are his crampons," Laura says. Which point up. "He could be up there being a Revenant up at the top. He could be in Alaska. It's a real mind fuck.

"They just won't go there," she says. "As humans we care. As a corporate entity, you're a number." Laura doesn't wallow in what authorities aren't doing; rather she travels to the Sol Duc as often as possible to continue the search. Usually she meets up with Tanya—the two have become close friends.

"You can't shake it off—you're left in this no-man's land," Laura says as she surveys the landscape—treescape—of Olympic National Park for the umpteenth time. She's still able to smile and laugh, and I can sense that even if this is Jacob's end, she's proud of her son for having chosen such a wild and beautiful place. "If he does show up I'm gonna shoot him in the knees."

There's a lot of "meanwhile" for a family of missing persons. The Oregon coroner's office called Randy about a couple cadavers— or parts of cadavers—found in Oregon. The office called him to ask for dental records and DNA. They were waiting six to eight months for DNA results to get back from the lab. One body wore size twelve shoes—much too large for Jacob, who wore a nine and a half or ten. The other, at China Beach, near the Oregon-California border, was a foot and partial leg and a hand. The body parts were from a young, white male. China Beach is off Highway 101—the same highway that winds through the northern border of Olympic National Park, but it's five hundred miles south of where Jacob's bike was found. In these cases lines on the map get traced a long way. Randy did send the coroner dental records and DNA. I could tell from talking with him that it ate at him. It seemed to me an unnecessary worry—Oregon is off the charts when it comes to missing persons. Randy would much rather hear from law enforcement that someone reported seeing a young man who resembles Jacob, not that they found a cadaver with big feet who had no more in common with Jacob than that they were young and white.

My friend Chris Solomon has written for *Outside* about the phenomenon of human feet—still in shoes—washing up on the shores of the Salish Sea in Washington and British Columbia. It's not just a couple of shoes, it's dozens. Some come in pairs, some don't. And disarticulated feet have been a thing for decades, though fairly recent changes in the foams of athletic shoes have caused the newer feet to float. Some of the feet have been matched with accident victims. Some have been thought to have drifted all the way from Japan following the Kyoto nuclear disaster.

Randy's familiar with the strange story of the feet washing up in shoes, but now every time a beachcomber finds a New Balance with a foot inside, it's another catalyst for another bad dream.

Search days bleed together and are sometimes forgotten, sometimes remembered by a single event. One afternoon during a foot search near the Sol Duc, a two-hundred-foot-tall deadfall Sitka spruce nearly crushes Tanya. She laughs the incident off back at the Bigfoot Barn, though she could feel the whoosh of wind the tree made and the shudder of the earth when it hit. The next evening Randy and Tanya come back from a hike above Sol Duc Falls proverbially looking like they've seen a ghost.

The day was hot, high eighties. They were headed back to the truck after a long day of combing through country they'd been in, but wanted to check out more thoroughly. Both were doing that tired downslope lope that is most efficient after a long shift. They came up to a big Western hemlock, over two hundred feet tall and six feet in diameter. Far from unique, but the tree split the route, and the path of least resistance was for each of them to take a different side. They circumvented left and right respectively, headed for a typical convergence, when they both felt a sudden pressure drop in their chest. "The temperature spiked twenty degrees," Tanya says.

"It was like we walked into a sauna."

"It's like all the air was sucked away," Randy says. "It was *weirrrrrd*." But just two steps further and things were cool and oxygen-rich again. Tanya insists it was not a breeze but felt more like they walked through a wall. They backtracked and hesitantly tried four times to recreate the event but couldn't.

Tanya Barba contacted Laurie McQuary, an Oregon psychic whom she'd worked with before, and asked her if what they walked through could have been a human spirit. McQuary responded that it must be a vortex area "that souls pass through when done here on earth," and that her experience was "unique, positive evidence."

Vortices are one of the more prominent paranormal explanations for missing persons in the wild. Some Native Americans talk about similar things, and the ancient pagan Celts told of "thin places," a Lapland between heaven and earth. "I don't know what it was," Randy says. "I'll show ya."

The next day Randy took me to the area to try to recreate the barometric and thermal phenomenon they'd experienced—he couldn't find the exact tree.

CHAPTER 13

FRONT RANGE, COLORADO

The only thing two dog handlers will ever agree
on is that the third one is doing it wrong.
                                           —*SAR saying*

IT'S DOWN TO Alan Duffy, nickname Duff. "You don't need a hundred people to find someone," Duff says. "You just need one or two dedicated ones." There are five of us in the Jeep if you count Duff, the bloodhounds, and the dead girl named Molly. It's a bluebird, sunny Front Range day, April 2017, and the Jeep is warm inside so that the smell is tear-making and I can't find the window toggle so I'm getting hotboxed. "Settle down, settle down," says Duff, who is wearing a dirty golf cap over his bald head. He isn't a tall man, and with his patchy white beard he resembles—another handler told me—a leprechaun. Duff glides his liquids when he speaks so that "Settle down" comes out "set her down, set her down!"

Molly is a child-sized mannequin with dark hair and blue eyes that Duff has infused with his proprietary recipe of pig blood, human hair, fingernails, toenails, a little urine. Molly—Duff's version of a CPR training dummy—is stuffed into an old military duffel bag. I'm riding shotgun while a hound drools in my ear. The smell in the Jeep—an old white Liberty—is so thick that I taste the glandular funk of bloodhounds and dog piss and slobber. I'm also smelling—tasting—cadaver. "Some describe it as an earthy smell, like moldy grass clippings," says Duff. "I think it smells like passion fruit." So maybe I smell cadaver, but also the dogs underlying the plug-in Glade air fresheners clipped to the vents on the dash. I haven't had lunch, and I don't care to ever eat again.

We park in the lot of an industrial complex, and five minutes later Duff's tethered to his newest charge, Mindy Amber, a ten-month-old red bloodhound puppy, by a twelve-foot nylon rope tied to a leather weight-lifting belt around his waist. It looks like some sort of water-skijoring setup. We duck the fence and are headed toward the weedy shore of Hidden Lake in the Denver suburb of Westminster, north of downtown. Rush hour traffic on US 287 and Interstate 270 is winding up so that Duff nearly has to shout over it. "The guy in that house over there called the cops on us last time." He points across the water to the far shore, maybe a hundred yards, to a neighborhood where people don't want corpses on their waterfront. "Says we'd give the neighborhood a bad reputation." A Westminster Police Department black-and-white cruises by—today the officers must think it's just an odd old man walking his dog. But you don't really walk a bloodhound in the standard sense any more than you walk a rhinoceros. A bloodhound on a search is liable to break free and follow a scent into traffic or over a cliff. A blood-hound follows its nose, which doesn't play in the dog park. Their droopy ears and wrinkled muzzles are by design. They form a sort of veterinarian's "cone of shame" that scoops and cultivates invisible scent molecules into the dog's turbo-powered olfactory system.

"Gizmo!" Duff says. That's Mindy's cue for cadaver mode—her assignment is to find a body. Or three, which is how many Duff believes are in here. "Go check it out, check it!" But first the lanky pup finds something else—a dried dead carp on the bank. "Leave it! Leave it, come on," Duff says.

He starts training his puppies at six weeks, no time to lose. "Some handlers wait a year, but that's just time wasted." Duff explains that bloodhounds are susceptible to bloat, which often kills them as young as eight years old. He gives the lead a tug, and she drops the old fish and makes her way to the water. This is training, and he wants her to focus—what she should be after is out there, at the bottom of the lake. "Gizmo! Atta girl."

She splashes in, and soon the sixty-pound hound is up to her elbows and stifles in the lake, sticking her muzzle in, duck-style, biting at the mud and silt and rocks at her submerged paws. "She's tasting cadaver," says Duff. The case—which had been reported in Denver media as a botched drug deal turned violent—is cold and nearly twenty years old, and authorities aren't sure where the bodies are, let alone in the lake. We stare at the middle like we're waiting for the Loch Ness Monster—or the man in the house on the other side who called the cops—to emerge. Duff's convinced cadavers can give off scent molecules for a century, even longer—even above water and underwater. "Scent works like gasoline in water, it rainbows outward," he says. R. C., a veteran now at four years old, waits in the Jeep—he's already hit on this case and it's the pup's turn to win. Duff beams as if his granddaughter just scored a goal in peewee soccer. "She's not thirsty, she's not getting a drink." He's got a relaxed hand on her lead, and he squints from the glare off the water. "She tastes cadaver. There are three bodies in there," says Duff. "You can't get the average dog handler to believe it. It's unexplainable, so there's no explanation." He pauses and looks at the water like a seer. "One of these days a body is gonna come floating up. The case is twenty years old—the dog is still hitting and she's never been here."

Duff studies these cases and advocates for more dogs on them, and bloodhounds at that. These old and cold cases don't become irrelevant for him. In fact, the opposite is true. This is ideal real-world training. "They're weighted down. Wrapped separately. See how she's biting the bottom?" Three of Duff's dead bloodhounds "hit" the lake in the same way. There was Suzie Q, Babes, and his horse-thief-chasing D. C. Annie. "One of these days something's gonna wash ashore." Eventually Misty Amber turns back toward the bank and her desiccated carp. "She's happy," says Duff. "She's sayin', 'I'm done. I wanna play. I did what I was supposed to do.'"

Duff assisted with a hip replacement that morning—his day job as a surgical technician sends him on-call at all hours all over the Denver area, so the traffic doesn't faze him. Spending all his vocational time in surgery, I wonder if it's affected his sense of smell and that's why he doesn't mind the hell-houndy atmosphere in the Jeep, but every time one of them farts—silently—he looks at me and says, "That's why people don't want a bloodhound. That's why people want a shepherd."

Dog people can and do argue which breeds make the best SAR scent dogs, but technology hasn't come close to the abilities of a bloodhound. A dog fitting the description of a bloodhound is first noted in literature in *Historia Animalium* by the third-century Roman scholar Aelian. Five centuries later, Belgian monks refined the breed. Every monastery in Europe had a kennel, and the hounds came to be called *blooded hounds* because of their aristocratic blood. They were an early status symbol, employed in hunting deer and boar. Since the Middle Ages they've been used to track people. In pre–Civil War America they were used to find runaway slaves. They're almost as iconic as Paul Newman in the movie *Cool Hand Luke*, wherein bloodhounds chase escaped inmates through timber and swamps. My dad was born and raised in Fort Madison, Iowa, where the high school mascot is the Bloodhound, since Fort Madison is home of the Iowa State Penitentiary.

When the article I wrote on Joe Keller dropped, I got some notes of support, but also some notes from readers who were upset. This was mostly search-and-rescue people who feel I misrepresented their efforts or didn't give them enough credit. The most slighted were the dog handlers. This is a paragraph from Chuck Wooters and his German shepherd Quake, members of Search & Rescue Dogs of Pennsylvania:

> Also, I take exception to the addition of the boasting by the Bloodhound handler on "who's going to find you, not a shepherd." Please look at the hundreds, if not thousands of K9's working in SAR, as well as protecting our streets in America and our troops in war zones by tracking down bad guys, drugs, bombs and missing people. Obviously this handler is out of touch but please don't misguide the public with this misinformation, especially since he had no success in finding Joe. Yes, we all felt that the most likely scenario was that Joe was somewhere nearby.

Duff doesn't have a smartphone or a computer—he relies on a pager. Unlike every other tracker I've talked with, Duff doesn't record GPS tracks of his dog missions. He doesn't care what anyone else thinks of his hounds' findings. It's enough for him to know the dogs proved out. After all, the dogs know.

Mindy Amber is named in honor of a 2010 possible homicide case down in Woodland Park that Duff and R. C. have been working for the last year. Mindy Lee is the victim and Amber is her daughter. We're spending the afternoon giving the hounds a little shakedown exercise before we take them down to Woodland Park on Friday to meet up with Mindy Lee's mother, Vicki White, and Bobby Brown, the bail bondsman and retired homicide detective made semi-famous on the reality show *Dog the Bounty Hunter*.

I'm a little carsick, and I have a strong stomach. R. C. slathers my left ear with drool. The hounds belong, really, in the bed of a pickup truck with a dog box or a camper shell. Something you can hose down at the car wash once a week. But then Duff couldn't sing to his dogs. "Set-her down! Set-her down!" Duff is a bit of a dog himself, and he fairly bathes in the smell of bloodhound and bloodhound fart and the bad perfume of chemical air fresheners covered in dust and dog hair. R. C. and Mindy Amber hate motorcycles, and when they thunder up behind us, Mindy Amber barks sharply and pisses the cargo area like a little circus elephant. These are not pets.

"Shepherds might be fine dogs, but they aren't tracking dogs—they're guard dogs," says Duff. "It's what law enforcement used before they had tasers. They let loose a couple German shepherds." Duff is dressed like the little guy on *MythBusters*, but we're more like *History Detectives*, backtracking over cold cases, dog on dog, hound on shepherd, in an overlay that Duff calls his *exercises*. The tenor of his voice changes when he mentions shepherds. "You can put lipstick on a pig, but that don't make it kissable."

This morning, Duff schooled me on cadavers and gave a thorough show-and-tell lesson of his homemade training tools. I was surprised. For a dead human, I was expecting a variation on roadkill deer. "Human is human," he says. "Animal is animal." Instead, cadavers emit death esters, a disorientingly sweet smell. But to me it's less passion fruit and more like fish sauce mixed with Lucky You perfume. "Most dog handlers don't go to the extent I do to train the dog," says Duff. I ask him why he named the mannequin Molly. "I don't know," he says.

We go through a show-and-tell of sniffing and touching and guessing. He unwraps a two-foot-tall skeleton of a child. This can't be real, though I don't know that it *isn't*—it sure appears real. It's been packed in some sort of goo. Duff smiles. "It's a Halloween decoration." The dogs don't necessarily need the visual authenticity, but hey, why not. Some of Duff's samples are forty years old—he made them when he moved to Colorado in the early eighties, soon after his brother was found dead. "Ninety percent is all hog product. I invented this system," says Duff. "I'm the only guy in the States who has as much hog product material as I do."

He gives a trickster's grin. "When I die the police are gonna be taking a look here." Besides the hog, there's the human hair and nail clippings. He shows me a chunk of human femur bone that a friend at a medical research lab gave him. Duff gets his pig blood—the closest thing to human blood makeup—at the Asian grocery store down the street. Hair is easy to come by at the local Great Clips, and fingernails are free at the manicure joint on the corner. He uses tampons, too. Where do you get those? I ask. "Just people I know," he says. "They know what I use 'em for." Some stuff is wrapped in plastic and duct taped. Some is stored in a Walgreens bag. There's something in a bag marked BIOHAZARD from his day job. He shows me a Vicks VapoRub jar with cadaver jelly in it. "The scent of the Vicks can't mask it," he says. He likes to set materials in plaster of paris—"environment," he calls it. One tool he shows me is white PVC plumbing pipe sealed with a cap. The pipe has turned red from the cadaver sauce leaching to the outside. "Nothing is airtight," says Duff.

"They're not gonna find a piece of bone," he says. "They're gonna find the *environment*." By "environment" he means whatever material the body has begun to decompose into: soil, carpet, plywood, cement, a vinyl purse socked full of plaster of paris–infused faux-cadaver. Duff uses a purse to plant in a public place—say a bus station—and sees if the hound can hone in on it. Pity the purse snatcher who races home with Duff's dummy purse. He also has a generic-seeming flashlight that he can plant inconspicuously inside a building—it's full of Duff's cadaver sauce, too.

I get a little queasy from smelling cadaver. Duff is just getting warmed up. "Here, smell this one," he says, holding up another something untoward. It's clear he can go on all day, and it occurs to me just how sheltered I'd been that I'd never smelled a dead human before—at least I hadn't known it. And then to find out dead human smells like passion fruit, or at least a urinal cake. I think about the lime the townspeople spread around Miss Emily's house in Faulkner's "A Rose for Emily" and now I'm thinking, why bother.

It's not like Duff would be out golfing or fly-fishing if I hadn't come to town. This is what he does—he goes to work and he works his dogs. His reality is human tissue, whether it's in surgery or in the field. It's what he's done since 1978 when he went searching for his brother David in the San Gabriel Mountains near Azusa, California. Duff is one of nine brothers and three sisters. I ask if he's Catholic. He laughs. "No, but Mom and Dad—every Saturday night." When David went missing Duff took the family dog—a Heinz 57 mix—and hiked the mountains searching for his brother, with no results. Some kids stumbled upon David's body six weeks after he'd disappeared. "He was covered in maggots," Duff says. "The coroner put him in a canoe. I don't know why, but the coroner wouldn't even allow him in the mortuary." Duff doesn't wince, but I do. "He was moving—the maggots. The only thing not eaten away was a bone graft on his ring finger." A year later Duff got the right tool for the job, his first bloodhound, Suzie Q. "It takes a hound," he says.

For months I'd wanted to see R. C., the four-year-old black-and-tan bloodhound that is Duff's current flagship dog, work. R. C. worked the Joe Keller case five different times. We cram into the Jeep and zip from Duff's home and kennel in Broomfield to the public space a mile from his house Duff calls the Killing Fields.

We're headed into the field for an afternoon of training. Duff is too excited to eat lunch, and I don't have much of an appetite after the morning of smelling cadaver samples as if I were shopping for a Mother's Day gift at hell's Bath and Body Works. When not working a live mission or a historic case, this is where he trains, where he's hidden his homemade cadaver concoctions, buried in the weeds and under rocks.

Our prize now is a Mr. Clean bottle filled with one of Duff's corpse potions. "Gizmo! Check it out, R. C. What do you wanna do? What do you wanna do."

R. C.'s tail is up. "He's happy," Duff says. "Now he's working it." He sweeps back and forth the trail like a minesweeper or a divining switch. Watching the hound and his handler work seems both scientifically pragmatic and, well, a little magical perhaps, like a psychic. Duff in his golf cap. "He likes to work side to side." A woman and a Labrador jog up the path toward us and Duff chokes up on the lead and commands R. C. to sit. R. C. doesn't pay any attention to the Lab.

"Okay, R. C.," he says when she passes. "Work it. Check it, check it!" R. C. cost $1,000. He's not neutered, and Duff is considering breeding him with Mindy Amber. I have to walk at a pace that is almost a jog to keep up. Then R. C. stops abruptly to take an enormous dump. Back online, they sweep a trail intersection. "Work it, R. C., work it." On the far side of the little lake, we're in the cottonwoods and cattails. "R. C., where is it? Check. What do you want to do, R. C.? What do you want to do?"

R. C. walks over two dead ten-pound carp dessicating in the grass—unlike Mindy Amber, he couldn't care less. He's interested in the prize, the bottle full of cadaver sauce Duff had hidden under a rock. R. C. hadn't been here in six months.

R. C. finds his man—Mr. Clean. The event is celebratory, and Duff turns to R. C.'s reward. "I let him be a dog," says Duff. "That's the prize." The big galoot romps and rolls in the cattails in the swampy shallows. Back on the bank he enjoys a horse turd.

"I don't treat my dogs," says Duff. "That's the first thing an attorney will ask, 'Do you treat your dogs? What do you give 'em, M&Ms, Snickers, what? Oh, he did it for the treat.' So I don't do it. I just let them be a dog as their reward."

R. C. wallows like a hippopotamus for a few minutes. Then Duff commands, "Okay, R. C., take me home."

"It's not tracking—it's called mantrailing. It's not called a sniffer dog—I'm embarrassed when I hear that." But his hounds have found lots of stuff. Duff's dogs have detected cancer. "A friend of mine wondered why my dogs kept sniffing his ass—I told him he better get a rectal. Sure enough." His hounds have collared a graffiti artist. "We found his stoop—he confessed before he knew what we were after." His dogs even busted a cheating spouse. "I didn't want to do that one, but finally, okay, we smelled their bed and the dog took me to a car always parked down the street. I had to tell him, 'Yeah, your wife's got a friend.'"

It's 5:30 a.m. on Friday and we're headed down Interstate 25 to Woodland Park, to try to catch a murderer. I need coffee, but the air in the Jeep makes it unappealing. Duff gives a comprehensive homicide and missing person tour of the Front Range on the nearly two-hour drive as the sun comes up over the prairie to our left. Between Colorado Springs and Woodland Park, he pulls over and unloads R. C. in order to demonstrate their car tracking technique. The general concept is that bloodhounds are capable of "Interstate" tracking scents that may be months, even years old. This seems the biggest stretch for me, but Duff isn't the only believer. Duff worked with Colorado and Wyoming brand inspectors some years ago in order to track some stolen polo horses from Northglenn to

Laramie County, over a hundred miles. They stopped at each over-
pass to let the hound, D. C. Annie, work for direction. Apparently
there's more to it than K9 spin-the-bottle. After eight hours the dog
led them to a polo grounds near Cheyenne. To me it looks a lot
like R. C. is simply sniffing trash along the highway. R. C. wants
to climb an embankment through thick weeds, so Duff loads him
back into the Jeep. "You get the idea," says Duff.

We rendezvous at the Woodland Park McDonald's with Vicki
White, her husband, Jay Cribbs, and Bobby Brown, perhaps the
most famous bail bondsman in the country, who grew up in Colorado Springs. Bobby is just a few days away from appearing on a
podcast with Nancy Grace that may blow this case open. There's
also a good chance that it'll be met with podland crickets. Bobby
Brown does pro bono investigative work on cases he finds intrigu-
ing. "This woman is the best detective I've ever worked with,"
Bobby says of Vicki. "It's a shame she has to do her own police work
for her own daughter."

On the books, Mindy Lee's case was closed, declared accidental,
a combination of drugs and cold. Duff, Vicki, Jay, and Bobby feel
there's either a serial killer or a ring of related murders in Teller
County. Another woman was found just a few blocks away from
where Mindy Lee was found—her case was ruled hypothermia, too.
A man was found decomposed and upside down in the chimney of
an abandoned cabin. The head of Teller County Search and Rescue's
daughter was murdered three years ago. There are others.

This is the Colorado the tourism board does not want you to
think about. Statistically Colorado suffers the third-highest rate of
drug-related crimes in the country. The legalization of marijuana
seems to have done nothing to mute drug crimes. In fact, it would
appear that the opposite is true. Methamphetamine, opioid abuse,
and the heroin trade seem to be thriving. These little towns at the
joint between the high plains and the Rocky Mountains serve as

micro-hubs, with access to I-25, I-70, and lots of places to hide in the hills. The Teller County–El Paso County line is a dead body dumping ground, and in some cases authorities argue over which side of the line a corpse is found.

The problem is, we can't be sure Mindy Lee was murdered. The police closed the case as hypothermia brought on by an accidental overdose. Grief-stricken mothers are driven to excessive behaviors. But I agree that several things just don't square in her case, and that's why the group is together. Bobby Brown wants Duff's dogs to take one more pass at the crime layout—a bloodhound testimony.

On Thanksgiving 2010, thirty-three-year-old Mindy Lee was reported missing, having allegedly jumped from a vehicle carrying friends and her four-year-old daughter Amber at 1131 Parkview Place and run across the frozen ground barefoot.

"Stevie Wonder coulda found her," says Bobby Brown. He's pointing to the shed behind the athletic field behind the high school. Five days passed between the time Mindy Lee was reported missing and when the school cop found her body. It seems most strange to Bobby Brown—and I concur—that they didn't find Mindy sooner. There wasn't much snow and Teller County Search and Rescue—including bloodhounds—would have honed in on the shed, just a couple blocks from where she purportedly jumped out of the SUV.

We're in the neighborhood behind the high school. They were told by a Woodland Park Police Officer they'd be arrested if they entered school grounds with Duff's dogs. A dog on the scene in 2010—a bloodhound from Teller County Search and Rescue—hit a house with a blue roof ten times. A psychic also said she had a vision of Mindy's footprints here. R. C. has fact-checked the Teller County dog before, according to Duff, to a T. "He knows more than I know—that's why you have to let him lead."

Vicki and Jay had gone to Conejos Canyon in the search for Joe Keller. Vicki felt a connection with Neal, whom she'd met at an event in Colorado Springs for families of missing persons. She and Jay were with Duff when Duff explained to the folks at the Rainbow Trout Ranch that R. C. believes there is cadaver material buried under a shed on the ranch grounds. Duff was asked to leave and not come back. Of course he was still free to run the hounds on the national forest that surrounds the ranch buildings, but he was no longer welcome at the ranch.

While Duff and R. C. work the athletic field and the property behind it, Bobby Brown takes out a cardboard box of eight-by-ten crime photos and starts spreading them out on the tailgate of Jay's truck. They're graphic. Vicki walks around the corner, sees them, gasps, and spins away. Bobby Brown doesn't flinch. "Look at her feet," he says. "You think you could run across this ground in winter and your feet still look like that." There are no marks on her feet. Her blood contained eight times the lethal limit for methamphetamine, and a bag of meth was found in her vagina.

"I'm not saying she didn't dabble in it," Vicki says. "But she wasn't an addict. Her teeth were perfect." Even in the crime photos she has the teeth of a toothpaste model. While she was still missing, the police presented Vicki with a pair of shoes they said were Mindy's—Vicki, who saw her daughter every day, claims there's no way those ugly sneakers were Mindy's. Vicki also claims that when her body was found, her daughter was wearing someone else's old clothes. The coroner claims Mindy Lee was dead within four hours of her disappearance. "So where was she for five days?" asks Bobby Brown. "They had her on ice?"

Mindy's phone pinged in Texas, where a lot of the Colorado drug trade traffics. A psychic described a bathtub. Mindy's body was discovered at the shed just minutes before another large search of the area was about to commence. "Ten minutes before the major search is supposed to start," says Bobby Brown.

"Something happened here," says Duff.

Mindy Lee's friends lived in a rural housing development called Sherwood Forest, just outside of the village of Divide, so we head the seven miles up the road, west, in the direction of Cripple Creek. This is where Mindy's acquaintances lived and where Mindy's car was left. The psychic prompted them to check a basement here.

There's an alleged drug house on a road named Will Scarlet. "R. C. laid in the yard," says Duff, "Amber stopped there." *Here's the man in the golf cap again, just casually exercising his pets.* They wouldn't have been more conspicuous if he'd been playing bagpipes and shooting bottle rockets. If nothing else, the field day has validated things—the bloodhounds have validated things, at least to Duff and Bobby Brown—so that Bobby Brown has more ammo when he talks with Nancy Grace.

Like Wimpy, the Popeye character, Duff trades in hamburgers. "Once in a while I get a tank of gas," says Duff. "Maybe they'll buy me a hamburger. I don't do this for the money. In forty years I've maybe made twenty dollars." We end the day at Wendy's, Duff's favorite joint. He likes the burgers fine, but the real draw is that— pro tip—they offer dog burgers for fifty cents each. They're old burgers that have been sitting on the grill, drying out. And though he has a zero-treat rule, the burgers don't count.

"The evidence is still there," says Duff. "Today was an interesting day. To actually see a dog reproduce what he did six months ago, a year ago, is actually pretty factual. He had a purpose—go to the shed. He was pulling me. He checked out where the body had been dumped. He sat at the fence, then tried to go through it three times. That was one heckuva scent the victim put out. She musta really suffered. She knew she was gonna die."

"Dogs have their bad days, just like people. Today R. C. had a great day."

A hundred miles north and west from Woodland Park is the historic mining town of Silver Plume. I'd been thinking about it because for some time I'd been intrigued by the case of Keith Reinhard. Largely, I think, because he was a reporter—a writer—for the *Daily Herald*. The forty-nine-year-old sportswriter moved to Silver Plume, Colorado, in 1987 as a reset. Silver Plume is a living ghost town butted up against the mountain. He opened a little antique shop and lived in an abandoned Catholic church. I moved back to the west as a reset, too, and my wife—when she was still my girlfriend—and I moved into an old church in Kemmerer, Wyoming, another living ghost town. I felt something of a connection to him. So I was more than game when Duff suggested we head up-country to look for the writer.

"It's just like if your favorite was apple pie—you know what it is." Duff is talking about cadaver scent to a dog. "Could it be as weird as the ghost of the person is what they're picking up on? It sounds strange, but who knows? Maybe their spirit is trying to tell you something." Another thing that makes what he does mysterious is that a bloodhound can't tell you who the cadaver belongs to, only that there's cadaver present.

The mountains shutter the sun, and it gets dark early in that canyon. The story is that Reinhard took off late—4:30 p.m.—with the goal of hiking to the top of 12,275-foot Pendleton Mountain, on the south side of town, across Interstate 70.

What's strange about it is that Tom Young had disappeared from here just a year earlier. Young ran a bookstore out of the same space Keith rented to sell antiques. Young and his dog, Gus, went for a walk and never came back. When Keith went missing he was working on a novel based on Young's story. But earlier that summer, '88, Young and his dog were found on the mountain, both with bullet holes in their heads.

"Search dog coming through!" calls Duff. An older woman stood at her window, not sure what to make of the scene. She didn't seem to mind enough to step outside.

Duff took the fall line up and through a couple bands of snow until the going—without snowshoes—got too tough. "Let's go over to the road," he said. Good idea. I turned with Mindy Amber and headed downhill. At the woman's yard she backed up and slipped her collar. Fuck! She had all of the Arapaho National Forest to escape into. Hell, she had all the Rocky Mountains to go missing in. Forget that she's a thousand-dollar dog—Duff had invested ten months of training with mannequins and cadaver sauce and historic overlays in the field. I ran back toward Duff in hope he'd know what to do. Luckily, Mindy Amber only wanted to see what R. C. was up to and ran toward her partner and Duff.

We traded dogs so I could get a sense what handling a seasoned pro is like. We hike up the same fire road that Reinhard said he was taking the afternoon he vanished. At the first elbow Duff sits on a rock. "I'm just letting the pup rest a little," he says. "You and R. C. go on up ahead." At a cliffy cut below the road R. C. squares up his stern and lifts his nose above the drop-off. He's marking. "Yep, he's picking up cadaver," says Duff, still breathing hard after resting Misty Amber. "Might be Keith Reinhard, could be a hobo who wandered off the interstate."

Duff lives twelve miles from the infamous JonBenét Ramsey house in Boulder. When the dust from the initial law enforcement investigations settled on the ground, Duff took different dogs to the neighborhood and put them up against what he read in the papers. It would be inconceivable now for us to not swing by the neighborhood, seeing as how we're coming down from the mountain and—

hey—it's right there. "Someone else lives there," Duff says. I have more images of traipsing through someone's yard, Duff calling, "Search dogs coming through," and that's pretty much what would happen. "I think the house is on the historical register," he said. For some reason that made me feel a little better.

We parked on 15th Street, a block away. "We're just gonna walk our dog." I was hoping he wouldn't suggest I take Mindy Amber and risk her slipping her collar and running into Boulder traffic, which he didn't. Just as unfortunate in my mind was the image of stomping over flowers at a historic crime scene with a puerile bloodhound while the family who live there just want to enjoy a sunny Saturday afternoon.

Duff unloaded R. C. as incognito as he could—R. C. certainly appears to weigh the same as Duff. "Let's go gizmo—gizmo, R. C.!" I held back a bit, and when Duff and R. C. crossed to the far side of the street, I stayed on the east side, pretending to have something important to do on my phone. There was a woman and a kid inside the gated yard that did not have a fence or gate when the crime happened on Christmas in 1996. John and Patsy Ramsey moved away soon after the murder. The house was bought by the daughter of televangelist Robert Schuller. She and her family lived there for about two years, and now the place appears to be something of a pine-tar baby they can't sell, even though it's listed at a million dollars under market value.

I watch R. C. nose into the shrubbery. I see Duff wave and call, "Hi, ma'am, just walkin' my dog." When you have to claim you're just walking your dog, you're not just walking your dog. And I'd become more aware than ever that you don't just walk a bloodhound—it walks you. When Duff and R. C. got to the border of the neighbor's yard to the north, Duff waved at me. This means that R. C. hit on a scent there. A twenty-five-year-old scent. From where R. C. hit you can easily see the basement window that was an alleged ingress/egress for the killer. As we walk—ever so slowly—down the block, Duff and R. C. on one side, me badly acting on the other, I see the woman walk into the street and watch Duff and R. C. I consider how often this must happen—you could never have peace, living in the most notable murder house in the country. Wouldn't you pour your coffee and think, *What fresh hell reminder will we have today?*

"Violent death gives off a different body chemical," says Duff. "He's probably also picking up the negative scent of the person who did the killing."

We weren't finished. I'd hoped that now we could just circle back to the Jeep, but Duff wanted another pass at the house. The woman was waiting. "Do you live in this neighborhood?" she asks. "If not, I'm calling the police."

"We're just doing some historical scent tracking," Duff Duff-splains.

"I don't want to hear it," the woman says, holding up her palm. "People live here."

"All right, we're leaving," says Duff. "You have a nice evening."

Cheap yoga mats smell like my grandfather's 1972 Volvo sedan. Struggling into my homely downward dog always brings a memory-triggering scent that takes me back to age four. I'm concerned for when a smell triggers Duff's cadaver sauce, and it's started to happen. A woman's cheap perfume on the elevator. The blue stuff they use in airplane lavatories. The Glade plug-in in my sister-in-law's Toyota. The dogs in the Jeep have hundreds—thousands—of scent memories in their hard drives. Invisible as ghosts. *Gizmos.* Duff and I point out good places to hide a body. I ponder how appropriate it is to get this excited about the missing. I guess I appreciate that the hounds are that excited about it.

As the sun drops and we make the short drive back to Broomfield,

I can sense that Duff is thinking of another historic case to work, to show me. He's worked hundreds of cases and, conceivably, we could be out here for weeks. And though I have to take Duff's word and others that the hounds *hit* on these places, I find myself drawn in. This beats metal-detecting on the beach any day.

I thought the prompt *gizmo* was odd when I'd reported on the Joe Keller case. *Why gizmo?* I ask him now.

"It's a name no one would probably ever use," he says, as if it were obvious.

One thing is for certain—when Duff does enter the Happy Killing Fields, his wife will never be able to sell this Jeep. She'll have to salvage it, have it melted down. R. C. and Misty Amber will still be able to find the iron ingot it makes.

CHAPTER 14

PACIFIC NORTHWEST

Hope is a horrible thing, you know. I don't know who decided to package hope as a virtue, because it's not. It's a plague. It's like walking around with a fishhook in your mouth and somebody just keeps pulling it and pulling it.

—Ann Patchett

CHRISTMAS DAY IS an oddly pleasant day to fly. In December 2017, Randy picks me up at the San Jose airport in his gigantic Dodge and Arctic Fox slide-in camper—he slows outside the terminal, and a traffic cop yells at us as I throw my bag in the cab and jump in. Randy smiles and waves—there are few things Randy can't fix with his smile and wave, and if that doesn't work he throws in a *shaka*.

He gives me the tour on the way back to Santa Cruz. We drive by the homeless camp along the railroad tracks. Randy says the number of homeless in Santa Cruz has exploded in the last few years. We drive by his old house, the house Jacob grew up in. "Best house in Santa Cruz," Randy calls it. "Look, we had our own palm trees." It's 4,000 square feet on three-quarters of an acre. There's a pool. "Best house." Randy and Laura still own some Thomas Kinkade paintings that he'll cash in one day if he remembers.

The sun has burnt through the coastal fog in Santa Cruz. "Sun's out, school's out," Randy says, because they'd played hooky on those days to surf. Randy has been living with his sister, Judy Baldwin. She's visiting her kids in Nevada, and Randy and I take a couple days to gear up at Judy's for the trip to the Olympic Peninsula. The town smells like briny saltwater, fish, and marijuana smoke.

He introduces me to friends and takes me surfing. When I say Randy takes me surfing, I mean he allows me to follow him into the famous Steamer Lane, while I cling to a kelp bed and watch him drop in with his surf buddies. I will learn later that a total grom like me should have had his ass kicked for even paddling out into the local's way, but it was okay because I was with Randy Gray.

That's not to say anyone pities Randy, and therefore lets his friend from the Upper Peninsula clog up their surfing. Randy is respected in Santa Cruz, one of the old-school locals. A surfer, a builder, a father. One thing I found remarkable is that so many of his surf-community friends will light up when they see Randy, shake his hand and pull him into a bro-hug. But they hadn't heard about Jacob. His closest friends, Kim, Jon, and Joey Thomas, the reknowned surfboard shaper, know, of course, but hordes of locals have to hear about it for the first time while I'm with Randy, and I see them break into tears. *This shouldn't happen to a guy like Randy Gray.*

"Yeah," Randy tells them, "I've been pretty much living up in Washington, traveling back and forth. We're going back up tomorrow to check out some places Jacob might have wanted to visit." It's a plan. It's proactive. The faces of old friends say *this isn't good, this likely won't end well, but Randy Gray is no typical father.* In the short time I'm with Randy in Santa Cruz, he hears from three old friends he runs into along the beach who've had sons die from drug overdoses.

Four a.m., we head north and stop in Oakland to have a predawn breakfast with Dani Campbell and Dave, her husband, who also helped search in the weeks following Jacob's vanish. Dave is a fit guy, and I was relieved when he told me he had a hella difficult time just keeping Randy in sight while following him through the forest. The breakfast was one of the best I've ever had—eggs, bacon, tomatoes, toast, strong dark roast coffee. Randy and I were back in the rig and headed north before sunrise.

Tom Petty's "Runnin' Down a Dream," plays on the satellite radio as Randy wears more grooves into Interstate 5.

In Siskiyou County we pass Mount Shasta, which is a legendary now-dormant volcano of myth and magic and missing persons. It rises to 14,179 feet, the second-highest peak in the Cascade Range. The mountain is a sacred site to the Winnemem Wintu tribe, indigenous to the area, as well as the Modoc, Achomawi, Atsuwegi, and Shasta peoples.

Bigfoot has been seen here for years—dozens of them. Some Native Americans claim a species of tiny, evil people live above the treeline on Mount Shasta and throw rocks at humans who get too close.

Some people say Mount Shasta is atop Lemuria, coined by a seventeen-year-old named Frederick Spencer Oliver in 1883, who held the wild belief that lemurs traveled this lost continent as a portal from India to Madagascar. The lost city of Telos is purportedly under the volcano. Some locals claim to have seen cloud-shaped UFOs going into and out of the mountain. Some locals claim to have seen robed Lemurians shopping in the town of Mount Shasta.

In September 2011, a three-year-old boy was missing for five hours on the shoulder of Mount Shasta. The boy claims he was kidnapped by a robot that was a double of his grandmother—the robot grandma took him to a cave filled with spiders, guns, and purses.

While in the cave he was examined by robot humanoids and told he was put inside his mother's stomach by them, who are from outer space. After a few hours they placed him by a river to be found. He was found by Siskiyou County Sheriff's Deputy Sam Kubowitz and his K9, Tom, a three-year-old Dutch shepherd. The grandmother whom the boy believes had a robot double said she was somehow removed from her tent and sleeping bag and woke up facedown in the dirt. She felt sick that day and suffered a puncture wound on the back of her head—as if she'd been bitten by a spider.

That same month a Pacific Crest Trail hiker from Los Angeles claims he was lured off-trail by the beautiful voice of a siren. The siren was a beautiful woman with otherworldly-blue eyes. He was held captive in a cave and given secret information by the woman. He returned to the world and changed his name to Lord Kalki, who, he claims, is a Hindu god.

Later that fall, on November 11, 2011, another Los Angeles man, Michael Falvo, age nineteen, had been on the mountain meditating with a spiritual group. He took off his shoes and started hiking to the summit in order to place a rock there. He didn't return, and his meditation friends called authorities. A winter storm blew in and delayed the search. His body was found the next day at 9,600 feet.

It's an immense pyramid of vortices and ley lines, healing waters and fairies. To venture above treeline on Mount Shasta is said to be entering the realm of the dead.

In May of 1999 a sixty-nine-year-old Bay-area mountaineer named Carl Landers was on a trek to summit Mount Shasta with two friends. Landers had been there the year before and had almost made the summit when he turned back, and he vowed to reach it this time. He wasn't feeling well and had been taking Diamox, an altitude-sickness medication. His friends, Milton Gaines and Barry Gillmore, claim he left his tent at 50/50 Flat, the popular camping spot halfway between Horse Camp and Lake Helen, several times the night prior to his vanishing due to diarrhea. But the men were experienced and well equipped and planned to keep climbing. Landers started up the trail ahead of his friends in order to get a head start, as he knew he'd be slow. From Lake Helen, where a backcountry ranger hadn't seen him, he should have been in sight, essentially all the way to the summit. No one has seen him since.

Above the treeline there are vast faces and snowfields wherein a person would be most visible not only from a helicopter but from the ground. There was a winter's worth of snow on the ground, but no tracks that deviated from the trail. Landers simply vanished.

The sheriff's department quickly got two helicopters in the air, as well as an extensive ground search that included dogs. Not only could they not find Landers's tracks, they couldn't find any clues in the form of clothing or equipment.

The search leader, a man named Grizz Adams, who had been involved in searches on Mount Shasta for thirty-five years, told David Paulides in an interview, "…he either went up, or in—but he's not on it."

I think about Landers as we drive through Shasta's shadow on a bluebird day, but I don't mention it to Randy. Instead we talk about surfing, Randy's childhood, construction, Jacob, places Randy's traveled to, including Africa and the Middle East, classic rock trivia.

Most interesting to me are all the paddle-outs, the surfers' sea burial of ashes that Randy has organized and participated in. Dozens. A flotilla of surfers will paddle out past the break, circle, say prayers, and send the dead on. It seems a beautiful way to pass. On June 2, 2017, Jack O'Neill died. You've seen O'Neill surfwear, if not boards and wetsuits. He was an eyepatch-wearing surf-pirate legend not only in Santa Cruz, but the entire world of surfing and surf culture, and a close friend to Randy's dad, Bill. Jack was ninety-four when he died, not even two months after Jacob vanished. But

Randy made sure to make it back to Santa Cruz for Jack's paddle-out, which consisted of hundreds of surfers.

I don't bring up many other missing persons while we're driving, though I'm saddled with the knowledge that there are myriad cases in every county we motor through on our way up to Washington; I don't think there's much comfort in knowing it happens more than most people think. That sentiment is as hollow as Mount Shasta.

Every so often Randy, who has been driving and thinking, thinking and driving, will say something that may seem out of left field, but I've spent too many hours with him to be surprised. Also, my favorite place to put a person whose story I'm trying to capture is behind the wheel of a vehicle. Years ago I did a magazine profile of a professional skier-turned-pimp (there was more money in the escort business). I shadowed him as he did his workaday drill in Denver. Most of that time consisted of driving through traffic in his Subaru Outback and collecting cash and credit card receipts from his small workforce—hours of driving. I'm convinced there wasn't much he didn't tell me. The steering wheel is Wonder Woman's golden lasso of truth.

"I could see Jacob being adopted by a family of Bigfoot," Randy says. "Hanging with them, you know. Which would be good." It's not so much that Randy is certain Bigfoot exits. Rather, it's that he's certain that he *can't* know that Bigfoot *doesn't* exist. "There's gotta be something out there. *Gooottttaaaa. We're* here. We don't even know everything at the bottom of the ocean, you know what I mean? *Come ooooon.*"

On one trip back to Santa Cruz Randy fell asleep at the wheel and ended up in the barrow pit. He's lucky he didn't kill himself or someone else. Part of my job, I think, is to keep him company, at least keep him awake. The accelerator position hurts Randy's knee, and he uses the cruise control even in traffic. Sometimes he's coordinating between the speed controls, his phone, and the wheel at once. I find myself being the annoying shotgun passenger who tenses up and points out brake lights ahead. "He's stopping!" Of course Randy is a California driver, and the technique is a little different.

"I got it, bro," Randy says.

"Good," I say. "I don't want to have to do a paddle-out for you. You've seen me, I'm not very good on a surfboard."

We pull into a rest area near Olympia and climb into the back of the Arctic Fox. There's a peaceful white noise of idling diesel trucks and tires buzzing on the highway. Randy sleeps with bear spray in arm's reach, and I just hope he doesn't accidentally trigger it in the confines of the camper. We're both out fast. Mallory mines the computer back in Santa Cruz. She's the Internet research wizard this kind of search needs. She acts as a type of dispatcher for Randy in the mobile unit, the Arctic Fox. Every now and then she'll text something we should check out. She's been doing some research on a lake called Lord's Lake, south of Sequim—she's intrigued by the name and how it may fit into Jacob's mind-set. That's where we're headed. "I'm going to give Jacob this camper when I find him," he says. "He'll love it! We can strap the surfboards on top and just live at the beach."

It's still dark five or so hours later when Randy says, "Good morning," and reaches to light the stove for coffee. In half an hour we're on the road. Randy watches his speed closely, uses the cruise control, because he's one more ticket away from landing back in traffic school. There's a Sirius station called Deep Tracks, and we play a game of Guess the Artist. Small Faces? Jefferson Airplane? Canned Heat? James Gang? Blind Faith? When I'm ahead he can always best me by reminding me he's seen the group they're playing live.

We meet with Brandon Nelson, who was one of the first Olympic

Peninsula residents to help search for Jacob in those early days last April, at a café. Brandon is a RZR side-by-side—essentially a light turbo dune buggy—enthusiast. He got his RZR club involved in the search in the Olympic National Forest and spent days on end helping Randy in the Sol Duc River. It's thirty-four degrees and sunny in Sequim when we meet Brandon at the Mariner Café, where we look at maps and hash out a game plan.

After breakfast we climb into Brandon's Toyota Tacoma four-by-four pickup and head south into the mountains. We hit snow quickly after we start to climb. Lord's Lake is fenced off as a municipal water source, but we make the loop.

We tie back into Highway 101 near the 7 Cedars Casino outside of Sequim. Randy recently got a call from a psychic, who has become a friend, who heard a drunk Olympic National Park employee blab about Jacob's case. "It's not what everyone thinks," he says. "He's not dead." But that's all she could get out of him.

These kinds of things are maddening. A hang-up phone call. A drunk park employee at a party. But Randy's got to take these things seriously. And there's an element of hope in them—both suggest that Jacob may be anecdotally alive. The psychic thought she might see the employee again at a New Year's Eve party at the casino. She'd talk to him and try to get him to say more. But Randy knows he can't put too much stock in hearsay.

"The parks are like the Vatican," Randy says. That's a pretty fair analogy, considering the autonomy with which they operate.

There's a spillover of Seattle's homeless population in Port Angeles—for a town of just 20,000 it's palpable. Sometimes we walk around Port Angeles. Sometimes we drive. Looking for that silhouette. That gait. "I look at everybody," Randy says. "There's a reason you go everywhere—you just never know. He could be out there thinking no one wants him around. No one's looking for him. We don't love him. Doesn't want to be a burden on anybody."

Randy has contacted mental hospitals—but because of confidentiality laws they're limited in what information they can reveal. He doesn't think it's likely Jacob is in one anyway.

We wheel into the Port Angeles Texaco just uphill from downtown on the 101. The convenience store is tweaker central. They keep the two front doors open so it never gets comfortable enough inside to encourage hanging out. The manager has no teeth, and the several times I've been in there he's wearing a Seahawks mascot hat that resembles, well—a giant seahawk. The manager is nice enough, though a little nervous. Behind the counter there are printouts of security photos of people who have shoplifted the place. Randy has talked to him before, back in April. He says he saw a guy who looked like Jacob come in about the time Jacob vanished. Said the young man wore a blue jacket with a hood. "He bought some expensive bottled water," the manager said.

"Jacob would do that," Randy told him.

Seahawk guy remembered Randy. Without a transition he mentioned Alex Jones, who has a lot more traction with the underground than I'd given him credit for.

A woman also with no teeth and a yappy dog walked in from the cold, into the cold. She's a regular. Randy recognized her from last summer, when she'd just gotten out of surgery and there was gauze sticking out of a fresh wound on her side. "I'll help ya look for him," she told him.

There's been a spate of young suicides in Port Townsend, teenagers jumping off a local bridge. The population of the young homeless seems disproportionate here. Some dress warmly in baggy insulated Carhartt work clothing, some dress like skateboarders, some are goth and fitting of the vampire scene just sixty miles west down Highway 101. Most are pierced and tattooed. They must spend most of their time cold, as now the damp blows through you as if you're a skeleton.

Seahawk shows us the frequently updated rogues' gallery of shoplifters, but last summer they couldn't pull up any shots of Jacob coming in to buy expensive water.

We roll on, westward, toward the Sol Duc and the Bigfoot Barn. The sight of Lake Crescent triggers Randy to tell me what a psychic named Lauren saw. "Lauren had a vision Jacob left his bike in a clearing and walked out on a dock," he says. "Lake Crescent? It's the only dock close by. But we have his bike. We have Jacob's bike. It doesn't make sense."

We stop at Storm King, the ranger station on the west end of the lake. The ranger station is an old rock and log building right out of a Disney movie. There's a ranger named Peter Maggio there, just transferred in. Maggio has a standard-issue mustache. He doesn't know anything new, not much at all about Jacob's story but what they'd told him around the water cooler.

A different psychic also put Jacob on the beach at La Push, on the reservation where the Sol Duc meets with the Calawah and finally flows into the Pacific Ocean. Randy's been there a half dozen times. He'll keep going.

We hit Forks for supplies, groceries mostly, though Randy picks up some ammunition for his pistol here at the combination IGA and Ace Hardware. The fact that the *Twilight* series is set here is more irony—like the Bigfoot Barn becoming the ad hoc search HQ—that Jacob vanished near here. Sasquatch and vampires.

CHAPTER 15

OLYMPIC PENINSULA

*All the world loves a ghost. The evidence of that
simple statement can be found by looking in nearly
every direction.*

—Aberjhani

LA PUSH IS French for, roughly, the mouth. The Quillayute River
flushes into the Pacific here; the Quillayute begins just a few miles
upstream, where the confluence of the Sol Duc, the Bogachiel, and
the Calawah rivers form the Quillayute. The Dickey River flows
into the Quillayute just above the beach here. The name may be
Quileute for *wolves*, though the last known speaker of the language
died in 1999.

Deep Tracks plays a song called "Prehistoric Rhythm" by the
Native American band Redbone. I'd recently become fascinated
with the drums and read that Redbone's early drummer, Peter
DePoe, is from this part of the Olympic Peninsula, the tip of the
wolf's ear of the Lower 48.

It's New Year's Eve, and we drive against the arrows of the
Tsunami Evacuation Route.

Randy parks the Arctic Fox on the sliver of Quileute gravel parking lot at Rialto Beach—just off the Olympic National Park lot.

Randy narrates the tide and the swell as if he's in it. He's reading it. He's *ionized* just by being on the beach, smelling the surf. This has become Jacob's Coast. We aren't supposed to camp here, but that's the beauty of being self-contained—no one knows whether we're camping or just parking with the two other vehicles of backpackers who are spending New Year's Eve in the coastal backcountry.

We hike out to Hole in the Rock Cave. We have to catwalk some slick logs over swampy areas with water several feet deep. It takes all my concentration to not slip, not fall, while Randy fairly dances down the logs. At the formation—an impressive rock wicket—there are a couple photographers and a man painting *plein air*.

This is where Jacob's ex-girlfriend, Makenzie, told Randy she and Jacob liked to go surfing. Their break was a religious thing Randy doesn't entirely understand, but it involved Makenzie's parents not approving of the relationship if it progressed beyond friendship.

"What was he like before he took off?" Randy asked her.

"Nothing unusual," Makenzie told him. "He seemed really happy when he was here."

Randy is hopeful that 2018 is going to bring good news, that they'll find Jacob—or at least get some answers as to where he's gotten off to. We eat tacos back at the Arctic Fox at Rialto Beach. I picked up an IPA in Forks, but Randy doesn't drink, not even on New Year's Eve—you get the sense Randy would like to drink, he's just not very good at it. The stars are out. There are a few fireworks from La Push, across the river, but mostly it's just the sound of the surf that washes in the new year.

The next bluebird sky morning all is quiet on New Year's Day, as the U2 songs goes. Nothing changes on New Year's Day. Before coffee, Randy is outside. He climbs the ladder and stands atop the Arctic Fox and watches the swell—ten-foot beach breaks. From my bunk I heard them thump the beach then whoosh back out, then thump again like footfalls of a giant. I can feel the truck move as

Randy walks the top of the camper like he walks his surfboard—lithe, catlike on the balls of his feet.

"Cistern," Randy says. This, now, has been eating at him. Another psychic—always a psychic—was persistent about a well, or a cistern. A desperate father could either dismiss it or follow up; and anything a desperate father dismisses is gonna dig at your temples at two in the morning. So Randy follows up. We're headed east, back toward the Sol Duc. He turns south, up the Olympic National Forest Road 2918—the west side of the river. He narrates the last two organized searches as we drive upriver. Here's the locked gate that the Park Service refused to open so they could access the Sol Duc Hot Springs Road without having to drive around. "That would have saved us a half hour each time," he says. "At least just give us the key." The Park Service threw up one roadblock after another. "We didn't let it rest," Randy says. "Elise got on Facebook, and that's when things started to happen. Without that nothing would ever have happened. We're gonna just do it. We've gotta do what we're not doing."

He parks at the end of the road, which had climbed steadily for 3,000 feet or so. Sometimes I fall into laziness wherein I follow Randy into the wilderness without bringing so much as a bottle of water, and this is one of those times. Randy is a whirlwind and, though I always know better, sometimes I get caught. We hike an old logging road that is mostly grown over. Randy sees an old blanket that I can tell from a distance has been there since further back than April. But he drops down a steep embankment anyway, just to let it go from his mind. He still thinks it's possible Jacob would have abandoned his bike to just *live* off the forest. He drags the rotten blanket up the steep slope to show me, have me validate that this blanket is in no way related to his son.

He can't pass a game trail, a small creek, or an old overgrown logging road up the Sol Duc without searching it to the end. It's the only way to shut the psychics up. The only way to clear the chatter, the static in his mind. A lot of things feel like wasted time. But then the only thing that would seem truly productive would be finding Jacob. Everything less than that is mowing the lawn.

"You gotta check it out," Randy says. "Then you can check it off."

There's a hot spring on the map over the ridge, but it would be twelve miles of hard hiking to get to it. It's a place Randy had thought might be a destination for Jacob, but he and Tanya and Derek and James have canvassed the area. Something made him want to come back up here this evening.

It's getting dark, so we plan dinner as we walk a grown-over jeep trail back toward the Arctic Fox. There's something ahead, something industrial. Randy picks up his pace. It's an old green steel government water tank, a relic from some water diversion project. There's a tiny stream trickling into it and a twelve-inch boom pipe running out the far end. *Fuck.* I feel like I've entered the psychic's dream. This hike was a bit of a fringe whim anyway, and now we run smack dab into what could be argued is a type of *cistern.*

"Wait here," Randy says and runs downhill to the truck a quarter mile away and brings back a flashlight. He's not gone five minutes, comes running back uphill. We have to scramble up an eroded bank by pulling on spruce roots. Randy chins-up atop the big steel tank, which is the size of a UPS truck, maybe holds 2,000 gallons. It's nearly dark when he opens up a lid on top like a submarine hatch. My heart's pounding, and I know his is, too. This is too much like a bad movie. *Scooby-Doo.* My mind races to what I'm gonna do for Randy when he shines the light inside and there's his dead son. My irrational, winded, adrenalined, hungry, illogical, fiction-writer self thinks for a moment that this is it, it's been foretold. This time the psychic wins, they told him where he could find Jacob. He shines the light inside.

Randy doesn't talk other than to say, "Toss me a stick." He jabs into the tank with the stick, feeling for his son. Then he redirects the flashlight. His head disappears down the opening.

I've seen Randy go into this trance before. A zone. It's like a drug dog at work. His movements quicken, he gets quiet. He's not overthinking, rather reacting reflexively, like an athlete. Search-and-rescue tai chi.

"The bottom's full of sediment," he says. He goes for another angle on the stick. His arms are soaked with rusty water. I'm a little concerned he might disappear into the tank entirely, hold his breath and dive into the dark gackwater. I realize I'm on land holding my breath for him. He stands up, tosses the stick away, then hops down. Jacob's not in the tank. We skitter down the scarp and walk back to the truck.

That night we camp along the Sol Duc, on the forest. We've traded the calming sounds of the Pacific Ocean for the gentle river sounds of the Sol Duc. He's closer to Jacob here, I can tell. Searching the green water tank was not a waste of effort—it served to help Randy cross *cistern* off his psychic burden list. Soon I hear Randy snoring. Calmly. Like a little kid.

The next morning is thirty-eight degrees and overcast. We're driving up to Hurricane Ridge and can intermittently see snow through the clouds. Randy calls Stacey, the woman who reported seeing Jacob riding two miles up the Sol Duc Road on the sixth of April, at ten a.m., and seeing his bike and trailer between the road and the river on her way down that afternoon. He's talked to Stacey several times before, but when something is chewing on him he'll back up and make a call and ask the person to repeat what they'd told him. In this way he's like a gentle cop.

Randy puts her on speakerphone. "It was a crappy day," Stacey says. "It's cold, it's April. It was foggy, cold, and rainy." Then she gets to what's eating *her*. "Why would he have a bow and arrows? I mean, I don't know what kind of kid he is. Something's not right."

Randy explains that he was an adventurous outdoorsman, that he liked to shoot archery—it wasn't hunting season.

"It looked pretty disheveled," Stacey says. "I said to my girlfriend, I hope there's not a dog in there, in the trailer."

"They would have found his body downstream," Randy says, "if he fell into the river and couldn't get out."

"It's very suspicious, isn't it," Stacey says.

It's strange that Jacob did not stop at the pullover—if this is an area he wanted to stop in. Instead, he pulls over a hundred yards above—past—the pullover. There's seemingly nothing there to pull over for—nothing but weeds and ferns and brush and devil's club. I too am haunted by the four arrows.

"The weather wouldn't have affected Jacob as much as other people," Randy says. "Same thing with surfing. He'd *trunk it* in winter. Shoot. He surfed the Fukushima tsunami." The waves reached Santa Cruz. "I had to work, but Jacob surfed it. That was freakin' bitchin'!"

Randy tells her cadaver dogs may have hit on a logjam. The closest thing to a signal from dogs in this vanish. "I dove the logjam twice and found nothing," Randy says.

"Honestly," Stacey says, "I think it was aliens. I think he was abducted."

"Why not a Bigfoot out there," Randy says. "Heck, I'm out there." I love that evidence of Randy Gray is also probable evidence of Sasquatch. "I think it'd be fun having one as a friend."

It's safe discussing the paranormal with Stacey, but the conversation doesn't end with it. "I think he's hiding out or something," Randy tells Stacey. The parking lot of the ski area at Hurricane Ridge is full when we get there, and we're turned around. Just one more of a thousand dead ends.

Randy pulls into a coffee shack. The blond woman who must be nineteen or twenty takes our order, mocha for Randy, Americano for me. "I have a mocha every day," Randy says. "Jacob and I used to. That was our thing. It keeps me in that mind-set."

Taped next to the drive-thru window is a missing persons poster of Jacob. "That's my son," Randy tells the young woman. "We're up here looking for him."

"Oh, I'm so sorry," she says. "He's cute—I'd remember him for sure. Good luck finding him."

The Coast Guard is forecasting a ten-foot swell at a wave period of fifteen seconds—good surfing, Randy says. Fifteen-second waves, measured by the distance between two waves passing through a stationary point, typically arrive from far offshore without the storm that birthed them. The generator on the Arctic Fox won't start. Battery is run down. Randy is still learning about the power systems on the rig.

The day keeps deteriorating. Randy sees that Laura deleted him from the group text celebrating Micah's promotion with the Coast Guard; the text included video of the ceremony. "Why would she do that?" Randy says. "Why does she have to be mean?"

To Laura's credit, it's entirely possible that Randy just missed something with his thumbs on his phone, and Laura hadn't deleted Randy from any group texts.

There seem to be two main ways to weather this type of malign loss. You can take Randy's approach and dive into the cold water headfirst. Or you can shell up and pull your head in. This is what most people do. They don't have the physical or financial resources of Randy Gray.

Randy's mom, Jimmie Jean, died when he was nine years old. His brother Ronnie fell off a ladder and died at forty-two, while stringing Christmas lights, in 1989. Those losses, shocking as they were, are nothing like this. But then, Randy tells himself, maybe this isn't a loss at all, rather a temporary misplacement. So he searches.

On January 3 we hike into the "quietest square inch" in America: the Hoh River Trail. This is a backway route up to the High Divide, Hoh Lake, the Sol Duc, and the headwaters of the Bogachiel River. Searchers hiked it in April, but Randy wanted to see the backside of the map for himself. There are only a couple vehicles at the trailhead.

But as for the quietest square inch of America, not so much. Jets on the descent for Vancouver and Seattle roar overhead. Military aircraft sometimes perform exercises over the park, even as they were so hesitant to scramble a Coast Guard helicopter in search of a missing cyclist. A couple of trail volunteers are drinking water at the quietest square inch. There is no sign, but they winkingly confirmed we were there, pretty much. "*Heeeeck*," Randy says. "Some professor is scamming people with his book about this being quiet." They laugh, then Randy unfolds an eight-and-a-half by eleven-inch poster of Jacob.

"We're very aware of it," the man says. "We keep looking, keeping the word out. Hopefully you'll get some resolution soon."

We turn around before the snowline. As we near the trailhead, across a small creek, we hear a ruckus in the water. Otters maybe— much splashing. Rather, it's Coho salmon, and they're spawning. They're the size of border collies, and it's so shallow their fins stick out of the water. You could grab one, though it would be illegal and a rotten thing to do. The new salmon will hatch in spring and make their way to the Hoh River. At three years old they'll return. Randy is so excited he dances to the parking lot, waving hikers to the spot. "Check it out," he orders. "You gotta check it out!" The cycle of life. What nags is that the Coho's life cycle makes sense.

* * *

Randy insists on driving me to Bainbridge Island to catch the ferry to Seattle so I can fly back home to the U.P. I sometimes forget I have a life back home. I want to stay with Randy until he finds Jacob. I tell him I'll be back out, but that implies that Jacob won't be found by then. We head east on 101. But first we have to see Bob Chung at Port Townsend Cyclery. Randy buys a used Cayne folding mountain bike with twenty-inch knobby tires. It's a mini-me version of the bike Jacob rode the last time anyone reported seeing him. The small red three-speed will be handy to take on ferries or just ride around little towns when he parks the Arctic Fox. We tuck the little bike into the Arctic Fox. Cyclist searching for a cyclist. Jacob would appreciate this mode of searching.

Some of the dead ends are on islands. My friend Scott Dorsch used to work an organic farm in Bellingham, goats and chickens. Scott tells me there are dozens of farms on the San Juans, so I tell Randy. "'That's where I'd go,' he says." And that's where Randy goes.

"Jacob's not intimidated by big water. It's second nature to him. Jacob would kayak to them." He means the San Juans, maybe the Gulf Islands.

"You know when you're kids playing hide-and-seek. With boundaries. Well, I'm playing hide-and-seek now, but there's no boundaries. No boundaries."

Randy studies shapes. As a father I get this—in a crowd of school kids, I recognize my son Sam's walk, the way he moves his long arms, the way he holds his head. A tourist family from England sent the Grays a video of a young man they'd picked up hitchhiking in Washington. The vacationing Brits were sure they'd given Jacob a ride. "It looked like him, but I could tell by the shape of his head it wasn't Jacob," Randy says. "Even if Jacob has a beard now I'll know it's him."

CHAPTER 16

IDAHO, NEVADA, CALIFORNIA, NEW MEXICO, NUNAVUT

My heart shoots into my throat every time I think
I see his loping walk, or catch sight of some floppy
brown hair on a boy—but it's never him, and each
time it isn't, my heart does a reverse trajectory
down into the very pit of my stomach.

—Lauren Oliver

"IN MY MIND, that's the national disgrace. It's not cancer. Everybody knows someone with cancer, but it's a minority who know someone gone missing," David Francis tells me over the phone from his office in Stillwater, Minnesota. "Typically, adults are most likely to be abandoned by the public sector, abandoned in the wilderness." Francis is the founder of the Jon Francis Foundation, which he founded in 2007. As I write this, the JFF has helped nearly fifty families who would otherwise have been left to their own humble resources or nothing at all. Francis's son, Jon, vanished on July 15, 2006, in the Sawtooth Range, Custer County, Idaho.

"We try to wrap our arms around the victims' families and provide some grief support," Francis says. "When a loved one's missing a child, that really messes up a person's brain. It's called unresolved loss."

I was introduced to the Jon Francis Foundation when they supported a spring 2016 search in Conejos County, Colorado, for Joe Keller. They organized twenty people and eleven dogs from points across the country. Though they didn't find Joe, it was a thorough, highly professional push that helped eliminate some possibilities.

I'd first talked with Francis before Jacob had gone missing in Olympic National Park. He had a different take on going missing within the boundary of a national park. "Those people who go missing on a national park are lucky. National parks are the gold standard as far as missing persons cases go. A county sheriff doesn't have the experience or funding or resources. That's the national disgrace."

And it depends on *who you are*, as well as *where you were*, according to Francis. "For example, the *New York Times* reported that the State of Nevada spent over $600,000 on their months-long search for millionaire Steve Fossett. Based on our search cost experience, Custer County, Idaho, spent about $10,000 and twenty-nine hours searching for Jon Francis." Ten grand is double their SAR budget, still a drop in the bucket.

"Fossett was the biggest case. There was a lot of inequity. If you go missing in a poor county, you're gonna get a short, somewhat sloppy search."

I did not tell David Francis that I was on part of the search for Steve Fossett, who disappeared from the Nevada desert in September 2007. The following summer I'd heard about a hyperfit PhD and his band of hard-core athlete searchers. The concept was to combine smarts with human performance in the pursuit of the missing.

Simon Donato, thirty-two at the time, and his crew have turned searching into both a science and a sport. Since the search for Fossett, Donato's Esquire Network adventure racing show *Boundless* has turned him into an almost-household name in Canada, but his real passion remains looking for needles in extreme haystacks.

Team Adventure Science, they're called. The members form a phalanx, keeping within shouting distance of each other while fanning out into the Sierra Nevada scrub. A half dozen of North America's top adventure racers, strapped with heart-rate monitors and slathered with Body Glide, synchronize their compass watches and set out at high speed across ridges, down canyons, and over bare mineral earth, all while keeping critical spacing and overlapping visuals to achieve a probability of detection (POD) of at least 70 percent.

They cover the ground like grasshoppers. "Simon, there's something shiny at two o'clock to your left, a hundred meters up," says Paul "Turbocock" Trebilcock. Donato, clad in a multipocketed racing vest and camo surf trunks, is the team leader and founder of the Canadian Adventure Racing Association. He sprints over to what turns out to be a white PVC mining-claim post. Not what he was hoping for.

What we are looking for, Donato told us at base camp the hot July 2008 night we arrived, is probably the size of two crumpled shopping carts: a hunk of steel frame, maybe an engine block, and possibly some human remains. Donato let me shadow the team of six athletes and three support crew that he'd gathered for a grueling week of scrambling through the area surrounding Bridgeport, California, near the Nevada state line.

The goal is to go at 60 percent of maximum exertion for eleven hours a day. Their heart rates, mileage, elevation, ground coverage, calorie consumption—all valuable measurements—would go into a database to help Donato assess what works and what doesn't. The immediate objective is to find a clue, any clue, to the biggest mystery in American aviation since skyjacker D. B. Cooper stepped out of a 727 over Washington State in 1971: the whereabouts of lost adventurer Steve Fossett, last seen somewhere over Nevada on September 3, 2007.

The search grid spread over 20,000 square miles after Fossett's plane vanished. Twenty percent of that original search terrain, Donato figures, is ideal adventure-racer habitat—forbidding ground where the wreckage could be hidden under a juniper canopy or some cliffy bit of geological chicanery. He zeroes in on a rough circle, with a sixty-two-mile radius, about 130 miles south of Reno. By Donato's own calculations, the odds of finding the millionaire or his airplane are less than 1 percent. But for the team, the wreckage has become the ultimate geocache, a corporeal Eco-Challenge with Steve Fossett as the prize.

But it is not simply racing on a grand scale. "When you're racing, you're not looking," says team member Jim Mandelli. "We're not just playing and training in the mountains. We're looking."

It was a clear Labor Day morning when sixty-three-year-old Steve Fossett told his pal Barron Hilton—whose million-acre Flying M Ranch, near Hawthorne, Nevada, he was visiting—that he was going for a spin. He took off just before nine a.m. in Hilton's Bellanca Super Decathlon, an athletic high-wing designed more for aerobatics than any long-distance flying. The plan was to be back for lunch. A soybean tycoon from Chicago, Fossett could take care of himself; the man was the first to pilot both a hot-air balloon and a jet around the world; he'd swum the English Channel, mushed the Iditarod, and finished the Ironman Triathlon. But when he didn't come back by nightfall, Hilton and Fossett's wife, Peggy, launched what would become the largest and most expensive search-and-rescue operation in American history, one that would ultimately eat up $1.6 million in public and $1.2 million in private funds.

For more than a month, the search dragged on. They went big: Civil Air Patrollers filled the desert and subalpine sky. Walker

Lake, the only big blue spot anywhere near the ranch, was seined with high-tech electronics. Expensive high-resolution photographs were fed into computers looking for anomalies. Meanwhile, amateur geeks from Switzerland and New Zealand looked for Fossett's plane on their coffee breaks, via Google Earth. But on February 15, 2008, after the ATVs and the satellites and the dogs and the geeks turned up nothing, the rich adventurer was declared dead.

Conspiracy theories brewed: His financial ship was sinking, Fossett had faked his disappearance and was living on a tropical island.

Fossett had only recently "checked out" on that particular aircraft, not an easy one to fly. There was debate over whether or not the plane was topped off with fuel. The Flying M staff pilot was the only one who saw him take off, then—maybe—a cowboy saw the plane south of the runway. Donato heard Fossett told people at the Flying M that he planned to fly Highway 395 and may have been vectoring toward Yosemite—in the vicinity of Amelia Earhart Peak. But no one knew where he was going, or why the emergency transponder didn't go off.

The mystery and media exposure fit Donato's big personality. He put himself through McMaster University in part by modeling for Harlequin romance covers—naughty-dancing with Photoshop partners on the paperback *Beyond Daring*, and holding a baby and smiling on *An Honorable Texan,* as if he'd just found the little guy in the woods and, hey, no prob, it's what I do.

A petroleum stratigrapher by training, Donato's résumé is also stuffed with sufferfests from Eco-Challenge Fiji to Raid the North Extreme, Newfoundland. His idea with Adventure Science is that their fitness allows human eyeballs to canvass vast and rough country that turns back four-by-fours and ATVs—and in a tenth of the time it takes classic foot searchers. "I had an epiphany several years ago while conducting my geology PhD field work in Oman.

I realized that doing things 'the easy way'—i.e., driving instead of walking—sometimes meant that crucial details were overlooked. Obviously, the high-tech method to find Fossett has failed, so it only makes sense to put the fastest and fittest people I could find on the ground to search the most difficult areas."

Fossett himself would probably have found it pretty cool that he could still disappear somewhere in wild America, that it was still feral enough down there to swallow an airplane. He also would likely have approved of Donato's sporting search methods. "My competitive nature," Fossett wrote in his 2006 autobiography, *Chasing the Wind,* "combined with the methodical use of statistical probabilities, added up to a winning formula."

Donato's biggest challenge was selecting a specific search area that fit his team's skill set. He spent the winter studying maps and talking with pilots, aeronautical engineers, and search-and-rescue personnel, as well as "Clairvoyant Kim" Dennis, a Calgary medium who'd supposedly reached out to Fossett in the spirit world and discovered he'd crash-landed in a marsh.

Ultimately, Donato decided that Fossett was most likely "on the edge of the Sierra Nevada, where difficult winds, steep drainages, and generally more-dense vegetation could conceal the wreckage." In May, Donato hired a pilot to fly him over this chunk of high desert. Fossett had many hours of flying gliders there, famous for massive thermals.

Torn between an area to the north, around Bridgeport, and a stretch of wild terrain to the south, closer to the national park, Donato chose north. This is where we found ourselves during the first team briefing, sitting under an E-Z UP tent in base camp at the Bridgeport RV Park under a waxing moon. Donato had assembled an elite team of jocks. In addition to "Turbocock" Trebilcock, a former Canadian ultramarathon national champion also known as "Carpenter Paul" for his role on the Canuck version of the TV show *Trading Spaces*, there was Mandelli, a Lions Bay, British Columbia, structural architect and veteran of the Raid Galoises; Derek Caveney, a Toyota scientist and mountain biker; Greg Marshall, a high-school teacher who went to grade school with Donato; and Gary Hudson, a massage therapist and world-class duathlete.

Supporting the athletes were camp manager Keith Szlater, a Calgary-based SAR coordinator; and Tyler LeBlanc, a Whitehorse paramedic toting a kit full of drugs and bandages. The lone American was Greg Francek, a former Primal Quest race director and Amador County, California, Search and Rescue deputy who'd been confined to field support after a fall from his roof.

"We're looking for plane wreckage," Donato told his team as they shoveled in spaghetti, carbo-loading for the day ahead. "We're not looking for a body." Everyone nodded. "And no photos when we find him. It's about respect."

Every morning at the RV park, we'd wake at dawn for breakfast—during which Donato blasted "Run to the Hills" from his laptop while we ate oatmeal. At seven o'clock sharp, Team Alpha loaded into Mobile One, Mandelli's Xterra, and motored out to search territory. There, we fanned out, performed radio checks, and spent the day hunting for an airplane. The physiological data went back to McMaster University, Donato's alma mater.

What nobody brought up is the possibility of not finding Fossett. These athletes were used to winning, and they'd visualized success, practiced finding Fossett in their minds. As a leader, Donato exuded less hope, really, rather probability and relativity.

Still, the pressure was on Donato. Everyone had paid their own way there and given up vacation time for the cause. Hopes were high, not just for the glory of solving the Fossett mystery or for the looming documentary being filmed by Donato's fraternity brother

Lindsay Robles, but for the promise of Adventure Science itself. Adventure racing, poised to go big when *Survivor* producer Mark Burnett began airing Eco-Challenge races on the Discovery Channel in the nineties, dropped off the popularity radar. Here was a benevolent application; even if the team didn't find a stick of evidence, they might still spawn something of a new extreme sport.

Midmorning day one and we already had a break. Base-camp manager Keith Szlater, with a Calgary cowboy mustache that fit right in on the Nevada line, is frantic on the radio. "We've got a very interesting development here." A white Jeep with California plates growled into the day's search site, near the ghost town of Chemung Mine, where the team was eating a lunch of trail mix and V8. Szlater was riding shotgun with a local named Tom who drank a midmorning Miller High Life while he told us he had been up here cutting firewood last Labor Day, the day Fossett disappeared. He and his buddy were taking a cigarette break with the saws off and heard a small plane sputtering.

The guy appeared legit. "I guarantee nobody searched in there on the ground," he said, pointing southward toward a canyon especially thick with piñon and juniper. "It's a real tough area to get into. You could land a 727 in there and no one would ever see it." Tom said he told the Mono County Sheriff's Department, but they didn't seem too interested.

But the tip is a bust. By the end of two hot, grueling days, all the team has found is a windscreen from a snowmobile, many old beer cans, an arrowhead, an antique Canadian whiskey bottle, and a boot. They were sunburned, blistered, and scratched from sagebrush and alder sharp as punji sticks.

The next day, at 10,000 feet on the eastern shoulder of snowcapped Mount Patterson, Donato found a battered aluminum door. He carried it out of the trees as if it were a Roman shield. The door was full of bullet holes.

"If that's his door," Turbocock joked, "it's proof that Steve Fossett was shot down." The door appeared to me to be from a snowcat—there's a rusty hinge and the handle isn't recessed for aerodynamics. At best it's a military antique. But when Donato posted the discovery on the Team Adventure Science website, the news that they'd found an airplane door made the newswires. A search-and-rescue version of Telephone. The door wasn't a clue, but it was a symbol, a reminder that Fossett really could be close by.

By the end of the week Team Adventure Science had combed sixty-two miles, climbed and descended thousands of feet, and consumed a case of Costco canned salmon. No sign of Fossett, but the area could be crossed off the map with semi-scientific confidence.

I got the news in September from Donato that Preston Morrow, the manager of Kittredge Sports in Mammoth Lakes, California, had found Fossett's pilot's license and a weathered wad of hundred-dollar bills in pine needles off a goat path seven miles west of the Mammoth Mountain ski resort. This was sixty miles from where we'd been searching on the Nevada border; at least Donato had chipped the search area down from 20,000 square miles to within sixty miles of the bull's-eye. His instincts were right. He was eating an apple at his desk, taking a break from studying the crash site on Google Earth. "This is five kilometers from where I'd wanted to go next, if we'd had more time and money."

A flurry of emails landed in my box from all the Team Adventure Science members. They were chomping at the bit to be out there with crews from the Madero County Sheriff's Department, above 9,000 feet, searching for the wreckage in terrain not accessible by anything with wheels. Greg Francek, the Amador County deputy, was headed up to the command center to assist in the search-and-recovery operation. There was no schadenfreude, rather something much closer to sportsmanship.

The mass of the wreckage was, true to high-speed impact form, the size of a couple of crumpled shopping carts. "I'm most glad they found Steve," Donato said. "If we can help search-and-rescue methodology in the future, great."

In March of 2012, Micah True—nickname Caballo Blanco—went missing while running in the Gila Wilderness of southern New Mexico. Donato wrote on his blog for *Canadian Running* magazine: *There are a lot of tweets offering hopes and prayers, but only boots on the ground will result in a happy ending here.* The happy ending never happened. True, who was fifty-eight and was made famous in the Chris McDougall book *Born to Run*, was found by runners. Donato flew down and searched in running gear. Three days after he went missing, True's corpse was found by three searchers, True's friends, Ray Molina, and friends Jessica Haines and Dean Bannon, with his feet dangling in a small drainage called Little Creek. The main trails had been thoroughly searched, and Molina and the others got frustrated with official search protocols and decided to follow a hunch. It appeared that True had suffered a bad fall—he was scraped up, bloody, and his finger was bent back at an unnatural angle. After finding True, Molina, Haines, and Bannon walked out to search headquarters with the news. Donato and former Army captain Tim Puetz volunteered to walk and run up the creek and watch the body overnight against bears, mountain lions, and the threat of a flash flood washing the body downstream. The next morning a trio of pack horses brought True's body out.

In the summer of 2018 Puetz joined Donato in the Arctic for a historical search for another famous missing person, Captain Sir John Franklin. The British Royal Navy officer led the ill-fated

1845 expedition to the Arctic in search of the Northwest Passage with two ships, HMS *Erebus* and HMS *Terror*. He was known in England as *The Man Who Ate His Shoes* after a previous infamous Arctic expedition. *Erebus* and *Terror* became icebound off the coast of King William Island. Franklin and 128 other men—the entire expedition—were lost.

A vast sea search followed in 1848. The British Royal Navy offered a reward for finding the ships; by 1850 the search included eleven British ships and two ships flying the American flag. Graves of three crewmen were found off the east coast of Beechey Island. It's believed the expedition devolved into cannibalism.

In 2014 a Canadian search team found *Erebus* on the ocean floor in eastern Queen Maud Gulf. In 2016 *Terror* was located south of King William Island. But no Sir John Franklin.

Donato is determined to find him. In a twelve-day expedition in late July and early August, Donato and Puetz, along with Myron Tetreault and Oliver Hubert-Benoit, fast-packed from Cape Felix to Terror Bay, over a hundred miles. The crew trekked a short distance from the shore, but farther inland than it's believed previous searches had taken place. They found artifacts, including multiple cairns, but no Franklin. They saw wolves and caribou and all manner of weather. Currently, Donato is analyzing the expedition's data for another attempt.

CHAPTER 17

SAN JUAN ISLANDS & UTAH

Loneliness adds beauty to life. It puts a special burn
on sunsets and makes night air smell better.
—*Henry Rollins*

RANDY SEARCHED THE farms of the San Juan Island chain in
February 2018. But Jacob had been interested in Canada—without
a passport it would have been possible for him to buy a beat-up
fifty-dollar kayak and paddle to Canada undetected. Not easy, not
safe, not advised, but possible. If the seas or a ship didn't get
him on his way across, the Canadian Border Services Agency—
the CBSA—might. Or he might have crossed Puget Sound on a
ferry and walked across the border in the forest. Again, not easy,
but possible.

Not incidentally, more than a few persons have disappeared without a trace on Vancouver Island—most notably fifty-nine-year-old
Robin Penwarn, a former search-and-rescue volunteer who went
missing in January of 2014 in East Sooke Regional Park, an area
she knew intimately, while on a routine day hike.

Jacob's athleticism and skill set compound the difficulty in finding him. If there is one kid who could slip into a swift river and *not*
drown, it's Jacob. If there's a kid who could kayak across saltwater

to Canada, it's Jacob. If there's a kid who could fend off an attacker with his cache of martial arts powers, it's Jacob.

And if there's one kid who could grow a beard and assimilate into a homeless population, hop a freight train across the Grain Belt, or hit the trail of itinerant organic farmers, that seemed to be Jacob, too. A kid like Jacob makes the search area much, much bigger.

It's not easy to disappear. There are, of course, some persons who want to stay missing, but can't. Before his arrest in April of 2013, survivalist Troy James Knapp, aka the Mountain Man, then forty-five, lived off the fat of the landowners. For nearly seven years, the Mountain Man had played hide-and-seek on a huge scale in the southern half of Utah, breaking into cabins, stealing firearms, and roaming on foot between 3,000 and 10,000 feet in a nine-county area the size of Delaware—wild country made wilder by winter mountain weather. South to north, his territory covered 180 miles. In the southwestern counties of Iron, Kane, and Garfield—his main range for much of that time—Knapp was suspected of dozens of cabin burglaries. He faced nineteen felony charges and ten misdemeanor burglary and theft charges in those three counties alone. Knapp is currently cooling his heels in United States Penitentiary Lee in Pennington Gap, Virginia, where's he's serving a ten-and-a-half-year sentence.

Antler hunting is a popular pursuit in remote Utah in the spring; on March 29, 2013, Good Friday, Dale Fuller and his fifteen-year-old son, Jordan, were scouting for shed elk antlers below Skyline Ridge on the eastern side of the 10,000-foot Wasatch Plateau in Emery County. While walking down the narrow Dairy Trail, they came across a man loaded for bear and headed upcountry. Mid-forties, a gray-and-blond beard, lean and weathered. He shouldered a fully loaded pack. His sidearm was not unusual in Utah, but the Fullers noted the assault rifle slung over one shoulder. Jordan's two-year-old brown Lab, Duke, growled—and continued growling for the whole encounter, even after Jordan tried to quiet him.

"The guy seemed way friendly," Jordan told me. They talked about snowpack levels—this area was at 60 percent of normal, and the trail was an Easter succotash of mud, corn snow, and vegetation—and whether or not they'd seen anyone else in the area. Dale asked what he was doing headed into the high country. "Going camping," he replied. "I'm the Mountain Man. I don't plan on shooting you guys." Knapp continued up the trail when Duke would not stop growling.

Of course the Fullers—who were armed themselves, but lightly in comparison to the assault rifle—had heard of the Mountain Man, and when they got within cell service, they called a friend who is married to an Emery County sheriff's deputy; the deputy forwarded them photos. The photos of Knapp confirmed what the Fullers already knew. It was him all right.

Over the Easter weekend several Emery County residents opening up their cabins after the winter discovered evidence of an unwanted guest. Investigators fingered Knapp for a break-in near Joe's Valley Reservoir—about fifteen miles north of the Fullers' encounter, near the border with Sanpete County—where a crowbar was left at the scene. On Easter Sunday, they responded to another break-in report in the same area; this time guns had been taken.

The Fullers' sighting gave authorities the fresh lead they needed. Officers on snowshoes slowly tracked Knapp over three days and fifteen miles; his bearpaw tracks led into Sanpete County and to a cluster of thirteen cabins near 9,000 feet at Ferron Reservoir, on the shoulder of Ferron Mountain.

On Monday, April Fool's Day, a fifty-person task force that included members of seven county sheriff departments, the Utah Department of Public Safety (DPS), Adult Probation and Parole, and a half dozen federal agents from the U.S. Marshals Service, gathered at the Sanpete County Sheriff's Department to strategize. Emery County detective Garrett Conover told me that they discussed the February cabin standoff in California that ended with the death of ex–Los Angeles policeman-turned-murderer Christopher Dorner. When authorities located Dorner in a cabin near Big Bear Lake, a firefight ensued; tear-gas canisters caused a fire that burned the structure to the ground. Dorner was found dead. That's the scenario the Utah team most wanted to avoid.

The next morning, April 2, just after midnight, the lawmen headed into Ferron Canyon in snowcats and on snowmobiles with two Utah DPS helicopters at the ready, then quietly took position on snowshoes in the frozen dark. They weren't yet sure which of the cabins Knapp was inhabiting. They couldn't be positive he was there at all.

But part of the plan was that the racket from one of the helicopters would alert Knapp. It did. The first helicopter came in from the east; they could see Knapp on a cabin's porch. "At about nine in the morning, Knapp is out chopping wood for his morning fire when this big-ass bird comes in over the trees," U.S. Marshal Michael Wingert, the lead federal agent assigned to Knapp's case, told me on the phone. "He grabs his rifle and shoots at the bird."

Knapp squeezed off several rifle rounds. The men in the helicopter saw him reload. The fugitive strapped into his snowshoes, grabbed his rifle, and took off running to the south. After an exhausting hundred-yard dash, he encountered Emery County sheriff Greg Funk. Knapp raised his rifle. Funk fired and missed. Knapp broke back to the north and ran into a line of lawmen. He realized he was heavily outgunned—and surrendered.

"You got me," Knapp told arresting officers. "Nice job."

But for seven years, Knapp had had an incredible run in the

wilderness. Here was a lone man on snowshoes running circles around sheriffs and marshals with little but his physical fitness and backcountry savvy—an alpine athlete living on rabbit and Dinty Moore stew. He'd earned a sort of grudging admiration from the men on his tail; Knapp seemed to understand that you didn't have to outrun the dogs, you merely had to outrun the handlers. He was good at staying ahead of the handlers.

Wanted posters are more rare than missing persons posters. The posters of Knapp recharged southern Utah with an Old West quality; they'd been tacked up in gas stations from Kanab to Payson. Hikers and hunters were leery of heading into the high country, and families became shy about visiting their weekend cabins. The fugitive had even acquired a Facebook page, set up by an admirer, filled with mountain-man poetry and clumsy odes to outlaws and Waylon Jennings. The name Unabomber was bandied about. Some recalled the Olympic Park Bomber, Eric Rudolph, who hid for five years in the North Carolina woods, dumpster diving and swiping vegetables from gardens. Or fellow Utah fugitive Lance Leeroy Arellano, who disappeared into the desert in his silver Pontiac after shooting a state ranger in 2010.

Knapp didn't have a known history of that kind of violence, but he commanded respect. "I could take every cop in Utah who's comfortable on a pair of snowshoes up there right now and not find him," Wingert told me. In a year and a half of tailing Knapp, Wingert became the Pat Garrett to his Billy the Kid. "You give this guy a day and he's fifteen or twenty miles away. There's people who can survive a night out—say they break a snowshoe binding or lose the track on a snowmobile," Wingert said, "but to actually stay out there for months and months and years on end—this guy is as close to Jim Bridger as we're ever gonna see."

In summer, Knapp lived in his own homemade camps; over

the years deputies found bivouacs, usually with a blue tarp, in the aspen trees, stocked with guns and, in one, a copy of *Into the Wild*. Several of his high camps were discovered by cougar hunters, who hunt in high, rocky terrain. As far up as 9,000 feet, they were relatively sophisticated shelters with framed doors and rocks and wood and earth.

In winter, the Mountain Man made himself at home. His usual mode of entry was to break a window or door pane, twist the lock, and let himself in. Sometimes he'd wipe his boots, sometimes he wouldn't. He made soup from cans and helped himself to coffee. Knapp liked sardines, mayonnaise, and especially liquor—if there was a bottle of spirits, he might drink it and rend the place with bullet holes. He might replace the firewood he burned. Sometimes he did his dishes, but he never put them away. He liked to steal radios, listening on local AM stations to erroneous reports of his own whereabouts.

In early 2012, when Knapp's identity was verified by investigators and reported by local media, his reputation as a harmless survivalist began to slide. In the cabin owned by a former Las Vegas police officer, he made a crucifix with knives on the bed. At times he appeared angry at Latter Day Saints—he shot holes in a portrait of Joseph Smith and ripped up the Book of Mormon. He cost one cabin owner thousands of dollars in smoke damage when he closed the flue before vamoosing. He traded guns with another—leaving his old .303 British and taking a sexier Remington. He crowbarred into a gun safe, laid all the arms on a table, and took none. In another cabin, he removed the grips from all the guns, but left them. He placed food cans behind kitchen drawers so they wouldn't close. He defecated on a porch; he also shat in a pan and left it on somebody's kitchen floor.

Authorities labeled him "armed and dangerous" in January 2012, reporting that the Mountain Man had been leaving threatening notes in cabins or outside scrawled in the dirt. The tune was always the same: "Get off my mountain."

For most of those seven years, lawmen were hunting a ghost. As early as 2007, they suspected that one man was breaking into properties over a big area, but damned if they knew who. "Even when we got a tip, we were always one week behind," Kane County Chief Deputy Tracy Glover said. The Mountain Man stuck to ridge tops, avoiding established trails. He walked on vegetation to avoid leaving an easy track. He slipped from heavy hunting boots into size ten sneakers to minimize his footprints.

Knapp mainly roamed 1,000 square miles of southwestern Utah, from the Arizona border north into Zion National Park and onto Cedar Mountain above Cedar City. His habitat ranged from alpine forests to the sparsely populated desert. He was known to walk to town—St. George and Cedar City—and hang out with the home-less population and make phone calls to his mother in Moscow, Idaho, then head back into the wild.

Then investigators got a break in December 2011, when a motion-activated camera outside a cabin in Kane County captured the image of a man with neck and hand tattoos and a ginger goatee. The man wore forest-camo hunting outerwear that hung on him. A camo fleece beanie. A Remington 600 bolt-action rifle. A long hunt-ing knife in a leather sheath. Purple aluminum snowshoes. People captured with wildlife cameras have a spectral quality to them, like they don't belong in the frame, are out of place in the ecosystem.

The game cam photo alone couldn't positively identify the man, but fingerprints obtained from a broken windowpane in 2009 matched with Troy James Knapp, five feet ten inches tall, approximately 150 pounds, with hazel eyes. This led the cops to mug shots taken in Inyo County, California, in 2000. Knapp's hand and chain-link neck tattoos matched the Mountain Man's.

Knapp had been in trouble since his high-school-dropout days in Kalamazoo, Michigan, where in 1986 he was incarcerated for four years for breaking and entering and receiving stolen property. After that, he drifted, working odd jobs and living for a time with one girlfriend and then fathering a daughter with another in 1995. He was charged with harassment in Seattle in 1997 (that charge was eventually dismissed with prejudice). He lived briefly in Salt Lake City in 1999.

His stepdad, Bruce Knapp, a sportsman, had taught young Troy wilderness skills—hunting, trapping—and that became Knapp's MO. In September 2000, he began living the outlaw life in Inyo County, camping near the town of Bishop. There he was arrested on charges of felony burglary for stealing from the Inyo County solid waste facility and the Mount Whitney Fish Hatchery in Independence. The *Salt Lake Tribune* reported that Knapp stole a pair of boots from a game warden's pickup near the hatchery, even as they were looking for him. A deputy's report from 2000 quotes Knapp: "I did not want to hurt anyone." Then, in 2004, after spending four years in jail, Knapp broke parole.

Southern Utah, his next stop, is a lot like Inyo County: It is high alpine, but also full of slot canyons and rock chicanes and deserts side by side. One day it's sunburn, the next, frostbite. In Inyo County, the Sierras quickly drop to Death Valley. And the county had its own backcountry outlaw: the Ballarat Bandit, George Robert Johnston, who eluded law enforcement for years while camping and squatting in remote southeastern California and western Nevada before he shot himself in the head with a .22 in July 2004.

Utah authorities thought they were hot on Knapp's trail in late February 2012, when a resident shoveling snow spotted a camo-clad man with a large-caliber rifle slung over his shoulder. A two-day manhunt went down above Cedar City, including Iron County sheriff's deputies, Cedar City police, and even the campus cops from Southern Utah University. A helicopter scoured a ten-mile radius.

In the end, the manhunt only fueled the myth. Locals were left wondering how anyone could have eluded a helicopter with FLIR technology and thirty men on foot.

I grew up on stories of the Mad Trapper of Rat River, a legendary Canadian survivalist fugitive from the 1930s, and Claude Dallas, the poacher who evaded capture for over a year after killing two game wardens in 1981 on the Idaho–Nevada border. In the mid-nineties, Hilary and I lived in a remote cabin in northern Utah, where we'd ski up to and peer into the vacation cabins that hibernated over winter. What a resource, I thought, for a wayfarer with just a little wilderness savvy. If an uninvited guest was considerate enough, no one would even know they'd been there. Unless the cabin had a wildlife camera.

In April 2012, I traveled to Knapp country. At that point, I'd been tracking him—via wire stories and local knowledge—for nearly four months. I had a wall map full of enough Knapp sighting pins it looked like a game of Battleship. Photos on my desk showed him grow thinner from mug shot to game cam shots; he seemed to be working into fighting shape, which you need to be to hump a heavy pack over mountains for twenty miles a day.

Kane County is 4,000 square miles, the size of Hawaii's Big Island, but there are just over 7,000 people living there, half of them in the county seat of Kanab. The sheriff's department boasts thirteen sworn officers, not including the uniformed mannequins in the marked SUVs parked at the city limits of Mount Carmel and Orderville to discourage speeders. This part of the state has become Mexican cartel marijuana country, and I was reminded of what Wingert had told me before I arrived: "If we have trouble finding cartel-size grow operations in that country, imagine trying to find one camouflaged guy on foot who doesn't want to be caught."

The bull's-eye of Knapp country seemed to be the Cedar Mountain area above Cedar City, where hundreds of seasonal cabins are tightly surrounded by Dixie National Forest land. The area includes 11,307-foot Brian Head Peak, the Brian Head ski resort, and Duck Creek, a little village where you can hire four-wheelers or snowmobiles and a guide.

Since the first wanted posters went up in Duck Creek in January 2012, the Mountain Man had become something of a cross between Sasquatch and Jeremiah Johnson. Cougar hunters saw him walking a ridgetop before he vanished. A cowboy reported running into a "suspicious" mountain man packing his gear on a pair of mules. Strange campfires were seen on the mountain above Cedar City at night. Dozens of people saw the Mountain Man riding his mountain bike through town. Kids liked to spot him in trees. My favorite was a dog let outside at 4:30 every morning that returned at 6:30 reeking of campfire smoke.

Marshal Wingert ghosted me after I got off the plane in St. George, as law enforcement sometimes does, so I relied on local knowledge. In Duck Creek, a sledhead at a snowmobile shop told me that I needed to find Rosey Canyon, up the North Fork of the Virgin River, because that's where I'd find a guy named Ken Moffett, the caretaker for several cabins. Back in February, he said, Moffett had tracked the Mountain Man in the snow, on foot, for seven miles. This would make Moffett, at the time, the guy with the closest encounter with Knapp. "But honk your horn at the mouth of the canyon," I was warned, "otherwise he might think you're the Mountain Man and shoot ya."

The road led through Springdale, the gateway village to Zion National Park. At a bar and restaurant called the Spotted Dog, I met two forty-something cabin owners, Robert "Roberto" Dennis and his sister, Wendy Dennis. Like many of the locals, they were curious and a little anxious and wanted to check the family hunting cabin to see if anyone had broken in. "We keep guns up there," Wendy told me. "They're our shitguns, but still."

We climbed into Roberto's 1994 GMC pickup. Wendy took the jump seat; Duke, the Lab-pit mix, got the middle, where he slobbered on my maps. Southern Utahans do not leave home without some kind of firearm, but Roberto packed light—a toy-size .22 caliber short-barrel Beretta he called a hooker gun. We were headed twenty-five miles higher up, toward Cedar Mountain. It was drier than a Mormon wedding, and the truck left a veil of dust.

Roberto and Wendy had found something odd in the forest the hunting season before: a Hefty bag hanging in a forty-foot ponderosa pine. They thought it was trash, but the bag contained a knit beanie. Felt boot liners. A camo sleeping bag. A pair of nearly-new size ten sneakers. Matches and chainsaw sharpeners. This didn't say hunter or Boy Scout. It said transient—alpine homeless. Still, it's curious why it was up here, so far from Interstate 15.

Many of the cabins we passed were homogenous: attractive, clean, and new. The Dennis cabin was not, rather a cobbled utilitarian compound with a generator shed where they hang the venison and an antique propane refrigerator that sealed the silverware and some warm Budweisers from the mice.

Something had been inside the Dennis cabin for certain, but it wasn't human. There were rifle cartridges and Tammy Wynette eight-track-tape cartridges strung from hell to breakfast. Turds the size of licorice snaps were strewn all over the kitchen table, like a taunt. Wendy located a dusty green bottle of Jägermeister. "Gotta take a shot at the cabin," she said and did. The mood was one of light relief, but mostly disappointment—disappointment that a varmint had ransacked the place, but also that the infamous Mountain Man had skipped it for a stay-over.

We got back in the truck and turned upcountry to Rosey Canyon, driving fifteen more miles, over dirty snow drifts and through braided streams, until we came upon a man standing in the middle of the two-track road.

"Are you Moffett?" I said through the truck window.

"Yes, I am," he said.

Moffett was clean-shaven with long gray hair. "We've had a problem now for seven years," he said. His encounter had taken place six weeks prior, in mid-February, a week before Knapp was fingered by name. "I caught these weird tracks," Moffett said. "This guy was sneakin' around bushes," he said as he pointed up the road toward the neighbor's place. "Sure enough," Moffett said, "there's these tracks going around all their windows."

Moffett had hopped on his four-wheeler and motored up the road. "Went up to check on the Stuckers' place," he said. He'd walked the property and circled back. Then Moffett told us the strange thing. The mountain man had sent Moffett a message in the snow: "I noticed there were carefully placed snowshoe tracks on top of my boot tracks."

Moffett is the kind of Edward Abbey-esque character who might have appreciated Knapp's gift at surviving solo, but he too had tired of the Mountain Man's antics. "Give him a can of soup, who cares," Moffett said. "But I think he's getting more and more disturbed. He's progressively upped the ante here. It's like he's getting paranoid now. I don't wanna walk up on him, and I don't want one of my neighbors getting shot."

That seemed bound to happen, as Knapp got angrier and messier. After he was ID'd, he left several drunken notes, including this one from a cabin in Kane County: "Hey sheriff; fuck you! Gonna put you in the ground! It's better, these times, to be a ditch digger, septic cleaner than a pig." I was curious about his use of a semicolon.

Authorities were unsure, however, how violent Knapp was. Wingert told me about a homeless man in Washington County, along the Virgin River, who in 2010 said that he had been brutally beaten by Knapp with a rock over some camping gear. The man declined to press charges.

Knapp's time on Cedar Mountain also coincided with a strange, cold-case homicide straight out of a Coen brothers' movie. In 2007, during hunting season, the partially buried body of sixty-nine-year-old Kennard Martin Honore of San Clemente, California—who'd leased a cabin from the Forest Service—was found in the cinder pits near Navajo Lake, west of Duck Creek. Honore had died from a single gunshot wound from a small-caliber rifle and been hastily buried. Kane County deputies could find no motive and no sign of robbery. There were a lot of hunters in the area, so it could have been a stray round. But the small caliber doesn't make sense for deer, and the quick gravework doesn't make stray-shot sense. No evidence connects Knapp to the case except that he is believed to have been in the area at the time. Still, Wingert said, "It's kind of an unusual coincidence."

Before Knapp was apprehended, I spoke to criminal psychologist Eric Hickey, dean of the California School of Forensic Studies at Alliant International University in Fresno. "The isolation is probably costing him," said Hickey, who worked as a consultant on the Unabomber case. I told him how Knapp's behavior had seemed to escalate, about his threatening note to the sheriff and the pan of scat in the kitchen. "Most people are not good at being isolated like that. He's acting out. I suspect he has no control." Hickey said the scat in the pan was a signal. "This is a signature.

"The truth is," said Hickey, "if law enforcement decides to go after him, they can track him. I guarantee, if he hurts somebody they'll go after him." But he didn't, and Knapp's trail was cold all last summer.

Then, in October, he resurfaced. Knapp had moved north—almost 120 miles north. He was seen near Fish Lake Reservoir, a high-alpine lake on the Fishlake National Forest in southern Sevier County, and again north of there in Sanpete County, which borders on the Wasatch Front, the mountain playground for Salt Lake City. Gaunt and clean-shaven, he appeared on a security camera, this time at night so that his eyes glowed, waving his arms to feel out an alarm.

He broke in but took nothing. Then, in November, an elk hunter reported seeing Knapp in Sevier County. That sighting mustered a forty-officer cabin-to-cabin manhunt that again kicked up goose eggs. What followed was a long, cold winter of no news until the horn-hunting Fullers met the Mountain Man on the Dairy Trail.

Knapp is lucky he wasn't gunned down in the shadow of the Wasatch Plateau when he opened fire at the helicopter with an assault rifle, an outcome Detective Conover attributes to "dumb luck."

Shooting at a law-enforcement heli certainly amplified his woes, as did possessing a .357 Magnum when he was captured. Now, in addition to the six felonies and five misdemeanors he was charged with on April 4 in Sanpete County—including assorted counts of burglary, theft, criminal mischief, and unauthorized use of a firearm—he could face charges of assault on law-enforcement officers and discharging a weapon at an aircraft. "The cabin burglaries," Wingert said, "will turn out to be the least of his worries."

But Knapp seemed at peace with his capture. In wire photos he appeared relieved, even grinning at times. He told deputies he was tired of the elements—that he was getting older and the winters were getting colder—and that he didn't hate people, but he didn't especially like them, either. He mentioned Robin Hood by name, pointing out that he'd simply tapped resources—food, firewood, guns—that weren't being used.

Sanpete County authorities got him a shower, a new striped jumpsuit, and some pizza, then spread out the maps and let Knapp draw lines between all the places he'd been. When you haven't talked to many people other than your mother for nearly seven years, apparently it builds up. Knapp didn't appear concerned about lawyering up; he sang to officers like a proud jailbird.

Troy James Knapp had a closet full of baggage, I know, and I wish he was more Robin Hood and less just hood. I wish he'd only left thank-you notes instead of threats, and never shat in a pan. But his capture made me a little sad. Utah needs, as the Grateful Dead song goes, its friends of the devil spending the night in a cave—or cabin—up in the hills.

Some of the lawmen who participated in the manhunt don't think Knapp was trying to hit the chopper with his rifle—just deter it. Why do you say that? I asked Conover. Because that's what he told us, he said.

"It's a good thing you got me when you did," Knapp told the lawmen on the ground. "I was gonna move tomorrow."

CHAPTER 18

MOUNT RAINIER

*The inclination to believe in the fantastic may
strike some as a failure in logic, or gullibility, but
it's really a gift. A world that might have Bigfoot
and the Loch Ness Monster is clearly superior to
one that definitely does not.*

                             —*Chris Van Allsburg*

THE HOPPING OF the San Juan Islands was wet, lonely, and unproductive other than talking with farmers and baristas and passengers on the ferries, and pinning posters to community bulletin boards outside of small grocery stores and coffee sheds. Islands are societal compressors, and it would be unlikely for Jacob to go unnoticed in the San Juans. The little red folding bicycle wasn't much use there after all.

But the hanging of posters, the process, is a type of mantra—it becomes a ritual that feels like progress. Pinning posters is the most analog of reflexes when a person is missing. Jacob's picture is right there in front of you, what a winsome kid. All the memories, that are actually the memories of the last time you thought of a time—

the memory of a memory—reproduced like missing posters on a Xerox machine. Maybe Jacob will see his own poster and remember to call his parents.

Randy went back to Santa Cruz without Jacob, again.

On May 2, 2018, Randy forwarded me a Facebook message Mallory had sent him, from a person identifying herself as A——. Her last name is Native American or First Nations.

I know this sounds crazy and I don't want to give you any false hope but I feed a family of Sasquatch in Washington State one of them sent me a telepathic message and told me his name he also showed me Jacob Gray he was alive he was not free to go he was free to walk around that is all that I can tell you I know this is not conventional news or something that anyone want to hear but it is what was shown to me

A——

I live on Alder Lake and I have been feeding this family for two years. I don't want anything. I just needed to tell you what they have shown me

I am willing to take a lie detector test

A——

She gives her phone number.

The Find Jacob Gray Facebook page says this:

I'll pass your number on to my family

Thank you. I don't know any more info than I've provided. There is definitely something going on that's not natural or publicly known. And the Sasquatches are not involved.

A—

I knew the message from the Bigfoot feeder struck a chord with Randy, enough that he'd forward it to me. I could tell what he was thinking and made travel plans to meet him in Santa Cruz—we'd head back to the Pacific Northwest, and once again Bigfoot would be involved, this time more directly, it appeared, than the researchers and the Bigfoot Barn. This was a witness with information about Jacob.

Randy has a really hard time being a skeptic. He's childlike in his sense of wonder, a quality I admire. I can't help but think of the Mitch Hedberg bit: *I think Bigfoot is blurry, that's the problem. It's not the photographer's fault. Bigfoot is blurry, and that's extra scary to me. There's a large, out-of-focus monster roaming the countryside. Run, he's fuzzy, get out of here.* But I see the need for Randy to believe that there are things we don't understand, and one of those things may be the tie to finding Jacob. Sharks are a reality in Randy's water world—it's only natural, then, that Bigfoot should exist in Randy's terrestrial world.

There are strange species at the deepest depths of the ocean that we haven't ever seen, but scientists believe are there—maybe there are primate hominids that are invisible to trail cams. And trail cams are now everywhere.

The Clackamas Indians believe that adolescent Bigfeet must pass a test to become an adult member of the Bigfoot tribe. The young Sasquatch must leap in front of a human on the trail, and wave their huge hands in front of the human's face, without being seen. Invisible as a missing person.

*   *   *

I can't talk about Bigfoot without mentioning David Paulides. Paulides was angry with me after the story about Joe Keller was published. He thought I'd done him a disservice by both mentioning that his books are self-published and conflating his Bigfoot research with his missing persons research. He writes in an email:

> *It almost appears you want to diminish my sincerity and credibility by bringing up something that is categorically irrelevant, yet something that many readers believe is a joke. It appears to be a left handed attack at my credibility and thus takes away from our work with missing people and will push people away from our work in that arena...I don't understand why you did this. David Paulides*

Paulides is without a doubt the one who has brought the most attention to this phenomenon, all the unfound and unaccounted people missing in the wild. He's also a well-lubed marketing man, and from what I can glean doesn't directly give back or help search—his contribution to the underworld of the missing would be awareness. He's certainly a provocateur, at times a carnival barker, and a disruptor if you're the National Park Service. He's careful to remind his audiences, often at a UFO or cryptozoology conference, he's not saying UFOs or Bigfoot are causing people to vanish, but he also doesn't appear to say they're *not* responsible.

Randy and I drive by the ocean. There are people selling avocados eight for ninety-nine cents from their tailgates. Randy shows me the spot near Cowell's Beach where Randy and Jacob saved a kite surfer's life together. "It was a big, stormy day," Randy says. Kite boarding is dangerous enough on a flat day, dealing with lines and a wet kite. The guy was two hundred yards out in a big swell. "Big waves."

We go to the Longboard Union surfing contest. "I'll go out and surf for a day, I'll stay out eight hours," Randy says. "I gotta get back into it. When I find Jacob I'm gonna get back into it, surfing every day." Randy never did tell me Jacob sold his favorite surfboard— Laura told me that. That was a thing that really worried Randy, a bad sign.

We both buy raffle tickets to win a custom longboard, but neither has any luck. Randy introduces me to Frosty Hesson, the Santa Cruz surf legend who trained local kid Jay Moriarty, a fifteen-year-old Santa Cruz kid, to surf the famous Mavericks surf break, where in the winter waves can top out at a mountainous sixty feet. Randy tells me *training* for such epic waves consists of learning to hold your breath for a really long time. Gerard Butler plays Frosty and Jonny Weston plays Moriarty in the 2012 biopic *Chasing Mavericks*. Moriarty was twenty-two years old when he drowned in a freediving accident in the Indian Ocean in 2001.

"You want air so bad," Randy says. "Panic is not gonna help you. You just relax, let the wave do its thing."

Randy calls me *Grom*, a kid, so I call him *Kook*, a newbie surfer. Truth is, I'm more of a kook than a grom, and he's the opposite of a kook in the water, but acts like a grom in life—it's his childlike attitude, I think, that propels him to search the universe until he finds some answers in Jacob's vanish. His life goal now: "I just wanna go surfing with that sucker. That sucker." He's talking about Jacob. "We're gonna surf."

Randy is going undercover. He's growing his hair shoulder-length and making an attempt at growing a beard. The long hair comes naturally to him; the beard, not so much. It's wiry and thin, not unlike Shaggy on *Scooby-Doo*, though back in the day he could sport a grand mustache. The idea is that he can slip in and out of homeless camps and organic farms and not get too much attention, he tells me. And there's a cult in Canada that he wants to check out, one that Mallory told him about—the different look will be good camouflage. But I think he just needs to reinvent a part of himself, a different Randy Gray with all of Randy Gray's superpowers.

I realize he's less in denial and more in gear, moving forward; the nature of this type of trip is that you must take the long route. "You get the reality of what it means to find a needle in a haystack," Randy says. It's not a cliché, not a misplaced hammer gun at the jobsite. "I've been thinking. I'll need a tool on a construction site. I'll remember where I put it—I've just seen it, but I can't find it. I'll look for a day for it. And when I stop looking for it—there it is, I'll find it. I think it's maybe the same way looking for Jacob."

This time we fill the propane tanks and leave, headed north, in the evening. We grab dollar-menu burgers and camp in a rest area on the interstate near flooded rice fields in northern California.

In the morning Randy makes coffee in the Arctic Fox and we chew on Dr. Amen's Brain on Joy bars, dark chocolate and coconut. I have a family member who suffers schizophrenia, and I think about how *let's get you some help* could sound like *we're gonna have you committed* to him—the police used to talk to him through his television set.

"Impossibilities become possibilities," Randy says. Which is why we're going to meet an Indian who feeds a family of Sasquatch. "I got nothing else to go on. It's shooting in the dark. I need to not have an agenda. Is it logical what my son did? What the shit is logical?" There's nothing logical about the Bigfoot woman, but Randy wants to see what she has to say. Bigfoot is not going to walk out of the woods holding Jacob's hand, but then Randy might learn something there that leads him in the right direction—in this case

Bigfoot at Mount Rainier is the catalyst that gets him out of Santa Cruz and back on the search once again, when he'd exhausted every probability in the Olympic Peninsula.

Randy phones Derek Randles, this time solely because of his Bigfoot experience and knowledge. "What do you think about a woman who feeds a family of Sasquatch who got a telepathic message that they know where Jacob is?"

I can hear Derek take a deep breath on the speakerphone. "In all honesty, Randy, it's a load of horseshit."

"The Sasquatches told her Jacob was trying to get out, but couldn't. He was naked and dirty in the forest. He was scared."

"Yeah, well, I'm just telling you straight up," Derek says.

"Okay," Randy says. "Hey, I think we're gonna head your way after"—we lose the cell signal.

But not the satellite. "Ride Captain Ride (upon your mystery ship)" by the Blues Image plays on the Sirius XM. "This is the mystery ship," Randy says, referring to the big Dodge. It's getting dark, time to start looking for a place to camp.

"This is not normal," Randy says. I'm not sure if he's talking to me or to himself. "I'm not going through a normal part of my life right now. Nothing's normal about this." Randy is part Cherokee, maybe one-sixteenth, he guesses. That at least can't hurt to get him closer to Bigfoot.

"You gotta be attuned," Randy says. "This lady's gonna get me in tune."

Randy tells me that when he was eighteen his friend's parents— Christian Scientists—died from eating poisonous mushrooms. Randy had eaten some too, but just enough to make him sick, not kill him. "I hadn't thought about that in a long time," he says.

He loves martial arts and its symbiotic relationship to surfing. "Budo-Kai," he says. "Budo-Kai, karate. We trained with a Zen master who had us run through a dark house at night with masters throwing punches at us. They'd just pop up from behind a couch, behind a door, and *bam!*" I get the sense that searching for Jacob is a bit like running through a dark house at night.

When Randy was twenty-two years old—the same age Jacob was when he disappeared—he almost moved to Japan indefinitely to study karate. Instead, he accidentally started what he calls a half-way house in Santa Cruz. He owned a small house near the beach and let a friend going through a rough patch stay there rent-free. "It just kind of opened up to other people," he says. He kept letting people in and watching people move out, including Jessie Young, a soundman for local rockers the Doobie Brothers. Randy ran the house that way for a decade.

"Man, it was trashed at the end," he said. But it's representative of Randy's generosity. I've traveled with him enough to know it's genuine—his heart is huge.

It's after dark when we pull off the highway to camp on the Gifford Pinchot National Forest near Mount Rainier.

In the morning—it's a Wednesday in late May—he wakes up wanting to tell me about his dream, even before coffee. "I had a dream that I was piggybacking on one of those suckers!" Randy says. I can't tell if he's joking or not. By "suckers" he means Bigfoot. A crow is squawking outside the Arctic Fox.

Like some sort of drug deal where the drug is Bigfoot information, we plan to meet A——, Bigfoot Woman, in the parking lot of Rocky Point Recreation Area on Alder Lake. The sun is out, we can see snowcapped Mount Rainier, and Randy is snoring in the reclined driver's seat after eating a big steak and eggs breakfast at the local tavern. Randy is the ultimate optimist. He's wildly curious. The seeker from the Who song. "What else do I got?" he says. "What else can I do?" Psychics and Bigfoot people.

The psychics don't see anything alike with each other and

the Bigfoot people call bullshit on each other's theories. Meanwhile, Randy believes *something*—who knows what—could lead to *something*.

A— pulls up. She's wearing a cap that says BIGFOOT DOESN'T BELIEVE IN YOU EITHER. She seems shaken. Back at the general store in Elbe, there was a white van. A couple of "Amish-looking" women and a punk-rock girl. "It was strange," A— says. "They were like cult members. Something wasn't right, I got a bad feeling. I got their license number, AKC 397, but I didn't see what state it was."

She decides she can trust us, at least a little. She's half Cherokee and appreciates that Randy is a fraction. Besides, he's immediately trustworthy to everyone he meets. We follow her down the highway to her rented place. Her landlord, who I'll call Loretta, is there to scrutinize the Arctic Fox pulling into her driveway. She stumble-walks over to the driver's side; it's apparent she's half in the bag. "There's an RV campground down the road," she says. A— explains what's up, that we're here to commune with her Bigfoot family regarding Randy's missing son. Loretta says we can park the rig and spend the night.

We walk down the hill into a clearing. It's cool and Randy wears his Pearson Arrow hoodie, which also serves to keep the mosquitoes from biting his arms and neck. There are two motorhomes that look like they were just driven down the hill and abandoned, maybe twenty years ago, maybe last week. A— builds a fire in a firepit. The smoke is good against the bugs. She cracks a beer and we wait for dusk, when, she says, the Bigfoot family sneaks through the weeds to feed on the apples and powdered donuts she leaves in a hanging feeder that doubles as a bird feeder.

To the nonbeliever it would look a lot like the resident raccoon climbed out on a limb and grabbed the donuts. But to A— and Randy, it's another message.

There's a racket uphill, toward the house.

"She's drunk," A— says. "She's always drunk."

"What the hell is going on down there?" It's Loretta. There are other tenants who live in different parts of the house. I get the sense the place is dysfunctional, a house like something out of Ken Kesey's *Sometimes a Great Notion*.

"Go away, Sasquatch!" Loretta calls. Her voice is getting closer; here she comes. I hope she doesn't have a pistol. "This is my place. Look what I got—what do you got, Sasquatch! Get the fuck out of here!"

Randy tries to reason with Loretta, who has a slosh-crush on the shaggy-haired surfer with California plates on his mobile home who just came motoring into her life a couple hours before—*kismet*. Randy is good with drunks and street people. He's good with kids. I think he'll be good with Bigfoot. Then Drunk Loretta says this: "He's dead. Your son is dead."

"Go home, get the fuck out of here, you bitch!" A— yells. "How dare you!"

"I own this place, what do you have, you get the fuck out of here," Loretta slurs.

Instead of getting angry and flying off the handle at Loretta, the gentle surfer coaxes her back up the hill, redirects her like you're supposed to do in dog training. He makes sure she isn't going to fall down the hill, then returns to the clearing by the fire.

It's not that Randy, surfer-optimist that he is, truly expects a Bigfoot is going to tell him where Jacob is. That isn't the point. But the Sasquatch—even if it doesn't exist—could still lead him to Jacob. That's what Randy understands. Searching for a missing person, after that first week, is a believer's game. Hell, even having lost his son, Randy's glass is so full it's spilling over the rim. Even if Derek calls it horseshit, Randy's gonna go check out the horseshit. He has to.

"You've got to open your heart," A— tells Randy, if he wants to telepathically talk with the Bigfoot.

"I already have," Randy says.

It's pitch dark now. Randy sits in a lawn chair facing the donut birdfeeder and speaks in his warm, calm voice to the Sasquatch. "Stay-e-mah," he says, the word A— instructed him to use, their word for Sasquatch, Bigfoot. "Stay-e-mah. Stay-e-mah."

A— says, "This is Randy Gray, Jacob's dad. Aeeshee—friend." The Bigfoot word for friend.

"Aeeshee," Randy says into the night. "Aeeshee."

I walk back to the truck and let Randy communicate without me listening over his shoulder. This is private, between Randy and the Bigfoot family and A—, but I don't belong. I'm already concerned about how I'm going to write this and not misrepresent Randy or A—. I walk slowly back to the Arctic Fox, but I'm listening.

"Stay-e-mah. Aeeshee. My name is Randy Gray, Jacob's dad—"

I read in my bunk until I fall asleep. Randy climbs in some time later. "I think I heard a grunt," he says. "The donuts are gone too. A grunt." He wants so badly for Sasquatch to be sentient. His missing link. Biologists would find a lot of raccoons with cavities here. "A grunt."

I see another thing Randy is, in part, doing. Another psychic— always a psychic—had a vision that she'd seen Jacob, dead, along the Sol Duc River, downstream from where the bike and trailer were found, across from the fish hatchery. That's where Tanya and James and Derek and Laura are gonna search in a couple days, and we're supposed to meet them. Another psychic dream. He's trying to distract his mind from the river search on the Sol Duc, and Bigfoot is helping him do it. As far-fetched as another psychic vision is, Randy is thinking, *What if she's right?* The psychics don't tend to see visions of Jacob alive—at least the Bigfoot told A— Jacob's near them. It's far more hopeful that the Bigfoot say Jacob's alive, even if he can't go home.

The next morning Randy makes coffee and reaches me a cup while I'm still in my sleeping bag. "I'm gonna go find Loretta and thank her," he says. I'm not convinced that's a good idea, but what do you do. Randy walks toward the lake to search for evidence of Sasquatch. Ten minutes later I hear, "Motherfucker!" and it's on— Loretta is up. She's arguing with A—. Randy smooths her feathers. He climbs in and fires up the diesel.

"She's still drunk?" I ask.

"Yeah, still drunk," Randy says. "And drunk again." It's not even eight in the morning. "She's drinking beer. She said, 'Maybe Jacob doesn't want to be found. You have to find yourself.' Maybe. Maybe I'll do a little of that too."

CHAPTER 19

OLYMPIC PENINSULA & THE HOLY LAND

Then the man said, "Your name will no longer be Jacob, but Israel, because you have struggled with God and with humans and have overcome."
—Genesis 32:28

Best case scenario for us now is obviously that he's found alive. Or he's found. Worst case scenario is we never know.
—Matthew McAfee, Ollie's brother

MALLORY SENT ME the maps. She believes a mashup was going on in Jacob's mind. "Check out how similar these maps are," she says. "One of them is Israel's journey through the wilderness, and the other is Washington...Brings a new light? Canaan and Canada are mighty similar as well." Jacob's browsing history shows he was in the process of applying to go to Canada and may have explored ways of getting there without one.

Shuffled with the maps of Washington's Olympic Peninsula and Olympic National Park are historic maps of the Middle East showing deserts between ancient towns like Heliopolis and Memphis. Side by side, the Olympic Peninsula and the Holy Land conflate.

The Strait of Juan de Fuca and the Mediterranean Sea. The Sinai Peninsula and the Wilderness of Wandering. Humptulips and Zin. The Dead Sea and Angeles Lake.

A meteorological map illustrates Technicolor rain pattern images that resembled a Grateful Dead tie-dye tour shirt. There are bike tour maps, a United States Geological Survey Washington Water Science Center map that looks like some sort of nerd camouflage, and a *Go Northwest!* travel guide. I feel akin to Jacob in how I'm fueled by cartography.

Mallory also sent me a photo of her and Jacob's grandmother's painting. It's a trip. Wyoma's watercolor is a zoo-swirl of a winged lion and the lizard-like duck. Wyoma calls it *Olympic National Park*. There are horned sheep that resemble the mountain goats park officials are slowly removing by helicopter from the ONP high country because they're taking over. The *exotic* nonnative ungulates are thought to ruin park vegetation and can be aggressive—a hiker from Port Angeles was killed by a goat on Klahhane Ridge in 2010. There is a blue-and-green fish that may be a Sol Duc River salmon. There is a bear—an ONP black bear maybe.

Otherwise the painting seems less ONP and more Noah's ark or Book of Revelations even. There are familiar cattle, a pig, a rabbit, pigeons, and a cat and kitten that may be mountain lions. Green dinosauresque reptiles, a tan python-scale serpent, and a green dragon. A white bird—a cross between a dove and a goose—clings to the mane of a lion. The creatures don't seem menacing or frightened, rather at peace with their station in this world.

In the center of the painting is a woman with auburn hair cloaked in green clutching two ears of corn. She's looking down at the vortex of the scene, a blond-haired king with a gold crown riding a white horse bareback in water. The king is wearing a blue cloak and a gold crucifix on his chest. From atop the galloping horse the king dumps a clay jar of water into the water.

Perhaps most peculiar and easy to miss is the tiny brown naked man a third of the size of the pigeons—or maybe they're doves or grouse—at the bottom of the painting so that he appears to be standing on the rim of the easel.

It's an Old Testament acid dream of a painting, and Jacob studied it for hours.

I ask Mallory if she thought this was out of character for Jacob—I'm one who experiences art-museum fatigue after half an hour. "Not if he was experiencing a mental health issue," she says. "It would seem 'normal.' If I can notice the maps looking similar, maybe Jacob combined the similarities and came to the conclusion that his journey and his purpose was just that. Also, on a side note my grandmother is very…'spiritual.' She talked to Jacob about a portal somewhere in Olympic National Park."

I asked Marty Leger if his brother was deeply religious. No, he said. "You could say he was agnostic I guess. We grew up Catholic but never really practiced much." The reason I'm interested is that another cyclist disappeared in Israel in November of 2017, eight months after Jacob Gray. I explain that some psychologists believe twenty-nine-year-old Oliver "Ollie" McAfee from Dromore, Northern Ireland, may be suffering the strange and controversial condition called *Jerusalem syndrome*, a condition that amplifies an obsession with biblical scripture and geography and produces a type of messiah complex. Sufferers may or may not believe they are literally Jesus or another character from the bible. Although the syndrome is most often diagnosed in Israel, where travelers and pilgrims may be set going by their arrival in the holy land, Ollie's story is in many ways similar to Jacob's.

The devout Christian quit his landscape gardening job in Essex, England, in the spring for a bike tour of Europe. He wanted to see the Holy Land in Israel by bike and gave the trip five weeks—the plan was to be home for Christmas. By the time he arrived in Israel he'd already logged 8,700 miles across Europe, camping and pretty much living off his bike. *Wild camping*, it's called in Europe— riding all day with no reservations, then pitching a tent in a forest or sleeping under the stars in a vineyard. It's a style of economical travel that Jacob would appreciate, and by now Ollie was deft at it. He owned a Cannondale touring bicycle with panniers and had his system of packing and riding and navigating and eating and drinking and sleeping dialed. He planned to ride from the north, toward the Golan Heights, then south, along the Jerusalem Trail, eventually ending up at Eilat on the Red Sea, then end of the road.

An American cyclist gave him some water on the Israel National Trail near Mitzpe Ramon in the Negev Desert on November 21. They were the last person to see him. Backpackers in the Makhtesh Ramon crater—the world's largest volcanic erosion cirque (a non- impact crater)—found some things belonging to Ollie, including a tablet computer, keys, and his wallet, which contained fifty euros and two credit cards. A Bedouin camel trainer named Whahaldi found a bag belonging to Ollie—scattered about were his tooth- brush and some notebooks. He also found one of Ollie's shoes. Ollie's brother filed a missing persons report when Ollie didn't check in for his flight home. Police turned the search over to Search and Rescue, who found Ollie's bike, tent, and a digital camera. With the camera they were able to breadcrumb his trip down to the crater, his LKP, last known position.

Ollie took two photos each day. "Jordan," he told a barista who befriended him in Givat Harel. "I'm going to Jordan." He did, riding through the Jordan Valley. He circled the Sea of Galilee clockwise. On his eighth day of cycling the Holy Land a photo proves he went swimming in a Jordan estuary near Gesher Arik. Then onward to Ein Gev and the Golan Heights, Mount Hermon and Ramot Naftali. On November 5 he texted his good friend in Essex from Shlomi. Pedal, camp, repeat. Now he rode west, southwest, and down the coastal plain. A local of Gedera took Ollie's photo astride his bike. Next, after two and a half weeks of cycling through Israel, he rode into Jerusalem on his Cannondale. That's where the trajectory of the trip changed.

"After he left Jerusalem he was different," Meidad Goren of Har Hanegev Search and Rescue says. The photos became more abstract. "Suddenly he's documenting small and esoteric details. Suddenly he starts making all kinds of shapes near his camp. Hanging stones with ropes." It appears Ollie ripped pages from his bible and pinned them against the wind with stones. He dug a "temple" of sorts, the size of a grave. Especially odd is that he dug it with a tire lever from a bicycle multitool; searchers found the tool in the center of the excavation.

The last photo was dated November 19, 2017, two days before the American cyclist recalled seeing Ollie. The photo was a close-up of a hitchhiking station in Tsomet Tsihor.

The notebooks found scattered about document a confused struggle with God, Jesus, and existence. "Throw away all personal items, photos, destroying a little, it stops from destoying my whole self…to relieve me from the pain I feel." Searchers believe Ollie may have been fasting because they found food, including whole cans of sardines, among the items left behind. The desert was cold, especially at night.

"Look," Goren said, "it's rare nowadays for people to not leave any digital traces behind. This reinforces the fear that he is here in our region. We search carefully. So if he is not here, then where?" Israel may be the world's foremost surveillance state. The entire country, at 8,000 square miles, is half the size of the Upper Peninsula of Michigan. Much of Israel not bordered by the Mediterranean Sea is fenced, either with wire or technology.

Satellites, drones, and security cameras keep watch on nearly every inch. A foreigner doesn't simply cross in and out of Israel without notice.

One theory is that he fell in with Bedouins and is either living among the almost quarter million of them in one of their Negev villages or may have crossed into Egypt or Jordan with them and could be anywhere.

Two days after Oliver's bag was found, there was an incident at a military base along Road 40. At 3:48 a.m. a figure with a headlamp approached the base's security fence. A camera shows a silhouette in the glare of the light, but it's impossible to make out who it is. The figure disappeared. Ten minutes later a soldier hears screaming. "Ho! Yo!" she reported. "Ho! Yo!"

"Keep away from the fence," she instructed. The light switched off, and the figure disappeared into the dark desert. Locals know they could get shot approaching an Israeli military installation at night.

Sure, the Negev is a massive moonscape. Ollie could have crawled deep into a cave and died there. He could have fallen into a crevasse. But so much of that desert is visible from the air. Searchers will often use birds to indicate a carcass. Early on in the search for Ollie, Goren homed in on an eagle foraging on *something*. It turned out to be a dead camel.

Sufferers of Jerusalem syndrome often have a history of mental illness, but that's not always the case.

"We do have Oliver's journals from his travels, which don't strike us as anything being amiss," Angela McAfee, Oliver's sister-in-law, told me. "He reads the bible and often writes notes as he does, as many Christians do. He also journaled his physical travel through the country, and as you would imagine this journey did blend beautifully with his faith—he was in the Holy Land after all. From his writings, he does discuss preparing and making the trip to come home...There is nothing that we have read that sticks out as indicating that he was seeking to disappear."

A campsite was discovered some distance from the bike. Bible pages—scribbled on in McAfee's handwriting—were left pinned with small rocks, a sort of breadcrumb trail that led to a type of altar made of rocks and scratched out with a bike tool. Some authorities speculated Jerusalem syndrome. Although it would be foolish to rule it out, the Ollie clues—his expensive gear left behind, the bible-page trail, the altar dug in the dirt—just don't feel like foul play. Searchers in Israel believe it's quite possible Oliver is still alive. His sister-in-law speaks of him in the present tense. But there's just so little to go on. "Unfortunately the search for Oliver is very much at a standstill. There have been no confirming sightings, or clues as to his location," she says. A dog trainer in Jerusalem called to report having seen Oliver, but it turned out to be someone else, a pilgrim suffering delusions. That's pretty much the extent of clues following the discovery of the altar. "We fully appreciate it's virtually impossible to search for someone when you have no idea where to look."

"I think he's alive," says Detective Gabi Yifrach with the Israel police. "He lives somewhere in central Israel, the Jerusalem area. In my opinion, if he reached the road, so he wanted to live and must've hitched a ride, but that's just my gut feeling." Ollie's sleeping bag, phone, and passport have not been found.

Some psychiatrists believe one doesn't have to be in Israel to experience Jerusalem syndrome. Perhaps Jacob Gray was looking for God in Eden-like Olympic National Park.

"I think you're definitely on to something with the Jerusalem syndrome," Mallory says. I'm careful to tell her I'm not assigning or prescribing a condition to Jacob, and many psychiatrists and psychologists believe there is no such thing, Jerusalem syndrome is as fictional as Bigfoot and the Loch Ness Monster. "Being in his weak state he could have made connections to anything," she says. "That Canaan looks like Canada—he did try to go to Canada a couple times and couldn't because of no passport."

Robert Koester calls the condition "vision quest." "[Victims] tend to be younger individuals, twenties, thirties," he said. "They tend to suffer mental illness, diagnosed or not. They tend to show signs of despondency. They may not see any need to check in with family. They think they receive a message from God—they will climb the highest mountain, go into the woods."

Or the desert. Jacob may have been using his bicycle as a search engine.

CHAPTER 20

THE PACIFIC CREST TRAIL

The present is the only thing that has no end.
—*Erwin Schrödinger*

RANDY PUSHES BUTTONS on the in-dash screen. "This thing," he says. The map illuminates the cab. "Sometimes the GPS will just come on and I'll follow it—maybe it'll take me to Jacob." Now Randy fumbles with his phone. We're east of Puget Sound, where most of the state is, but it's not his usual Washington beat, so he wants to check in with Sally Fowler, Kris's—*Sherpa's*—mother. Kris "Sherpa" Fowler, a through-hiker, went missing somewhere on the Washington section of the Pacific Crest Trail six months before Jacob disappeared. Randy has befriended Sally, an advocate for similar persons, and her outreach even helped locate a Canadian hiker missing for three years—he was found, alive, in South America. For a short time there was confusion that the Canadian may have been her son.

Laura has become good friends with Sally Fowler. They share a state in common—and like Jacob, there is a stupefying lack of clues in Kris's disappearance. Randy keeps in regular contact with her, too.

"Hi, Randy," she says.

"You're *psychic*," Randy says.

"Well, your name comes up on my phone." Randy lets out with his sincere deep-lung laugh, a warm thing that puts you at ease and makes you like and trust Randy Gray.

"Kris never made it out of White Pass," she says. She's resigned. There was an epic storm, he was worn down to the point of being ill, he succumbed to hypothermia and made characteristic stumbling circles in the snow. But Randy still talks of Sherpa in the present tense, even when Sally doesn't.

He wants the possibility that Kris is alive. Or he simply believes that he is, and for the sake of Randy Gray's vantage on the world, both Kris and Jacob are out there doing the thing they need to be doing.

"He knew a big storm was coming; clearly he wasn't thinking like his mother wanted him to think," Sally says. "I talked to a lot of through-hikers who got depressed toward the end because they have to go back to the bright lights and big city."

Kris had packed the book *Wanderer*, Sterling Hayden's 1963 memoir about walking away from a rutted life. Sherpa had been recently divorced. He didn't have a career. He may have been dragging his heels on the last leg of his PCT journey, trying to avoid going back to a life, as Thoreau has it, of "quiet desperation." His dad passed away after Kris went missing.

"You have to have hope until there's no hope, and we don't know until we know," Sally says. "I sure hope he's still out there walking around in a daze, in a commune somewhere, growing broccoli." She speaks with a callous, resigned courage. She's also become a default aficionado on missing persons in the wild. She can laugh and sigh in the same breath. "He just didn't have a lot to run from. My heart hopes he's in a commune braiding hair, but my head says he's on the mountain."

Randy asks Sally if she knows of any cults that inhabit the PCT.

"The Twelve Tribes cult," Sally says. "They have a deli right across the street from where the hikers end up." Randy throws me a glance, and I know that's where we're headed.

"When we find him, I gotta talk to him," Randy says to Sally, referring to Sherpa. It's a positive affirmation. It doesn't work on Sally, but it works on Randy. He says the words. He sees the words in the air, tastes them after they leave his mouth. It probably won't come to pass, but positive statements are like protein to Randy Gray, and that sentence will fortify him for another day.

"He was very tired and thin," Sally says. "He knew a big storm was coming."

"Kris and Jacob aren't thinking logically," Randy says.

"Like Jacob," Sally says, "it's such a vast area to search. People have from time to time reported seeing him, but I don't know," she says. "There's an awful lot of thin, tall hikers with beards." There's a pause. "Someday I hope we both have answers, Randy. I'm ready for the answer, whatever it is. I'm ready for the next chapter."

Randy tells Sally how he's supposed to be back on the Sol Duc for a search near the salmon hatchery because a psychic— who contacted Laura—had a vision Jacob's body was above the river, across from the hatchery, at the edge of a horse farm. James Million scouted it, and a property across from the hatchery vaguely fits that description, so they planned to search the tangle-brush and high weeds there. Randy tells Sally he's supposed to rendezvous with them, but his heart isn't in it; psychics have exhausted him. "What the shit?" Randy says. Which is as good a question as any.

Sally Fowler is quit of psychics, too. "Ask them what the lottery numbers are tomorrow," she says.

Sally tells us about Trace Richardson, trail name Baptist, a PCT hiker who has devoted significant time and expense searching for Sherpa. Baptist had been leapfrogging with Sherpa and would drink beer with him in towns—that counts as trail buddies in the PCT world.

There is debate as to where the search for Fowler should center—some bear hunters reported seeing Sherpa near Blowout Mountain. Baptist is adamant Sherpa's remains are most likely some distance away, in the direction of White Pass, and he's moved from Phoenix to Portland to search for his friend.

We have plenty of windshield time, and Randy gives Baptist a buzz. "People have seen the movie *Wild*. It's a great fairy tale," Baptist says. "You have people escaping. *I quit my job. I divorced my wife.* A lot of people come seeking. It's not fixing all of your problems. It just gives you some perspective. But you often find things get harder off the trail. I think the PCT attracts a risk taker. But all the dirt that comes with the real world comes with the PCT."

Randy asks Baptist about the Twelve Tribes. Baptist says he recalls them from southern California. "They had something chocolate," he says. "That was primarily their draw, good food."

Baptist is gearing up to go back on another ground search for Sherpa. He and Randy talk about the pitfalls of searching, the online static. "There's a lot of people who post because they're attention seeking," Baptist says. "It brings false hope. It's cruel. A search is a mileage game—you have to cover ground.

"Some bear hunters said they saw Kris on October twenty-second at Chinook Pass. Nobody's going on purpose into a storm like that. It's such a low likelihood. It's like the ship sank, he swam to the island, then got food poisoning on the island and died."

The two talk about hypothermia, as likely in the Cascades as in or along the Sol Duc River. "It happens surfing," Randy says. Randy remembers his dad wearing wool sweaters to surf in the days before neoprene wetsuits. "I call it a Shangri La. You're in forty-degree water but then after a while you think you're warm."

"It's a hard death," Baptist says, "but it's a nicer exit. Moisture management is critical. You're not drying out in the Pacific Northwest. It can lead to a cascading failure of events.

"It can be a roller coaster," Baptist says. High highs and low lows. A through-hike is a magnifier of emotions. "You get to town, resupply, drink—it's really hard, maybe you leave with a bad hangover. Then the next day you'll be on this amazing height. There's a window of clarity that happens. Things can be more intense."

Sherpa maybe wasn't taking care of himself. He lost a week of mileage because he was ill. He wore sandals when he should have worn boots. He had blisters on his feet he wasn't attending to properly.

"We were racing winter," Baptist says. Late in the conversation he tells us how he got the trail name, because he accidentally pissed on a rattlesnake, baptizing it. "I got off on October second because I didn't want to die."

Sherpa got caught in the weather two days after he left, Baptist says. "Two years later they're searching sixty miles north of where they need to be."

Randy is a riverboat gambler when it comes to diners and greasy spoons, eschewing IHOP and Denny's for the mom-and-pop heartburn shacks. We stop for breakfast at a place in South Tacoma with the weakest, ropiest coffee in America. The place is red-lit and it feels like something from a David Lynch set. "Wichita Lineman" plays on the speakers—they don't actually have a jukebox. The corned beef hash is straight from a big can. Randy will always order a milkshake in these places, without fail, to arrive at his table when he's finished with his eggs and bacon, and for him that milkshake makes up for the bad coffee. Not me, but we'll stop at Starbucks in a few miles.

Maybe it's the milkshake and the Bigfoot and the Loretta psychic hangover, but after breakfast Randy says, "I don't wanna go to the

Sol Duc now. Let's go to Canada. Wouldn't that be something if Jacob's on a farm up there somewhere."

There are over a thousand farms in British Columbia alone. We watch Mount Adams through the dirty, bug-splattered windshield. "He wanted his passport," Randy says. "Why did he want his passport so bad? Jacob *wanted* to go to Canada."

I can tell it's settled. The lodestar points north instead of west. We're going to Canada.

"I think I'm done in the Sol Duc," he says. Again, he's talking to himself as much as to me. "I don't think there's anything more to search there. I swam the river one last time. Three or four miles down the river. I had my wetsuit, my snorkel and mask." Randy's litany. "When I got to a place that was deep I'd grab a rock and go to the bottom. Looking for a watch or anything. I found fishing lures, a compact disc. Jacob's not in there. He's not in the Sol Duc. Not in there. I bet he's in Canada."

CHAPTER 21

NEW MEXICO & AUSTRALIA

I'm sure that there are places in the deserts in Australia that could be similar to where we might want to go on Mars.

—Buzz Aldrin

STEPHEN CAREY, FIFTY-NINE, an El Segundo, California, resident and father of three, is missing in the Organ Mountains above Las Cruces, New Mexico. He checked out of his motel on July 8, 2019, and drove east toward the mountains. His 2007 Subaru Legacy was found three days later by New Mexico State Police parked at the Baylor Canyon trailhead with the keys inside. Carey's phone, wallet, and black Motobecane full-suspension mountain bike are missing. No fresh mountain bike tracks were found, but it had rained in the three days between checkout and discovery of the car.

In New Mexico the state police are in charge of search and rescue; on July 12 they organized a search for Carey of Baylor Canyon and surrounding ridges with the Dona Ana County Search and Rescue. That search lasted about six hours—it was called off when temperatures got too high.

The area is inside Desert Peaks National Monument, which is administered by the Bureau of Land Management. Desert Peaks is comprised of half a million acres, half of which is designated wilderness. It's possible for someone to travel through the monument and onto federal military property. A search larger in scope was complicated by being near the restricted lands and airspace of White Sands Missile Range. Carey's family had to struggle through federal red tape in order to be able to do any searching of the military space that covers parts of five counties and nearly 3,200 square miles. WSMR is not unlike a national park, and vice versa, when it comes to emergency searches for missing persons. Searches were conducted by WSMR personnel assisted by the El Paso, Texas, sector Border Patrol Search, Trauma and Rescue (BORSTAR). Carey's family eventually got permission to hire a professional drone operator—day and nighttime overflights showed no signs of Carey.

Virgin Galactic's Spaceport America is fifty miles north of Las Cruces—the area is gearing up to be ground zero for commercial space travel. I used to live in Las Cruces and mountain biked the high desert and Organ Mountains. Temperatures in July and August routinely get above a hundred degrees. The trails are filled with cactus and goatheads and sharp rocks that can puncture bike tires. I've never been to a place with so many rattlesnakes. Now the place fairly buzzes with Border Patrol four-by-fours so that you have to try pretty hard to vanish cold.

Talking with Robert Bogucki is like having a phone conversation with a bible character. In 1999, the thirty-three-year-old Alaska mover and volunteer firefighter cycle-toured Australia with his girlfriend, Janet North. While North flew home to the States, Bogucki had unfinished business down under and so set out to cross Australia's 300,000-square-kilometer Great Sandy Desert on his seven-speed Trek Calypso, a beach cruiser. What ensued is one of the great survival stories of all time. Furthermore, Bogucki may have experienced the spiritual, psychological, and emotional journey Ollie and Jacob are on.

Bogucki, like Jacob, is of the make-do-with-what-you-got mind-set—a beach cruiser is better suited for the sidewalks of Santa Cruz and not bikepacking across the Outback. He packed a week's worth of food—chocolate bars, ramen noodles, and canned tuna—and twenty-six liters of water. A week, he figured, would get him to the McLarty Hills, where he planned to fast and wait for God to visit him. After the meeting with God it would take him another week to pedal northward to the highway to Broome. The whole trip would be about six hundred kilometers. Piece of cake, can of corn. In essence, he was riding to God through a red desert on a blue bicycle.

There was no Plan B. The trip was predicated on the use of a bicycle, with no thought about what to do when that part of the equation evaporates. The roads on the map were hyperbole, used for definition by the cartographer because there wasn't much else to include in the blank space. The terrain—rolling hills of deep red sand, spinifex grass, and thorny tire-puncturing plants—became unrideable very quickly.

The choice of bike—the Trek Calypso, meant for tooling around town—wasn't rational. But neither, perhaps, just two days in, was the decision to abandon the bike and go forth on foot instead of doing a 180 and backtracking to the Great Northern Highway and civilization. Bogucki was on a mission.

To jettison the bicycle is to make a place fourfold more remote. Assume a person on foot in the desert walks at a pace of two or three miles an hour (which is faster than one could hope to *push* a loaded bike in that landscape). Now you have to calculate water and calories differently than if you could pedal, as you'll be out there days and weeks longer. But it made sense for Bogucki to leave the bike behind if he was going to continue his trek—he never really took the option of turning back seriously. "Dropping the bicycle is difficult, though," he writes in *One Way to Death and Heaven*, his self-published account of the quest that became an ordeal. "This thing I've depended on halfway around Australia will go no further, and this upsets me. Tears begin to fall. Initially I feel alone and sorry. Yet while sorting and packing the necessities, at a deeper level I feel like more is happening here."

He stuffed what he could into his knapsack. Food, water, a small blue tarp, his bible. He talks about the bible almost as if it's a spiritual version of the *Air Force Survival Manual*. "The bible is the inspired word of God," Bogucki writes. Eventually, though, he pitched it due to its weight. "Considering that, and the fact that I'm no longer reading it, I decide to drop the bible. If God wants me to know something he can tell me another way; I will hear."

When he ran out of food he began, by default, fasting. A human being might live for nearly a month without food. What's ethereal is Bogucki claims he went for more than twelve days without significant water—a thing that many physicians say is impossible. Most think a week without water is at the far end of survivability when it comes to severe dehydration. I question him about it one afternoon in May 2018; Bogucki is at home in Fairbanks. He's heard what the physiologists say time and again. "It's just scare tactics," he says. "You're not gonna hear that [you can go longer] in America. Look at how long some newborns survive in earthquakes."

Mucus built a puck on the back of his tongue that he'd have to scrape off and spit out. The water he did find had to be dug for under dry riverbeds. Digging for water under dry riverbeds takes energy and burns calories. The cycle was vicious, even aside from the twelve days of no water at all.

Two weeks after he lit out on foot, a group of four-wheel-drive enthusiasts found his blue bicycle and reported it. Authorities at first believed the bike belonged to an Asian tourist on account that they found cheap noodles and chopsticks with the bike. And in the sand were footprints made with dimple-soled flip-flops.

Jacob Gray appeared to have done the same thing as Robert Bogucki—abandon his bike on day two of his journey. A difference being that Jacob originally intended on keeping to rideable roads—it doesn't appear that he was forced to continue on foot.

When authorities realized the bike belonged to a missing American, the ensuing search became one of the largest search-and-rescue operations in Australian history.

Bogucki's journey of self-discovery sounds a bit cliché, but I can imagine no better way to find oneself than to see how you react to survival on the edge of this mortal plane. "My intention had been to spend time in a lonely unfamiliar landscape, to resolve some internal conflicts, to make God real in my life and clarify a desire to live," Bogucki writes. "And for this I decided to fast, to put my body through extreme hardship." It's an age-old concept, but few people have the sand Bogucki did. He hallucinated—voices told him where to dig for water. He experienced vivid dreams. He didn't have a bowel movement for a month. A desert flower that he sucked nectar from made him violently ill. "It was empty, but comforting," he said of his stomach. "I kinda thought about Jesus fasting in the desert and it was an inspiration. After dropping the bike I had the sense of elation that I could go on, and I was walking in the direction I'd planned." He averaged twenty kilometers a day on foot. He'd learned to find water like a lizard. He was becoming a desert dweller and was unsure he wanted to be rescued. At one point he pulled his blue tarp under a bush in order to not be seen from a small airplane that he'd later learn was searching for him.

An American Vietnam veteran named Garrison St. Claire, of a volunteer outfit called 1st Special Response Group, flew to Australia for the search. St. Claire is a uniformed, cigar-smoking musta-chioed larger-than-life character. News outlets in both Australia and the States covered the search, which had turned into a media circus.

It wasn't an Army or search-and-rescue helicopter, rather a news helicopter that spotted the skeletal wanderer forty-three days after he left the Great Northern Highway. Bogucki wrestled with the idea of being rescued, but was at his threshold. "A person can go so many days on a certain amount of faith," he writes, "and mine has reached its limit." The helicopter dropped off one of their crew so that Bogucki could fit in the chopper. He spent three days in the Broome hospital, where he got to meet St. Claire and the noted man tracker Joel Hardin, who runs tracking classes from his home base in Clearwater, Idaho.

Later there was some controversy as to whether or not Bogucki—even in his weakest state—had been eluding searchers on purpose.

I'd sent him a clip about Jacob Gray from the *Peninsula Daily News* and asked Bogucki what he thought of Jacob's story, what Jacob may have been thinking, doing. I also sent him a story on Ollie McAfee. Same questions. And did Jerusalem syndrome make any sense?

Talk switches to Ollie McAfee. Bogucki lived for a short time in Israel, in 1986, where he worked on a kibbutz. "Israel is not a big country—you're not going to get alone there like you would in Washington. [Ollie] wants to spend time being anonymous. How motivated was he to go there? In my mind it equates to his prospects for living through it.

"Jerusalem syndrome," Bogucki says. "I don't see it in response to an unreal thing. I compare it to really bad seasick. People say it's all in your head, no it's not." That's not to say Bogucki ever thought of himself as having a mental illness—the opposite. "Being in the Holy Land influenced me—history and things that are greater than your little life. I didn't consider it some fantasy thing where people think they're Jesus or John the Baptist or anything like that."

In his book he recalls his time in Israel. "Yea, I remember that trip," he writes. "The kibbutz, Yiftah. The drinking. The blood. The (first) intifada started soon after. An old war that is…Somewhere in time Abraham also sat on a hillside in an arid land, looking out over a valley below…his mind only on God and the land, must have felt like this…the way I do now."

I can tell that Bogucki shares a certain understanding with Jacob and Ollie. "That's what we try to do, get away from everybody."

Bogucki agrees with Randy, that it's unlikely Jacob fell in the river and stayed in—an accident at the river didn't end his spiritual quest. The kid would go into the wilderness—which is 95 percent of Olympic National Forest. In and up, toward the snow and peaks. "He's thinking, I'm going to do this, even if it kills me. The drive is there. Jesus—the spirit drove him into the wilderness. It's as much of a drive as a mother protecting her child. It's that strong."

As adamant as he is about the vision quest, Bogucki is a pragmatist about it. "If you're going to be out there for a while, you're gonna want to get yourself comfortable—it's gonna happen out of necessity. Some place you can sit and be at peace."

At the last outpost of civilization before he rode into the Great Sandy Desert, Bogucki sent his parents a postcard telling them he loves them. We talked about Jacob's last phone call to Laura Gray. "'Mom, I'm packed and ready to head out,'" Bogucki says. "He did his duty. That was his obligation. To me it sounds like he needed to go. He needed to look for something. He may not know what."

To Bogucki, fasting was a type of asceticism. "The more you're going without food, you're going by feelings," he says. "A beautiful sunrise will give you more strength than a drizzly morning."

Bogucki had nothing but beautiful sunrises in his forty-three-plus days in the desert—it never rained. I think of a thing Randy told me, of how he and Jacob would often get a mocha and go sit on the beach in Santa Cruz and watch the waves as the sun came up.

Bogucki would do deep breathing in the morning just to work up the drive and energy to stand up. "A ritual. That was my relaxing time, like having a cup of coffee in civilization. Anything to look forward to," he says. "That was the job, to get up and walk."

"[Jacob's] going on feelings with this," Bogucki says. "This guy has plenty of time."

Simplify is a word Bogucki likes, which is a theme straight from Thoreau, who was an imposter as a survivalist and adventurer. It was a simplification to leave his bike. "Fear gets phased out at the start," he says. "There was fear when I left the bike, but you're continually moving in the direction you want to move. It's not one big fear, it's a bunch of little fears. I don't need to worry about what happened because the survival manual is out the window already. All I have to do is walk."

Bogucki conflates his story and Jacob's story as we talk. "To clear the head, get away from demons, thoughts. If the thoughts aren't his, he can get away from them. The trouble comes when you think the thoughts are coming from you...with Jerusalem syndrome the thoughts aren't coming from him, not his own."

Jerusalem syndrome, or a vision quest, isn't necessarily a messiah complex—Ollie McAfee may not believe he's the world's savior. But what does manifest is an intense delusional curiosity and drive that pushes certain people toward irrational behavior. Ollie doesn't appear to have wanted to be found. I wonder if Jacob Gray wants to be found.

Jacob and his grandmother, Wyoma, read Revelations together. Jacob had talked with Wyoma about a portal to another dimension inside Olympic National Park. *Like arrows in the hand of a warrior are the sons born in one's youth*, reads Psalm 127:4 in the Holman Christian Standard Bible, though it says nothing of arrows stuck in the ground.

Furthermore, it's not lost on Randy that in Genesis 32:28, Jacob changes his name to Israel.

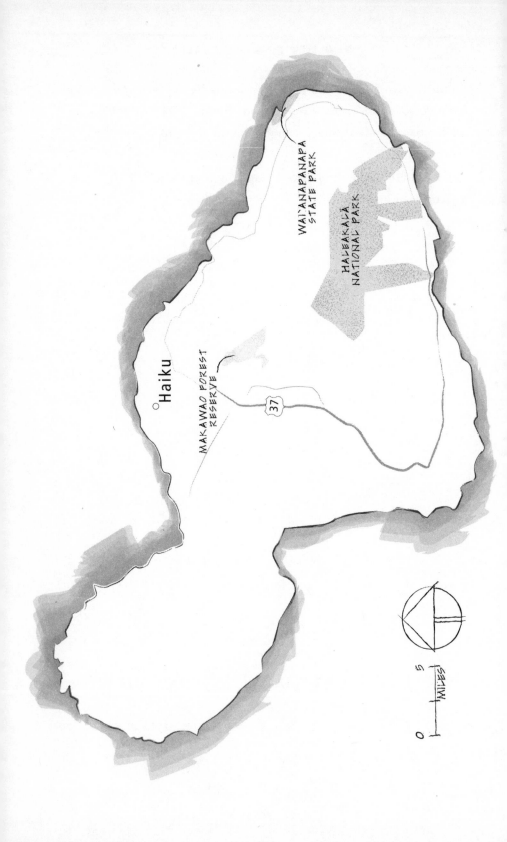

Haiku

MAKAWAO FOREST RESERVE

WAI'ANAPANAPA STATE PARK

HALEAKALĀ NATIONAL PARK

37

0   5
MILES

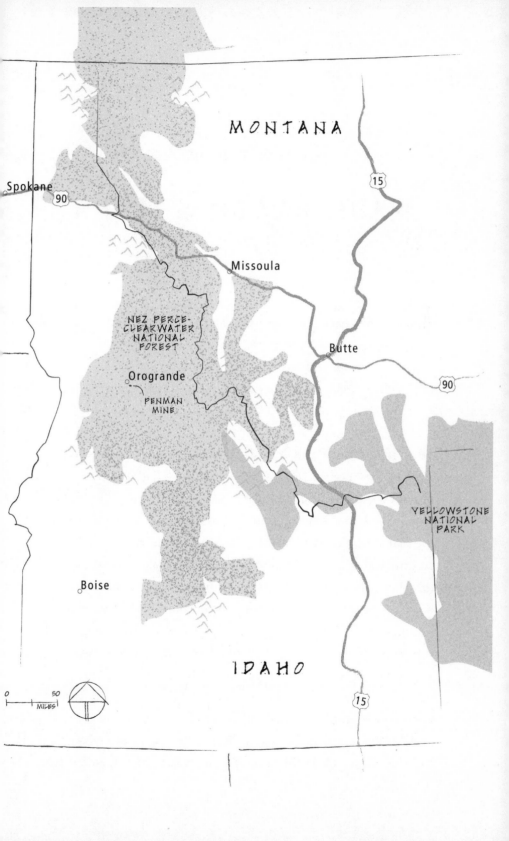

CHAPTER 22

MAUI, HAWAII & IDAHO

The brain uses the most energy. And even very simple calculations become difficult after three days without food.
—Guido Camida, a former chef who leads primal survival courses in Italy

TO PARAPHRASE PROFESSOR Rescue, a runner tends to run themselves out of the search area pretty fast. That's just what yoga instructor and physical therapist Amanda Eller, thirty-five, did on May 8, 2019. She'd intended to do a routine three-mile trail run in the Makawao Forest Reserve, 2,000 acres of non-native Cook pine and tropical ash that shoulders the towering Haleakala volcano on the Hawaiian island of Maui. Eller, who lives in Haiku, ducked down a little side path for a meditation break. When she stood up to continue on the main trail, she got turned around, forgetting which way she'd come in. And as outdoor athletes can and sometimes do, she pushed herself swiftly and confidently in the wrong direction, determined not to backtrack, so that her hourlong outing turned into a seventeen-day bushwhack from hell.

After her boyfriend, Benjamin Konkel, reported her missing to the Maui Police Department on the morning of May 9, authorities located Eller's white 2015 Toyota RAV4 at the Hunter's Trail trailhead. Her phone, wallet, and water bottle were locked inside the car. Her car key was found hidden behind a tire. This wasn't necessarily unusual—she wouldn't need her phone on a short familiar route, and the only thing you can do with an electronic car key in the forest is lose it. There was no immediate sign of foul play; Konkel took a lie-detector test and passed.

According to the federal National Missing and Unidentified Persons System (NamUs), Hawaii ranks eighth in the United States in number of missing persons. Whereas in most of the United States the county sheriff is in charge of search and rescue, here Maui County Department of Fire and Public Safety is in charge of search and rescue and commanded the search for Amanda. Maui Fire was joined by Maui Police as well as dog teams from the volunteer organization Maui Search and Rescue. In a matter of hours there were helicopters, drones, dogs, and trained boots on the ground. As word spread, dozens of volunteers showed up to help scour the trails.

"We would take anybody who could walk," says Sarah Haynes, a recent California transplant and friend of Konkel's who found herself helping organize the search and taking the role of family spokesperson while Eller's parents, John and Julie, were unreachable for the first two days while on a diving trip. Haynes's brother, Jon Truscott Haynes, vanished in Colorado in 1981 and has never been found.

At first all those searchers were organized under the direction of Maui Fire, who are well versed in incident command. But on May 11, mandated by a seventy-two-hour limit on rescue-personnel efforts, Maui Fire had to pull the plug on the official search.

In most cases, unless you're Steve Fossett, after the official search is called off and the incident command goes home, the effort is left to family, friends, and sometimes a handful of strangers who want to help. It's rare for searches to get a figurative shot of vitamin B when it looks more unlikely a person is still alive or still in the search area altogether. It's an unequal undertaking that sometimes seems based on pragmatism, sometimes chance, sometimes familial and demographic privilege.

The small nonprofits don't have the scale to fill the need for all the remote missing persons cases all over North America and beyond. Like the Jon Francis Foundation (JFF), the Minnesota-based outfit that helps families of persons missing in the wild, Texas EquuSearch (TES), which was in communication with Jacob's aunt Elise shortly after his disappearance, works missing persons cases in remote places and not necessarily with horses. TES searched for Natalee Holloway, the eighteen-year-old Alabama resident who went missing on Aruba in the spring of 2005; Holloway was declared dead in absentia in 2012. In most searches, there are conspiracies and gossip fueling the inertia—or lack thereof—but in some cases these are the period at the end of a sentence.

As of Sunday, May 12, volunteers looking for Amanda were on their own, an army without an officer, a gang without a gang leader. That's when arborist Chris Berquist and Javier Cantellops, a former Special Operations Army Ranger and free diver, stepped in. Cantellops had taught scuba to Amanda and heard his former student was missing. Berquist was on his way out the door to do some parasailing on a day off when he got a call that a woman was missing not far from where he lives and they needed help.

At first, after Maui Fire left the scene, things were as DIY as homemade soap. The hasty searches had already been conducted and what was vital now was organization and direction. "Chris showed up and the next thing you know he's on the other side of the table," Haynes says of Berquist. "It quickly exploded, and we got a small team of people together who then had hundreds of people under them."

* * *

"We need people who are comfortable being outside six to eight hours a day," Berquist told *Maui Now* from the operations yurt that was erected on site. As a search leader, he didn't appear to fit the official mold, with his scruffy blond beard and trucker hat, but it was clear Berquist understood the importance of the local media— he came off as calm, professional, and most of all, confident. The search took on the new energy of an *event*. Word spread throughout the island on what they call the *coconut wireless* that the search for the missing runner wasn't hitting the wall; 60 to 150 searchers showed up every day for two solid weeks. And the spirit was such that they would have kept showing up.

Soon the camp looked like an aid station at an ultramarathon— tables lined with electrolyte drinks and piled with energy bars and donated sandwiches from local restaurants. People shuttled in the most precious commodity for a tropical emergency like this: ice, to keep searchers cool in the humid ninety-degree heat. FAA-certified drone pilots flew cameras over the forest canopy. Experienced hikers and fast packers were able to cross off chunks of map. Rappellers spidered down cliffs; free divers checked ponds and pools. Hunters even killed boars and examined their intestines. Maui Search and Rescue ran dog teams.

Media attention that had by now gone global helped Amanda's GoFundMe search site raise more than $70,000 to help offset private helicopter costs, which can run over $1,000 an hour. And Berquist is quick to point out that members of Maui Fire were still assisting behind the scenes even after they had to officially step down.

It's mayhem if no one keeps track of all that activity, all that searching, all that has been searched and still needs to be searched. Berquist and Cantellops started with a flip phone and a legal pad. With the help of Haynes and Elena Pray, a rappelling guide for

Rappel Maui, they began by handing out paper "pirate maps"—X marks the spot, with a hairball problem of solving for X.

All volunteers needed to be checked in, accounted for, and checked out. Their routes and notes had to be logged and added to the map. Pray would be called to rappel into an area inaccessible to hikers. "One afternoon we assisted a group of searchers out of a deep gulch using technical rope gear just minutes shy of darkness," she told me. One volunteer, Stephie Garrett, went from yurt ops to being a search-team leader. A Swiss tourist named Susann Schuh spent her tropical vacation organizing data for stacked twelve-hour days.

Gradually computers were plugged into generators and the team utilized apps that allowed coordinators to color in specific areas that had been scoured. They were aided by the tech prowess of Amanda's brother Chris Eller and father, John Eller, who had worked a career as an engineer for the government, designing FLIR systems for the military, before founding the telematics company InSight Mobile Data. Eller's company coordinates communications and tracking information for such applications as shipping companies and emergency services like ambulances.

Troy Helmer, a local pig hunter, scouted the topography and con-sulted on the battle plan. "Troy knows that area better than anyone in Maui," Cantellops told me. One day searchers in the heli spotted a four-hundred-pound boar, the Maui version of a grizzly bear.

"They're aggressive," Berquist said. "You don't want to stumble across a sow with piglets." The wild ginger is so thick a human can hardly see through it, let alone walk through; the pigs make trails underneath, at the stalks.

The searchers found nothing for two weeks. Surveillance cameras at a grocery store in Haiku showed Eller shopping the morning of May 8. A time stamp on a package placed her at the post office. Police reviewed video footage from doorbell security cameras on the road from Haiku to Makawao to see if she had been abducted or followed. "She was alone in the car and having a normal day," Haynes says, "so we felt strongly that she took herself to the forest in unsuspicious circumstances." Hikers reported having seen Eller— they chatted briefly and she petted their dog—but that was walked back as a mistaken identity.

Media attention grew, this athletic woman missing in paradise, and it was impossible for outlets not to compare Amanda's story to missing women like Natalee Holloway.

Foul play was on the table fast, especially because no one could recall someone vanishing in the Makawao Forest Reserve and not eventually getting found by a hiker or a hunter or simply pushing through and hitting a road. *It's impossible to get lost in there* was a thing I was told by multiple people. When Occam's razor doesn't prove out quickly, speculation fills the void left by a vanished person pretty fast. Armchair investigators on Facebook and Websleuths figured that if she hadn't fallen down a lava tube or been eaten by wild pigs, she'd surely been abducted. The boyfriend must have offed her, they theorized, and cheated on the polygraph. Or it could have been an ex. A jealous coworker. She probably stumbled across an illegal marijuana operation. Maybe there was a serial killer on the loose.

As all these theories and leads swirled around him, Berquist kept focused. He was so dedicated to the search that his employer— a landscaping company—fired him for showing up to look for Amanda day after day. "We are nowhere close to stopping by any means," he told *Maui Now*. "We have so much more that we can do out here, we're gonna continue to push it."

Lost persons are often found—often deceased—within an original search area. In this case, the computer mapping allowed searchers to feel confident that they'd fairly saturated the original mile-and-a-half radius. They also incorporated lost person behavior into the search plan: upward of 80 percent of persons in a similar situation are found near rivers, in drainages. That's where they'd push on.

On the afternoon of Friday, May 24, Berquist realized he needed to plan for the Memorial Day weekend, when many more volunteers would show up to search. He thought they might need to move the yurt to another location, to venture beyond the radius they'd been focusing on for the past two weeks. He, Cantellops, and Helmer climbed into pilot Pete Vorhes's yellow Hughes 369D helicopter for a reconnaissance flight. That day, Amanda's family had upped reward money from $10,000 to $50,000 for information leading to her whereabouts.

With only fifteen minutes of fuel remaining, the men on the helicopter prepared to turn around. They were now well outside the boundary of Makawao Forest Reserve, about seven miles from where Amanda's car had been found. That's when they saw a woman on the riverbank, between two waterfalls, waving furiously.

Overnight, the story of Eller's ordeal would erupt on news sites and make the morning shows. "I just felt that she was alive, man," Cantellops told the *Today* show. "If we haven't found her and we haven't smelled her, that's because she's on the move, she's moving out and she's way farther out than we think she is."

Amanda had lost her route and didn't know where to backtrack and had decided to forge ahead. Day three is when she went from panicked, lost-person mode into survival mode, searching for clean water and foraging for food. It rained, and her running shoes got swept away in a flash flood. She fell twenty feet off a cliff, fracturing her leg and tearing the meniscus in her knee. Now she was reduced to crawling. Temperatures at night dipped to near sixty, potentially hypothermic conditions when it's wet. She had nothing but her yoga pants and a tank top. To keep warm, she covered herself with ferns, leaves, and forest duff. She slept in a boar's nest.

She ate plants she didn't know and wild strawberry guava when she could find them. For protein she swallowed an occasional moth. Maui waterfalls look fresh on postcards but can contain *Leptospira*, a genus of bacteria that causes a whole buffet of problems including meningitis, kidney failure, and death. But to not drink meant certain death. She lost almost twenty pounds in those seventeen days. In addition to her broken leg, Amanda had a severe skin infection from sunburn. She said she'd heard and seen several helicopters previously, but none had spotted her. "I looked up, and they were right on top of me. I was like, 'Oh, my God,' and I just broke down and started bawling." She had walked—and crawled—about thirty miles. Up, down, and in curves and spirals.

Searches are as unique as fingerprints in that no two are alike, but the hunt for Amanda Eller was significant only in part because she survived seventeen days lost and alone in the Hawaiian backcountry.

On Sunday, May 26, not forty-eight hours after Amanda was found, I got a text from Javier Cantellops. He couldn't talk, he said; they were getting in a helicopter to look for another missing person. A thirty-five-year-old local man, Noah "Kekai" Mina, disappeared on May 20 when he set out on the unmarked Kapilau Ridge Trail, also known as the Iao Valley Secret Trail, roughly twenty miles away from the command headquarters for the Eller search. As with Amanda, local authorities had searched for three days for Noah Mina. But because the terrain was so technical, Mina's father, Vincent, issued a statement advising against ordinary volunteers trying to find him. Searchers did find Mina's slippers—what the locals call flip-flops. But, Cantellops told me, "That's not unusual. A lot of locals here hike barefoot."

Outside sent me to Maui to cover the aftermath of Amanda's search and this new band of heroes who'd barely had time to do their laundry after Amanda's rescue before they deployed to help in the search for Mina. In the early morning hours of May 29, 2019, a helicopter circled Mauna Kahalawai, on the Hawaiian island of Maui, searching for Mina and deploying FLIR to detect any sign of life. The instrument is sensitive enough that the crew picked up axis deer, rodents, and beehives.

When I landed at LAX for my connecting flight later that morning, I got a text saying Mina's body had been found. "In the early morning hours of Wednesday, May 29," read a family statement issued on the public Facebook page Bring Kekai Home, "a crew of searchers aboard a helicopter spotted the body of missing hiker Noah 'Kekai' Mina. Mina was found about 300 feet below a fall line in the summit region of Mauna Kahalawai. Recovery efforts are currently underway."

Meanwhile, Amanda's story had become worldwide news. I'd landed in the fray of satellite trucks, my least favorite part of journalism. Family and friends were sheltering Amanda from reporters like me. Rumors on the island were that she was already busy negotiating major book and movie deals. The discovery of Mina's body made the local news, but that was about it.

I met with Berquist and Pray in the upcountry town of Makawao, which is more cowboys and mountain bikers than fishers and surfers. Berquist was on his way to the mainland. He told me it was for a well-deserved vacation, but he'd signed a nondisclosure agreement with John Eller's company regarding a new position in what would be called the STAT (Search Technology Advisory Team) Foundation, and I got the feeling it was a work trip, too. Technology was vital in Amanda's search. You could argue that without the computerized mapping done by the search team responsible for finding Amanda Eller, she would have perished in the Maui rainforest. But it was the brainpower, *human*, application of the technology that allowed Berquist's team to push past the original search area to where they found her. Even then, low on fuel, they were flying over a hunch when they spotted her. Noah Mina's tragedy was a sober reminder that many of these searches don't end well.

Berquist is careful not to overpromise. I ask him how the STAT Foundation might evolve their technology and search experience for a real-world application for the missing and murdered indigenous women and girls crisis (MMIWG, the acronym and hashtag, is an awareness movement for the epidemic and not an organization).

STAT is promising, especially, I think, if it can be *scaled up* to help address MMIWG in the U.S. and Canada. With all the people missing in national parks and other public lands, nothing comes close to the numbers regarding First Nations and Native American missing persons. For example, in Montana, indigenous peoples make up 7 percent of the population. Disproportionally, 32 percent of Montana's missing persons are Native Americans.

Outside the state level, the federal government does not collect cohesive data regarding MMIWG; a Southern Cheyenne scholar named Annita Lucchesi runs a database that does. "In terms of statistics—we have approx 4,000 cases documented across the U.S. and Canada, representing fifty-four states and provinces and over 450 tribal nations," Lucchesi told me. "Over half of those are murders, and a little over half are from the U.S." The database goes back to 1900, but 75 percent of the data is post-1980.

Though the problem is daunting, Berquist seemed intrigued with the concept. After all, finding Amanda alive in the rainforest was pretty daunting, too.

Cantellops and Pray met me at the Makawao Forest Preserve to show me where Amanda had disappeared. We parked where Amanda had parked that day. A pig hunter with his dogs walked by. The trails are largely unmarked, and there are pig trails that curl off into the forest. I had to object to the locals who claim no one can get lost in there—a person could absolutely get lost in there, including me.

Amanda's story caused a backlash on the island, especially after a press conference where she was seen in the hospital with a plumeria in her hair, talking about personal journeys and spiritual quests. She seemed to imply that the Maui Fire Department and Maui Search and Rescue hadn't tried hard enough or looked long enough, and it was only the efforts of the scrappy arborist, pig hunter, and scuba instructor that saved her.

Amanda's boyfriend, Ben Konkel, who didn't want to talk with me, is rumored to be a haoli shaman. Video surfaced on social media of him sitting on the beach a couple days after Amanda was found—he's babbling incoherently to himself. One commenter wrote, "The plot thickens."

While CNN and *People* magazine told a survivalist Cinderella story, some Maui residents claimed that Amanda was out there on a selfish trip—speculation included mushrooms, LSD, ayahuasca, and other hallucinogenics. A man called to tell me medical personnel, a friend of his, at the hospital confirmed she had drugs in her system. A Hawaiian native told me they had proof one of the main searchers had illegally guided tourists into the Bamboo Forest, near where they found Amanda, and that's how they knew where to plant her for the staged rescue. A common rumor had it that Cantellops had helped fake Amanda's disappearance so they could cash in on a movie deal. The Eller family did it for the GoFundMe money. A kid at a bike shop drew me a map of where to harvest my own psilocybin mushrooms in a cow paddock northeast of Paia. Milder talk at the Sip Me coffee shop, which I found the most convincing, had it that Amanda was simply underprepared, foolish, and should show a little more humility.

Just before I leave Maui, I stopped for a meal at a restaurant in Paia. Amanda Eller is there across the patio. She could play herself in the movie. She's tan, the trademark plumeria behind her ear. She's wearing a red caftan. I recognize John Eller, whom I'd talked with at a presser a couple days earlier, otherwise I might have not noticed Amanda at all. Her crutches lean against the patio wall. Her mother is there, too, and a young man who is not her boyfriend.

The journalistic equivalent of counting coup would be for me to stride over and ask her questions. But she's only been out of the jungle for a few days. I'm glad she can be there enjoying her family. The satellite trucks have gone, and I may be the last magazine hack on the island for her story. She's saving her story for the book and movie. Besides, what would I ask her? *How did you get so FUBAR lost on such a small island? What's it like to be a ghost? What do moths taste like?*

As soon as I got back from Maui in early June I learned that a writer, Davey Johnson, whose work I admire, had disappeared in a manner not dissimilar to Jacob Gray—but instead of a bicycle, Johnson was touring on a motorcycle. Johnson wrote for car and motorcycle magazines and was an Anthony Bourdain–type character in the gasoline-fueled media world. The road-weary forty-three-year-old was testing a new Honda CB1000R for *Motorcyclist* magazine. The bike—with the key still in the ignition—and his belongings were found along the Mokelumne River off Highway 49 in Calaveras County, California, in the Sierras. Soon after the bike was discovered abandoned—which was about three days since anyone had heard from him—a search including ground crews, drones, a helicopter, and dog teams ensued. A tracking dog indicated Johnson had gone into the cold, swollen river. An active search lasted for ten days before officials scaled it back. In this case *scaled back* wasn't a euphemism for canceling the search—four days later, on June 20, 2019, Calaveras County Sheriff's Department searchers found Johnson's body in the river.

A month later I got a message from a contact in Maui that another woman was missing on public land. Twenty-three-year-old Khiara Henry flew from the mainland to Maui by herself and rented a car on July 21, 2019. Her rental car was found in the gravel parking lot of Wai'anapanapa State Park near Hana on July 25, 2019. It's an area of lava rock, cliffs, caves, and waterfalls. Henry was described as five-foot-three, 120 pounds, with brown eyes and brown hair. She's Native American and black.

Chris Berquist and the STAT Foundation were called in. Maui Police and a small group of hikers did a hasty search of the main trails. A helicopter was dispatched to the search, then divers to check rivers and waterfalls. Henry's belongings were found in her car, but her keys and phone were not there, so presumably she had them. This area is more searchable by air than the heavily over-storied Makawao Forest where Amanda Eller went missing, but the heli crew found nothing.

I talked to one of the volunteer searchers, Judi Riley. Like Sarah Haynes, who was instrumental in the search for Amanda, Judi has also lost a brother. Forty-seven-year-old Jon Michael Riley disappeared without a trace in Ontario in April 2013.

Riley is circulating an online petition called Change Canadian Adult Missing Persons Police Protocol asking for "a law to be passed that requires all missing persons reports to be recorded, entered into CPIC (Canadian Police Information Centre), as well as the RCMP national database of missing persons." She says the family is awaiting DNA testing to see if Jon's disappearance is connected to serial killer Bruce McArthur, a grandfather, landscaper, and mall Santa charged in 2018 with killing two men in the Toronto area.

McArthur is believed to be responsible for the deaths of perhaps a dozen men.

Riley puts something in perspective that I hadn't thought of before. "Fear," she says. "Everyone searching has that. People really fear the unknown of the missing person. The seed of fear. The person on the milk carton." She assigns the conspiracy theories surrounding missing persons cases to fear. "That's how we protect the parts of us that are scared of the missing."

I'm reminded of Randy. "Early on, you're frantic, you want to find them," she says. But then time elapses and the chasm of the unknown gets bigger. "My brother and I were raised as twins. If he was dead I'd know. As time goes on, you almost don't want to know.

"You can't have closure," she says. "But you have to hang on to the belief. Otherwise it'd be giving up on the person."

Following the search for Amanda Eller, some native Hawaiians felt like the search infringed on their traditional lands and, because STAT was involved, this affected the search for Khiara Henry. Suspicion grew to the level of conspiracy theory that the Ellers were using the excuse of searches to topographically map the land. The STAT team had to search around areas deemed sacred by Hawaiians. STAT respectfully coordinated with the locals, who sent their own searchers into these areas.

Rains ahead of a tropical depression swelled the rivers and made searching treacherous. And while STAT was busy recruiting ground searchers and coordinating searches and aggregating search data for Henry, another person went missing. Craig Pitt, thirty-five, a Florida resident who frequently visited the Hawaiian islands to hike and seek out waterfalls, had failed to contact family. His rental car was found parked along the Hana Highway.

Pitt's body was found at the base of a waterfall on August 3 by Maui Police and Fire personnel. He'd fallen three hundred feet. There were still no clues regarding Khiara Henry—her family asked to suspend the search. Her GoFundMe had raised $2,590 when it was deactivated.

The Black and Missing Foundation's website gives FBI statistics from 2018 that of the 612,846 reported missing in the United States, 230,302 (or 38 percent) are minorities (Hispanics are included in the total count for white). As for how many black persons disappear on public land, in national parks and national forests, no one seems to know.

In July of 1999, Joseph "Joe" Wood, a former editor of the *Village Voice*, and author of the book *Blood Whispers and Color Lines*, flew to Seattle for a national minority journalists conference. On July 8 he drove from Seattle sixty miles southeast to Mount Rainier to do some birding. He entered at the Nisqually gate at 12:29 in the afternoon and drove to Longmire.

The weather was perfect, and he hadn't prepared for a long trek, just a three-hour hike with his binoculars and a field guide for birds.

After Wood was reported missing and rangers located his rental car, another hiker, Bruce Gaumond, later reported having talked with Wood at just below 5,000 feet (the summit of Mount Rainier is 14,411 feet), on the Rampart Ridge trail. The trail was still, even in midsummer, covered with five feet of hard snow.

There were some dangerous snow bridges, and Wood did have a heart condition. Rangers searched but after a few days figured he'd have to have succumbed to hypothermia. The snow continued to melt rapidly in the oncoming weeks, yet no body was ever found.

The notoriously treacherous Mount Rainier claims many alpinists, but not birders out for a hike on a placid summer day.

* * *

In September of 2010, Stuart Isaac, forty-eight, of Burtonsville, Maryland, vanished at Craig Pass, on the Continental Divide in Yellowstone National Park. His black 2009 Lexus sedan was found by rangers, unlocked with the keys inside, but Isaac, a native of the Pacific Island nation of Palau, is still missing. His case received almost no media attention.

Terrence Woods had been living a dream for any twenty-six-year-old who had wanted to make a living seeing the world. He worked as a videographer and production assistant for documentary film crews. He took a job on the crew of Raw TV, a British company behind the show *Gold Rush*. They'd filmed in Montana and were now, early October 2019, staying in Elk City, Idaho, where they filmed footage at the remote Penman Mine in the Nez Perce National Forest. Texts to his parents made things seem fairly normal, no problems, though the last text his father, Terrence Sr., received from his son stated he might come back home to Maryland early, cutting his work trip short. His mother would be having a medical procedure, and he told his crew he wanted to leave the project early to be with her.

A dozen crew members, plus locals helping with production, were on the scene of the Penman Gold Deposit, below the Penman Mine, near Orogrande, Idaho. It was late in the day, and they were wrapping up. Then things make little sense.

Reports are that Woods was talking with a local woman hired to shuttle the crew. Production manager Simon Gee was in the rental SUV finishing up the day's paperwork. The witnesses report Woods threw down his radio and ran over a fifteen-foot cliff, then just kept running down, through the forest, as fast as the lithe 130-pound man could run. The slope was steep and loose, and it's a wonder Woods didn't end up in a freefall. There were a dozen or so witnesses who offer no solid explanation.

It's speculated that Woods suffered a sort of panic attack or mental breakdown. Or that he may have arranged to meet someone, which seems even less likely considering the location. There are dozens of abandoned mine shafts in the surrounding terrain, and it's very possible to fall into one, permanently. Woods left behind his backpack, which included extra camera batteries, a three-inch folding knife, and a stun gun.

Local law enforcement, the Idaho County Sheriff's Department, does not suspect foul play, and the disappearance is not considered a crime, therefore the FBI has not been called in. A search, including dogs and helicopters, lasted a week. Temperatures each night dropped below freezing.

Terrence Woods Sr. believes his son was somehow bullied. After all, the day's shoot was over and they were getting ready to go back to town, where Woods could make his way to the airport to go back to Maryland. It's troubling and strange that he'd leave in a sprint without his backpack.

I talked to Joel Hardin, who lives in the county, about Terrence Woods's vanish. He said there's a road a thirty-minute hike downhill from the area where Terrence disappeared, the direction he was running. The search of the country between the mine and the road was thorough. Searchers don't believe he's there, in the search area. He caught a ride of some sort.

Some people disappear because they are lost. Some disappear and do not want to be found. But, like Jacob Gray, Terrence Woods would have called his mother.

CHAPTER 23

SOL DUC FALLS

CLAIRVOYANT, n. A person, commonly a woman, who has the power of seeing that which is invisible to her patron, namely, that he is a blockhead.

—Ambrose Bierce, author of The Devil's Dictionary, *who disappeared in Mexico in 1913*

THE TRAIL OF any missing person in the wild is paved with psychics. When Amanda Eller's case hit the news, out came the psychics. Most of them saw her dead. They saw men with tattoos. They saw her tied up and being thrown off a cliff. There was a phone number and a special email set up specifically for psychic tips.

@SteveConreaux, whose Twitter profile states "Predicting events is a gift from God. Also was a Kundalini awakening with some powerful internal energy. #Patriot #Psychic #Precognition #Chakra #Kundalini Columbus, Ohio," tweeted this:

#AmandaEller missing in Hawaii since Wed., I see she has passed away just a few minutes ago at 1:11 of her injuries sustained from a 75' fall. The 2 who threw her off Piiholo Rd. will suffer. I fear my tip this morning was too late.

@rachelholley6 replied:

Sadly, I think you're the one who deserves to suffer for tweeting this. You're no psychic, but you would communicate this kind of information which her family will see. If you have information this specific, you should go to the police, because it sounds like you're involved.

@Steve Conreaux:

Already contacted the police about it, sorry if my observation offended anyone. I did nail Kelsey Berreth's killer, day of murder and the murder weapon, the day the story broke. FBI has it all too, I never post until they've been contacted.

Kelsey Berreth was a twenty-nine-year-old mother from Woodland Park, Colorado, who went missing in November 2018. Police arrested her boyfriend, Patrick Frazee, and charged him with murder. They believe he killed Berreth, burned her body, and disposed of the remains in a landfill or river. But her remains have not been found.

It's said that a lie travels around the world while the truth is still pulling its boots on; you could say the psychics are *finding* missing persons while searchers are still pulling their boots on. Not only were the psychics not correct in their assessments that Amanda was a victim of foul play, one could argue that they were a dangerous distraction. "To my knowledge," Koester says, "psychics have never solved a missing persons case."

Stewart Krull, Zach Krull's father, got an email from a psychic shortly after the disappearance. The message stated that Zach was alive and near a body of water. It went on to claim that Zach had an injury on his leg that he was nursing, and that he was rationing food.

"People come out of the woodwork with crazy-ass ideas and psychics," Laura Gray told me. "The most reliable witness [Stacey, the woman who first saw Jacob cycling on the road] said, 'I think he was abducted by *aliens*.' She's our only real lead."

Tanya had emailed Laurie McQuary, the psychic, in May 2017 to ask if she could help with Jacob's case, but McQuary said the request had to come from a family member. Jacob's mother made the official request the next day, and Tanya and McQuary began an email correspondence that lasted for more than a year. McQuary decided not to charge for the case when Tanya wanted to pay her as McQuary thought it unethical since Tanya was not family to Jacob. One of the first emails was McQuary asking for Jacob's birthdate and a photo. A few minutes later, McQuary emailed again, "Tanya, how far is Sol Quel from the search area? And what is a contact # for you please, Laurie."

Over the next few weeks, the emails were frequent and specific.

From: Laurie
Sent: Wednesday, May 24, 2017 11:30 AM
To: Tanya
Subject: Re: Missing Hiker, Jacob Gray

Tanya, I try not to question a message, all morning I have been " hearing" by the pool, if there is a quiet area of a pool of water near the falls, might bear looking at, wish I had more, I will wait to hear from you, God bless, Laurie

---

From: Tanya
Sent: Wednesday, May 24, 2017 1:22 PM
To: Laurie
Subject: Re: Missing Hiker, Jacob Gray

We have just arrived. We passed a place called La Poel. It is just before the entrance to Sol Duc Road. Caught my eye, since you mentioned the word, "pool"

From: Tanya
Sent: Thursday, May 25, 2017 7:51 AM
To: Laurie
Subject: Re: Missing Hiker, Jacob Gray

One of the searchers googled Sol Quel and realized that there is a road in Santa Cruz that is called, Soquel. This is where Jacob is from, and where his journey started.

From: Laurie
Sent: Wednesday, May 25, 2017 8:18 AM
To: Tanya
Subject: Re: Missing Hiker, Jacob Gray

Tanya, good morning, are you staying up there another day or so? I believe he is within a mile of where he left his stuff. Interesting I got the name of his place he resided, means his energy is coming thru. I will be with clients this morning and out for part of the day, will check in with you later, prayers of recovery to all, Laurie

---

From: Laurie
Sent: Wednesday, May 25, 2017 2:10 PM
To: Tanya
Subject: Re: Missing Hiker, Jacob Gray

Tanya, I heard the word Falls, just before I got "pool" and I said, he is not in water, but quite near it. Yes, the thought he staged his own disappearance is possible, but I also felt he was deeply depressed, and leaving his bike (expensive item) personal effects behind, speaks to me of suicide, I sent an earlier E-mail to you, saying I felt he was within I mile of where he left his stuff. I spent an hour and a half yesterday, pouring over the few maps on-line, and 2 topagraphicals I have to come to my closest estimate, right now, nothing new is coming through. I felt very strongly about the Falls, be it Marymere or Sol Duc, God, Tanya, wish I had more. Did he carry or have a gun? I will stay on this, keep in touch if anything new comes up, Laurie

Tanya tells McQuary about being with her mother and seeing a young man in the grocery store in Forks who they were sure was Jacob. McQuary replied that it must have been a spirit. "Spirits sometimes use other beings to bring messages." A few days later McQuary emailed, "I really believe he is still there. The young, disconnected young man you saw, was real, a person being guided by the spirit of Jacob to tell you he is there."

Tanya shared Randy and Laura's concerns about Jacob's mental health. She also said Randy thought Jacob may have attempted to hike the High Divide. "On this Trail," she wrote, "just before Deer Lake, there is an unnamed waterfall, with a large tree that fell across it, during an avalanche. This avalanche took place, around the same time of Jacob's arrivals to the park. Myself and my two partners have hiked over 220 miles so far, and have found nothing, related to Jacob."

By July 2017, Tanya wrote, "as the water levels drop, and the environment changes with new plant growth, I was wondering if your vision of Jacob and his surroundings would have changed?"

The emails slowed down over the winter, and in June 2018, Tanya reached out again.

From: Tanya
Sent: Monday, June 4, 2018 7:12 PM
To: Laurie
Cc: Laura Gray; Tanya U
Subject: Re: Fwd: Jacob Gray (missing hiker)

Hi Laurie

I hope this email finds you well.

I am sending you a message in the hopes that you can provide me with some new direction or insight into the search for missing hiker, Jacob Gray. I am now entering the 14th month of looking for Jacob in the Olympic National Forest. Myself and my two partners have put over 570 miles on the ground, by foot, along the Sol Duc River and have come up with nothing. Jacob's mother was just in town this past weekend, and will be coming back in July.

McQuary responded that she still believed Jacob was not alive and that perhaps he had been taken from the area. She was about to go in for major surgery, and Tanya wished her well and said to contact her if she thought of anything as they were "desperate for information."

"When working a case, city or wilderness, I request three things—a map of the area, a photo and the birthday of the missing person, and where last seen," McQuary told me. "I then write my impressions, or *victimology* as I call it, a description of the person's life and attitude, plus what circumstances brought them to this situation. Being verified in my observances ensures me I have the correct information for the work, which is reading the energy."

David Francis, whose son Jon went missing in the Sawtooth Range in Idaho in 2006, says that psychics offered him information during his yearlong search, but nothing specific. "Families need to cling to anything, including psychics," he says. "I'd always tell the psychics, 'I appreciate your interest, but if you know where Jon is, please take me there.' They couldn't do that."

CHAPTER 24

BRITISH COLUMBIA

*Then Jacob made a vow: "If God will be with me
and watch over me on this journey, if He provides
me with food to eat and clothing to wear, and if
I return safely to my father's house, then the lord
will be my god."*

— *Genesis 28: 20–21*

SIX YEARS AGO my daughter Avalyn—seven then—and I were
leaving our local Marquette Walmart when I spotted the most
amazing bus I'd ever seen. It was vintage, with atomic-toaster lines,
but also seemingly carved out of driftwood. This bus wasn't *Further*,
Ken Kesey's 1939 International Harvester psychedelic school bus
made famous in Tom Wolfe's *The Electric Kool-Aid Acid Test*—this
bus was much better upholstered on the outside. It seemed sea-
worthy, airworthy, and roadworthy at the same time. Less Kesey,
more Tolkien. Its magic caused me to grab Avalyn's hand and nearly
jog across the parking lot. "What are we doing?" Avalyn said.

Avalyn and I circled it. Still holding my hand, she said, "I don't
want to go inside." On the back of the bus was a painted message:
We know the way, we'll bring you home.

A man with gold wire-rimmed glasses and dressed in an

outfit straight off the *Workingman's Dead* album cover told me all the technical specs. The bus is a forty-two-and-a-half-foot-long chopped-and-channeled 1949 General American Aerocoach married with a 1955 GMC Scenicruiser. She's powered with a Detroit diesel engine and an automatic transmission. *Peacemaker* reads the headsign, the sign above the windscreen that might tell you a Greyhound is bound for Denver.

Then the man asked if we'd like to climb aboard and check out the inside. Avalyn's hand was clammy as she squeezed mine. "Absolutely," I said. My daughter cried and said we shouldn't. I dragged her aboard anyway, even though she has a good sixth sense. One time we were hiking in the spring, and I wanted to take a snowbridge to Little Presque Isle in Lake Superior. There were many tracks in the dirty snow, which to me proved the snowbridge was safe. "I don't think this is a good idea," Avalyn said. It'll be fine, I said. "You can say you visited an island today." She pleaded to go back to the car the entire time. That afternoon when we were driving home I heard on the local NPR affiliate that the Coast Guard was called to rescue two dozen hikers who were stranded on Little Presque when the rotten snowbridge washed out.

The bus smelled of cedar, saddles, and pie. A pleasant woman in a muted-yellow calico dress and a braid led us through the cabin. The insides were hewn out of cedar and upholstered with leather. You climb and descend between three levels. There was a galley with a commercial range and books netted in, like a ship captain's library. No *Moby Dick*, the books were all religious titles. Avalyn sensed this was a kidnapping vessel—I smelled an adventure. Who *are* you? The woman handed me a tract. Then I recalled the Twelve Tribes' Yellow Deli in Oneonta, New York, I'd been to a couple years before, and the gears in my head meshed.

The Twelve Tribes was founded in Chattanooga, Tennessee, by Gene Spriggs, or Yoneq, now eighty-two. Yoneq was a wild kid who had partaken in the excesses of the sixties—he'd been married multiple times before getting swept up in the Jesus tide of the seventies when he visited California in his early thirties. The movement began when Yoneq moved back east with the vision of recreating the original first-century church of the Apostles. Early converts were drawn to the discipline of skilled work, an agrarian lifestyle, and close readings of the bible. Members work either in the delis, day jobs, or farms and surrender their earnings to the group. The Twelve Tribes currently claim 3,000 members all over the world. In 2013 they made headlines when two of their communities in Germany were raided by police who removed forty children for alleged abuse after spare-the-rod-spoil-the-child discipline tactics were secretly recorded by a TV reporter.

I learned this was the second custom-renovated bus, officially the *Peacemaker II,* and the crew were traveling the country, motoring to festivals and sharing the peace. They were in Marquette for the tall ships festival; the magic bus served as ground support for the Tribes' schooner barque, also christened *Peacemaker*, and on-land outreach in places like Walmart parking lots. This was not the Manson Family, not Heaven's Gate—if this is a cult maybe I'd underestimated cults.

Had I been a twenty-two-year-old single kid with an entire summer to shoot, I'd have been hard-pressed not to jump aboard, calico, homemade bread, and diesel exhaust. *We know the way, we'll bring you home.* How tempting that must be to travelers on life's highway.

Randy Gray cannot tell a lie, and so declares the two avocados rolling around somewhere in the back of the Arctic Fox when the customs agent asks if we have any produce. The agent pretends she doesn't hear him, hands our passports back, and welcomes us to Canada.

We drive through vineyards and the greater Vancouver area rush hour traffic to Chilliwack. The Whack—as the locals say—is the seventh-largest agglomeration in British Columbia: 85,000 people. It's not a large city, but has that odd urban-wilderness interface feel that many southern B.C. towns do. There are huddles of heroin addicts on the street corners, and the forests are littered with ripped nylon tents and abandoned shopping carts.

A few years ago some Mennonites—the religious group that eschews much modern technology—here were busted for trafficking cocaine from Chihuahua to western Canada. No one thinks Jacob ran off with Mennonites, but we talk about the movie that would make. We're in the Whack because of a similar sect, however, the Twelve Tribes. In Mallory's research on cults, she came across mention of them recruiting through-hikers on the Pacific Crest Trail. They operate organic farms, value trades, and are family-centered in an Old Testament sense. They operate a micro-chain of Yellow Delis across the U.S. and Canada, and we find one on Yale Road, the main drag through the Whack.

Raw barn beams support the roof, and the tables are carved from yellow pine. The light is filtered through umber stained glass, and the electric lights are a soft mustard yellow—it's the opposite of the Lynchian greasy spoon and rather feels like being inside a jar of brand new raw honey. Instrumental lute music that is almost bluegrass plays on the sound system.

Randy and I are both taken aback to be taken so *in*. Twelve Tribers are disciples of the Son of God—though they call him by a Hebrew name, Yahshua. Our server, a pretty woman with hair tied back, no makeup, and bright eyes named Hahyen, takes our order and disappears. She's wearing genie pants and leather clogs. The other diners speak at hushed levels, as if this were a library. I think Randy and I both half expect Jacob to walk out from the kitchen in an apron with a tray of goat cheese and a big grin among a grand beard. There are other pretty women dressed in genie pants and bell sleeves. I want to join this cult, now.

This is slow, deliberate, nourishing food. A locally raised lamb sandwich for Randy and homemade chili for me. Bearded men with ponytails flit here and there carrying trays and busing tables. It's like eating supper in *The Hobbit*. I can tell Randy is thinking, *I can see it, I can see Jacob finding this place and folding in—I can see it. This is what I would have done at twenty-two, heck yeah, I can see it.*

Hahyen hesitantly asks what we're up to in Chilliwack—she does not call it the Whack.

Randy is tractor-beamed by Hahyen's eyes. "My son is missing. We're looking at WWOOFing farms. Someone told us about the Twelve Tribes." He does not call it a cult.

"I'm so sorry," she says.

"His name is Jacob, but he may have changed his name to Israel," Randy explains. Of course Hahyen is familiar with Jacob's story in Genesis.

Randy is compelled to tell her his surfing name—his own tribe. "Udo," he says. "My brother was Stumbo because he was a big stumbling guy." Stumbo had an Irish setter named Panama Red who lived to be twenty-two years old even though—or because—Stumbo and his buddies would exhale pot smoke into his nose.

"You're welcome to stay with us," she says. "Let me call and see if there's space at our farm." She returns to tell us that it's too late to camp at the in-town farm, but since we're self-contained we're welcome to stay in the parking lot, right here in downtown Chilliwack.

"Perfect," Randy says. And it is.

"Please have breakfast with us in the morning," Hahyen says. "And I'll ask if anyone's seen Jacob or Israel."

Hahyen tells us about their farm on Vancouver Island. There is a Friday dance—though she doesn't call it a dance, rather a sunset celebration of the Sabbath—and we'd be welcome there. We could stay on the farm even—the Twelve Tribes are part of WWOOF. She wouldn't know everyone who came and went out there on the island, so sure, it's possible one of her family there has seen Jacob. *Israel*. That's where we'll go.

We wake up at four a.m. in order to beat the Vancouver traffic to the Nanaimo ferry. The Yellow Deli seems to be open twenty-four hours to serve the vulnerable who inhabit the Canadian night. In the spirit of Yahshua, the Tribers want to give us breakfast for free. So far, if this is a cult, we're buying all they're not selling. Shalom, our server and cook, is a big-bearded ginger. "I heard about your story," he says to Randy. Shalom is bashful, a man of few words. "Your son disappeared on a bike trip."

"Yeah, Jacob," Randy says. "Israel."

"I did that," Shalom says.

"Did your folks know?"

"I sort of told my parents." What he's saying to Randy is that, yes, of course he should worry, but also, do not give up hope. His quiet validation is buoying. The thing about Randy's quest is that the smallest morsel of *maybe* can fuel an entire week or more of searching—along with a spinach-and-egg breakfast sandwich called the Spinwich, Shalom has given him that.

It's 5:30 a.m. Randy is still inside the Yellow Deli (like the Hotel California, it's hard to leave). I'm in the truck cab writing in my notebook. I look up to see two young men squatting on the sidewalk near their bicycles and a shopping cart that seems to be hitched to one of the bikes like a trailer. There's a blinking red bike light on the shopping cart, which is full of flattened cardboard boxes. The man in a camouflage hoodie rolls up his sleeve, briskly rubs his forearm at the elbow, picks up a syringe, shakes it, jams it in his arm and plunges. The suburbs stretch all the way to the North Cascades in Chilliwack, an hour southeast of the downtown Vancouver and East Hastings, the heroin capital of North America. Shiploads of opium were trafficked through southwestern British Columbia in the mid-nineteenth century, and it appears the tradition lives on. Seattle, of course, has its homeless drug-addict issues, but the greater Vancouver area feels inundated with roaming homeless heroin junkies. Randy would pull the truck over to read the map or take a leak—step into the weeds and there'd be a tattered Canadian Tire tent or a wheelless shopping cart turned on its side among cigarette butts and toilet paper. The detritus is so prevalent that I made an effort to watch for used syringes whenever I wasn't on a sidewalk.

The country is huge and feral. And people go missing there every day.

But Jacob would have dug the Chilliwack Tribers. He could assume a new identity—Israel. No one has a cell phone, which he believed, correctly, was a Big Brother bug. The core of an existence was hard physical work, something he appreciated. He could assimilate and hide. And Tribers are shuffled around between communities all over the world. He fist-bumps the Tribers, surfer-style, then deploys the *shaka!* They understand this dance, speak this universal language.

"The search has become more spiritual," Randy says while merging onto the westbound 1, the Trans-Canada Highway. "Psychics, Bigfoot. Now this group." He means the Twelve Tribes. "Look at a map. It's over a year out. I need to pull away for a while."

He doesn't mean he's winding down the search. I don't think he even means the search is now more about what's going on inside him, Randy Gray, and that his quest has somehow grown more existential. What he's doing is justifying not meeting the

Olympic Response Group and Laura at the fish hatchery on the Sol
Duc River.

He's certainly keeping up the search, more and more on his own
terms—that's why we're in British Columbia. When the clues are
not literal, rather cerebral or ethereal, what remains is the spiritual.
This whole time there have been so few literal clues. Essentially,
a bicycle, a bible, four arrows stuck in the ground. That's just
about it.

"When it's physical you don't hear people," Randy says. Swimming the river, bushwhacking through the rainforest. "When that
slows down you listen to people and chew on what they say."
There's no shortage of people with things to say, especially with the
megaphone of the Internet, which Randy is just about as distanced
from as an American can be. "Still, you want to hear *something*.
Silence is deadly. I like hearing stuff, even if it's off-the-wall and
wacky. Someone's thinking of him, they're concerned."

Rush-hour traffic parts like the Red Sea, and we drive straight
onto the Nanaimo ferry. A guy in an optic yellow vest gives us the
shut-it-down sign. We're in the belly of the whale. The ferry is not
full; it's mostly service trucks and just a handful of commuters and
tourists. Randy climbs the stairs up to the observation deck near the
bow, stretches out across the chairs, and falls into a snoring sleep as
saltwater spray mists the glass.

A claxon sounds and we're on Vancouver Island. Randy's island
driving is as frightening as his mainland driving. The big Dodge
one-ton has been modified with pneumatic suspension, frame
braces, and stabilizer bars so—even at twelve and a half feet high—
it takes corners like a Super Bee. He doesn't text and drive, thank
goodness—he needs his thumbs for the throttle. The accelerator
pedal still makes his knee ache, so he drives with his thumbs on
the cruise control like a kid on a video game controller; he doesn't

like to brake because then he has to reset the cruising speed. So he doesn't brake much. He's an excellent driver when fully concentrating, but I alert him to brake lights ahead, at least twice averting a rear-ender. "So that's how it handles when the brakes lock up," he says after smoking them once. See, every occasion is an opportunity to learn.

The thing about an island—this is certainly true for me, and I think for Randy too—is that the first thing I want to do is either circle it or transect it. Size it up. See what makes this shore different from that shore. Roll through the place-poetry of the names of the little island villages. What's the weather over *there*?

When we disembark in Nanaimo and look at the map of Vancouver Island, Randy is pulled west, toward the Pacific coast, where the surfing is—"That's where Jacob would go," he says.

The sky is the color of gravy, and some of the clouds touch Highway 4 as we diesel past Port Alberni and wind westward on the Pacific Rim Highway. I'm a little carsick from Randy's fast corners on the snaking highway and if I hear "Marrakesh Express" one more time on Sirius XM I'm unbuckling and jumping out. Meanwhile I keep an eye out for deer, a bear, a cyclist.

This highway feels much like Highway 101 in the Olympic Peninsula, sided by mountains and water and muted by the fog. Sproat Lake, Taylor Arm Provincial Park, Winche Indian Reserve. Windshield wipers on, we pull in at the rest area at Wya Point, where the road T's—Tofino to the north, Ucluelet to the south—but we're essentially at the end of the road, the Pacific Ocean.

Three young women from Victoria are parked, their old Toyota van packed with camping gear. The driver asks Randy if he has any radiator coolant, it's been running hot since Port Alberni. No, but he takes a look while they try to decide if it's okay to add a little water, temporarily, to get them to a shop. There's a kiosk near the restrooms with a large public bulletin board. I read the notifications—couple lost dogs and church suppers—while Randy carefully tacks a *MISSING Jacob Gray* poster on the board, the first one on the island. "You never know," Randy says. "Maybe Jacob'll be walking by and see it. *Hey, Jacob, call home.*"

I notice there are already two posters there, three men. My mind immediately goes to timelines—all three men disappeared on the same day, May 16, 2018—just two weeks ago. We haven't been on the island three hours and are already in the world of the missing.

It's eerie to see multiple missing persons posters in such a sparsely populated, wild, rural place. The poster on the left shows photos of Dan Archbald, thirty-seven, and Ryan Daley, forty-three, who had flown to Panama, purchased a forty-eight-foot sailboat, *Astral Blue*, and spent eight weeks sailing it back to Canada. They were, according to the poster, last seen in Ucluelet.

To the right is the eight-and-a-half by eleven black-and-white poster for forty-one-year-old Ben Kilmer, who went missing on the southeast side of the island, near Duncan. Kilmer's work van was found parked and still running outside. His cell phone was found smashed, and there was blood in the van. Kilmer is the father of two.

All three men appear athletic, fit, and shown in photos on their Facebook missing pages as smiling and participating in outdoor pursuits. The Royal Canadian Mounted Police have announced they don't believe the vanishings are related, but it's mathematically possible to drive between Ucluelet and Duncan in the three hours' differences in the timeline. Furthermore, Duncan is on the probable route on the way to Jordan River, believed to be the destination of Archbald and Daley. It feels like we've landed on the Island of Missing Men.

We walk down the ramp at the Ucluelet Small Boats Harbour, and Randy asks a couple fishermen just getting in where the *Astral Blue* can be found. One points. "End of the dock, there."

"What do you think happened?" Randy asks.

"Don't know," the fisherman says, "other than they had a couple of big duffel bags. Maybe something interesting in the bags. Something somebody wanted. RCMP's been all over the dock, helicopter flying around yesterday."

Archbald and Daley spent two and a half days in port clearing customs. This wouldn't be that unusual since they had to undergo assessment on the newly purchased boat. They claimed to be starting a new charter business and paid for a month's mooring in cash. Surveillance footage captures them shouldering the large duffel bags and walking with intent off the screen, into a vanish.

Daley keeps an RV on three acres in Jordan River; it's curious why the men wouldn't have sailed the *Astral Blue* straight to Jordan River, or nearby Port Renfrew, both places that would allow them to avoid high mooring fees closer to Victoria. It's also curious that, after an eight-week trip, they wouldn't have had a ride arranged.

Most curious to me is why Archbald would want to go surfing with his shipmate, where the waves were, at the time, *junk*—a Randy word—after being away from his family for eight weeks.

"Doesn't wash," Randy says. "They were dead before they got on that boat."

On the Pacific Rim we're reminded again how searching for missing persons is still painstakingly analog. On the short drive to Tofino we passed literally dozens of eight-and-a-half by eleven flyers for Dan Archbald and Ryan Daley, and Ben Kilmer—they were stapled to creosoted utility poles, about as old-school as a wanted poster in the Old West. It appeared different persons were hanging the respective flyers, as some areas would be more Archbald and Daley canvassed, some heavy with Ben Kilmer. We had to pull over to actually read them, but there was such a draw to do so, to see who in fact it was for, to see if there might be another person missing, and another. Redundancy is out the window, too, in a search.

We're headed back east along the Alberni Highway, toward Highway 19, where we swing north toward Courtenay. We're on our way to the Twelve Tribes farm just east of town, between town and the Strait of Georgia. You can't see the saltwater from the farm, but you can smell it.

We roll through the front gate and into the lot of New Sprout Farm. There's a farmhouse and a meeting center. A barn and outbuildings and cabins where members live. There are late-model pickup trucks, a VW Vanagon, a backhoe, horse trailers, and various farm implements. Nothing about the place necessarily says cult, more typical organic farm. We're at ease here immediately.

The women are dressed like Hahyen, and the bearded men wear a uniform of carpenter jeans and plaid flannel shirts. Humble, comfortable, practical.

Jacob isn't here—*Israel* isn't either. A tall, bearded Quebecer with an easy grin and thick accent named Will asks if we've heard of Alex Supertramp, the pseudonym of Chris McCandless from *Into the Wild*.

Yes! He thinks Jacob may be on a similar quest as McCandless's. "The adventure is stronger than the need for family," he says. He says it like pointing out the grass is green, the sky is blue. He has a wife and a young son, has arrived at family, but with all the Tribesmen there's an air that many wild oats have been sown previously.

Randy surveys the farm under the overcast sky. "Time goes slow," he says. "It doesn't really mean anything. I never know what day it is."

It's Friday, I remind him. Dance night.

Randy puts on a clean button-up shirt and combs his hair with his fingers because we're going visiting. Tribesmen and women welcome us into the community building. There is a piano and a man playing an acoustic guitar. We are handed mugs of yerba maté tea, the preferred drink of the Tribes. The guitar player, who is also the children's music teacher, plays a song called "Are You Weary?" He's a good guitar player.

There are confessions of faith and brotherhood, fables and parabolic skits with the children. After much talking and a delicious, simple meal of beef gravy and noodles, Randy dances the Hebrew jigs while I sheepishly sit and read Twelve Tribes tracts. Randy has tapped into his Jesus-freak days and is having a great time.

I head back to the Arctic Fox, parked near the barn. I'm asleep when Randy gets back, having cut the rug and imbibed maté until eleven.

The next morning we talk with the owner of the VW Vanagon, Will. He's a young hippie living on the road and doesn't have a Hebrew name. A friend of the New Sprout Tribers, he isn't an official member but finds safe harbor here now and then, working and worshipping for hot meals. He listens intently as Randy tells him about Jacob.

"Salt Spring Island," Will says with conviction. "One of the Gulf Islands. Every drifting kid ends up there. Goths, artists, farmers. That's where I'd go."

I can tell by Randy's face we'll be going.

First, he wants to go to another end-of-the-road on Vancouver Island. "Jacob mentioned Jordan River," Randy says. "I didn't know where it was." I thought Randy was confusing Jordan River with the River Jordan, but the fact that Ryan Daley kept an RV there, and the two sailors were headed there when they vanished, jiggled his memory. "Jacob wanted to go there. He could see it on the map, across the Strait."

In Sooke we get a view across the Strait of Juan de Fuca at

the majestic Olympic Mountains from the north. Way over there, below the snowcapped mountains, is where the bicycle was found, the last trace of Jacob.

Jordan River is forty miles west of Victoria. Bob Dylan's "Black Diamond Bay" plays off the satellite. We cross over the signed Jacob's Creek, which Randy points out with excitement. There is very little traffic headed toward Jordan River. The little hamlet, still called River Jordan by some locals, is a former logging camp at the mouth of the river and is nearly directly north of the Sol Duc Road. With his fondness for maps and biblical places, Jacob may have noticed the Jordan on the map and decided to go there.

Israel won't stop coming up. I recall from Sunday school that the Israelites escaped slavery in Egypt by crossing the Jordan to the Promised Land. It's where John the Baptist baptized Jesus of Nazareth. The Jabbok River, where God wrestled Jacob through the night and his name was changed to Israel, is a tributary to the Jordan before it flows southward and through the Dead Sea. On the south shore of Vancouver Island, the river feeds into the Strait and, at times, is a popular surf break for Victorians. There are signs pointing out tsunami evacuation routes.

Twelve Tribes. Four arrows. I try to think of a mathematical connection but can't get past twelve divided by four.

Past Jordan River is Port Renfrew and another literal end of the road. But first we stop at Sombrio Beach and make the short hike down to the water in dusky light. We meet a few surfers carrying boards back to the trailhead. There's a jouncy suspension bridge over the Sombrio River that drops to an estuary of rocks and sand and trees, and Randy fairly jogs down it—he smells water and fire. Peppered everywhere are tents and scruffy backpackers sitting on beach logs, playing guitars and poking at things cooking. Randy is quiet, scanning for any young man with Jacob's posture, a silhouette of his son. There is laughter, young men, young women. Randy takes his time taking it in. I watch him, thinking, *If Jacob isn't here, he should be. He should be with young people, doing young person things like camping at the beach and cooking on an open fire.* When we return to the parking lot Randy pins a *MISSING Jacob Gray* poster to the information kiosk. He crosses out the number for the Santa Cruz Police Department and writes *Call Randy Gray (Dad) 831-247-6991* on the bottom. "Santa Cruz police didn't do anything," he says. "They won't even call me back."

Sunday. "I wonder if May sixteenth was a full moon," Randy says. He's been thinking of the three men gone missing on the island. I check on my phone; it was not—not even close. It wasn't a full moon when Jacob vanished a year ago, either. I recall Randy telling me that last summer he'd drive up in the Olympics, turn his headlights off, and watch meadows under full moons because cults were rumored to perform ceremonies in the Olympic Peninsula on full moon nights.

Randy explains to me his idea for a wetsuit specific to river searching. He's been thinking of it since the day of getting pinballed off the rocks of the North Fork of the Sol Duc. The suit would be complete with reinforced knees for kneeling against rock and gravel. He also has plans for a type of SAR boogie board, based off one he saw used by lifeguards in Hawaii. "But it's gotta be shorter," he says. "Shorter. And with more handles." It's clear he'd do it again today if needed. "More handles," he says. "You gotta have the right gear. Without the right gear it'll kill ya."

Jacob is Israel. He's not in the river. He's adrift on land. Somewhere. Other people can assign him to a deep hole in the Sol Duc, but Randy will not. He's not here at the Jordan River, either.

* * *

That afternoon Randy decides to take the quick open ferry to Salt Spring Island. We're in the ferry queue at Crofton an hour early, so we climb in back and I make huevos rancheros and Randy brews some French-press coffee. Out the window we watch traffic for other ferries. "We're just like ants, aren't we," Randy says. "Always busy, doing something. Ants are always busy. Just like ants."

The ferry vectors around several small arms and islands, then we watch Salt Spring Island get bigger and wonder what we're in for. Randy had met with island after island of disappointment in the San Juans last winter, and hoped against experience that the Canadian version could offer up anything, which would be something. Other vehicles motor off the ferry and onto Salt Spring at the little village of Vesuvius with purpose, like they know where they're going. We do not, but the island is small enough to drive completely around in an hour.

Yoga retreats and goat farms. Houses painted turquoise with sunroofs and solar panels. Signs: *EGGS FOR SALE.* In the little town of Ganges there's a homeless feed in the park, sponsored by a consortium of island churches. A young woman with blue hair and a top hat feeds a baby. Top hats are in fashion for the young people—there's a somewhat menacing man, a cross between Willy Wonka and Rob Zombie. Steampunk gone off the rails. Some of the homeless have dogs. The food—pastas and salads—looks good. Randy shows his *MISSING Jacob Gray* poster to church members, and some of the eaters gather around. No one has seen him. A woman in her late sixties says, "I'm sorry about your son—Jacob? I'm gonna pray to Saint Anthony—he's the patron saint of lost people."

We walk to another smaller park behind the bakery. There's a group of older homeless people drinking canned beer. They're drunk. "What are you, cops?" a disheveled man says. He laughs, then lunges at Randy. "I gotta frisk you in case you're wearing a wire." Randy sidesteps and stiff-arms him. The man's friends laugh. Randy moves at ease, but with the confidence of a martial artist. He's no stranger to homeless populations, no fool, but could defend himself in a tight spot.

This isn't Jacob's crowd. "The homeless problem in Santa Cruz really bothered Jacob," Randy says. "Really bothered him." But there are dozens of small farms on the island. Randy pins a poster to a bulletin board at the seaplane dock at Long Harbour. "What else can you do?" Randy says. "Hang up another poster. What else can you *do?*"

We queue up in line at the ferry back in Vesuvius. Randy idles, and I hop out to pin another poster outside the general store. When we inch onto the ferry, Randy sticks his head out the window to holler at a pretty woman driving a blue four-by-four diesel Mitsubishi Delica, a narrow van favored by Vancouver Islanders, farmers, and surfers.

"Your steering wheel is on the wrong side!" he calls.

She throws Randy an enormous grin and shakes her head. "It's on the *right* side."

They flirt about diesel engines and gas mileage, and I think I'm gonna have to make myself scarce tonight while the two have a date. Alas, no. I saw her on the ferry, sitting in the passenger seat, playing a ukulele and singing softly. It starts to rain.

She passes us, dodging in front, beeps the little Delica horn, waving, on the highway to Victoria. "I should have talked to her on the ferry," Randy says. "The *ferry.*"

I bet she wishes he'd talked to her, too.

Maybe we should have spent more time on Salt Spring Island; maybe we should have spent more time on Vancouver Island. The scale of a search is so big, galactic, incomprehensible. I'm realizing that every search is a hasty search, that Randy will always be in the Reflex Phase.

*   *   *

Randy steers through and around downtown Victoria traffic, sticks his torso out of the driver's side window and talks our way into the queue—we're the last vehicle to make the 7:30 p.m. ferry, the M.V. *Coho*, to Port Angeles—another forty seconds and we'd be spending another night on the island. A stevedore closes the gate behind. A U.S. Customs agent asks if we have any produce or weapons on board as he runs our passports. "We have two avocados. But we bought them in the States," Randy says.

"I didn't hear what you just said," the mustachioed agent says, handing back our passports. A stevedore waves us into the dark belly of the whale once again. The 341-foot-long M.V. *Coho* holds 115 vehicles and a thousand passengers and is full up of people wanting to go back to the United States after a weekend in Canada.

This Canada sortie could be looked upon as a colossal waste of time and diesel fuel. An empty caper, a wild Canada goose chase. Except it isn't. Every resource in a search gets smoked up, but that's what propels you to the next area and other possibilities. For Randy it would be mad-making to pace around his sister Judy's living room, talking to her parakeet and making calls. He needs to be out in the world, where searching is a literal, physical act.

The wind is blowing forty knots and there is considerable chop in the Strait of Juan de Fuca. There was a big triathlon in Victoria, and the ferry is filled with tired athletes. Nearly every passenger is inside the sheltered lounge area, staring into their phones, playing cards, napping, drinking beer or coffee. But Randy spends the entire hour-and-a-half ride at the prow, King of the World style. It's the best view, and he'll be the first of the thousand to reach Washington. His gray hair is flagged eastward; the wind buffets the skin on his face. There are only kids out here, it's that windy and cold, and even they don't stay out here long. But this is the vantage where you truly understand how magnificent the Olympic Mountains—

Olympic National Park—truly are. Hurricane Ridge, the northern vanguard of the Olympic Mountains, rises snowcapped and proud above a crown of clouds. Though it's windy, the sun is out in a cerulean sky.

The mountains slowly get bigger and bigger as the huge diesel engine pushes the ferry toward the far shore. Waves slap against the hull, and the big ferry cuts and bobs in the chop. "If he kayaked across he'd get wet," Randy says. "Pretty *wet.*"

That spot across this water is where Randy's life changed forever. Of course, that's not what he's thinking—Randy Gray is not thinking about himself. Randy is taciturn now. It's a stunning relief of scale, sea level to the heavens. It's hard not to think Jacob had a grand plan, a keen vision for a twenty-two-year-old kid. It's clear he's thinking that his son left his red bicycle on the green shoulder beneath those white peaks. That river that he now knows better than the briny surf off Santa Cruz. Those mountains, home of the gods and black bears. What a grand and glorious place to vanish. Randy has questions for Jacob when he sees him.

We're driving west on the 101, back to the Bigfoot Barn, where we'll get a hot shower and make some tacos. I ask Randy something I've been wondering for a long time: *Are you bitter about Washington, the Pacific Northwest? Has this place been poisoned for you?* I think I'd have a hard time loving the Pacific Northwest, Washington, national parks, or the outdoors at all if my son went missing without a trace out here.

"No way," he says. "I love this place. Because Jacob loved this place."

I notice it's the first time in the year I've known Randy that he's used the past tense in regard to Jacob. *Loved.*

"I feel at home here." When he says *at home* I expect him to say *at peace.* Of course that can't be, it isn't squared. I consider how you can be at home without being at peace, and for now that seems okay with Randy. "I'll come back here as long as it takes. Jacob lived here."

We get to the Bigfoot Barn. I pour myself a splash of whiskey from the Bigfoot Bar. "Let me have a shot with ya," Randy, who doesn't drink, says. I pour him a shot of Glenlivet 12.

Here's to finding Jacob.

I can tell it's medicinal to Randy, not in a good way, but in a taste and burn way. "Help ya sleep," I say.

"Yeah, but I won't need help for that," he says.

Over dinner he says, "How about those Twelve Tribes! I'm gonna join. I've got my circular saw, my nail gun, I can build stuff for 'em."

"The whiskey has gone to your head," I say. "Find you a wife up there at least."

"I don't need that," he says.

We talk about the missing men, Dan Archbald and Ryan Daley, Ben Kilmer, and speculate some more. So many mysteries in Canada.

On the drive to Port Renfro we crossed over Lost Shoe Creek, which caused me to think about the hiking boot with the human foot inside recently found washed up on Gabriola Island, one of the Gulf Islands. I emailed the B.C. coroner, Andy Watson, who sent me a photo. It's a Merrell light-hiking shoe, a size twelve. Again, much too big for Jacob. But if Jacob picked them up at Goodwill or someplace, Randy says, he could have worn shoes too big for him. That's highly unlikely, I tell him. Even if Jacob was suffering some level of mental malady, he knew better than to try to wear shoes three sizes too big. *It's not Jacob, Randy.*

A thing we did not know when we were standing in the bow of the M.V. *Coho,* coming back to Port Angeles, was that while we were crossing the Strait of San Juan de Fuca, a pregnant orca whale was out there. Orca whales—also called killer whales—are endangered. This resident whale, called J-35, gave birth in July to the first local calf in three years. The calf died shortly after birth, and the blubberless carcass sank. The mother dove to retrieve it and pushed it to the surface with her forehead. The mother carried it for twenty-four hours, in the direction of Saturna Island and San Juan Island.

CHAPTER 25

HUDSON BAY

Mosquitos covered their hands and necks like fur.
—*Annie Proulx,* Barkskins

MICHAEL NEIGER and I are in northern Ontario, the Arctic Ocean watershed that drains into Lower Hudson Bay. Neiger rhymes with tiger. It was a two-day drive from our homes in Marquette to Cochrane, Ontario, where we catch the Ontario Northland Polar Bear Express, the last whistle-stop train in Canada. We have full expedition packs and are headed into the boreal bush—paper birch, red maple, spruce, jack pine, and tamarack. I catalog the tree species so as to occupy my mind away from listing the mosquitoes and biting fly species. Neiger, even at sixty-four, is an aficionado of extremes, whether backcountry ski touring in minus-forty-degree winter or searching for a missing trapper in a half million hectares of the most mosquito-infested muskeg swamps in the world.

What are the chances that—as I was researching Amy Bechtel—I moved to the Upper Peninsula, Neiger's hometown and home base to his small, all-volunteer MiBSAR (Michigan Backcountry Search and Rescue). When I got interested in other missing persons cases I tried to find all the people who pursue cold cases in very weather-beaten, remote places. My search came up with Simon Donato and Michael Neiger. Though he's generous with naming skilled volunteers who have worked tirelessly with MiBSAR on searches, Neiger doesn't know of anyone else who is solely dedicated to cold cases in the back of beyond either, shrugs at the question, it's just what he does.

I once referred to him as an expert, and he stopped me in my tracks. "I'm not an expert," he says. "Searching doesn't work that way." Neiger is two decades older than Donato, but he's as physically fit—I'll often see him running the hills around Marquette or hitting the weights at our university's gym. He needs to stay in top shape to carry the voluminous trademark rucksack.

"It's like having a book you haven't read, you know," he says regarding why he does this. "I don't go in until everyone has gone home. I'd rather just blend in, be a mushroom picker."

Neiger is a twenty-six-year veteran of the Michigan State Police—he retired as detective sergeant. Now he keeps many balls in the air, working a dozen cases with varying intensities at any given time. He's involved in more than two dozen cases now, pins all over Michigan, Wisconsin, and Ontario, some warm, some downright cold. "You burn out on it. That's why I have a lot of cases, move around," he says. "I describe it as a continuum. A lot of times I'm helping people along that continuum. There's really no end to it. Days turn into weeks, weeks turn into years." I think about Randy's continuum.

Neiger has solved cases, but doesn't keep score that way. Right now, he's going back to work in search of Michael Joseph Linklater, a forty-four-year-old Cree man last positively seen in 2003. Neiger has been working the case since the summer of 2016.

Linklater had a drinking problem. Linklater's father and brother, John, had taken Michael to the family camp on the Abitibi River, below New Post Creek Falls, because they were concerned about him and thought it might help to dry him out. Michael didn't like the plan, went to the outhouse at six in the morning on July 13, 2003, and didn't come back. The next day, when Michael hadn't returned to camp, John canoed downriver a dozen miles, then walked to a phone in order to call the Ontario Provincial Police.

It's most likely Linklater is long dead, but not everyone believes so. Passengers on the Polar Bear Express see strange lights in the bush at night. And occasionally a figure along the tracks ducks into the roadless swamps as the train nears. There isn't anyone else who could be out there.

It's the twenty-first of June, 2018. In May I was searching in British Columbia with Randy. Neiger and I were supposed to have headed into the bush a couple weeks ago, but the Polar Bear Express suffered a derailment, cutting off the lifeline between Cochrane and the First Nations settlements of Moosonee and Moose Factory, two hundred miles to the north. The derailment was caused by intense heat warping the tracks; now, to avoid another derailment, the train is running at only twenty-five miles per hour.

The conductor sees from our tickets that we're jumping off at Ranoke, a siding ruin that barely qualifies as a ghost town. Ranoke is close to the Linklater camp, which is at mile 115—the most efficient way to mark our location is railway miles. "Twelve thirty-five p.m.," the conductor tells us.

Before this railway was built in the 1960s, dogsled mushers delivered the mail to Moosonee down the frozen Abitibi River. We get coffee and breakfast in the humble dining car. There are passengers drinking morning Molson's Lagers. We chat with an Ontario Provincial Police officer headed for a hitch in Moosonee. He asks what we're doing and Neiger tells him, then asks if he had heard of the Daniel Trask case. The officer had, though he didn't work it. Trask, twenty-eight, disappeared in the Temagami backcountry in the fall of 2011. He'd been living off the land in the 6,000-square-mile wilderness. Trask's mother contacted Neiger through his website and asked him to help. In 2013 MiBSAR volunteers Cathy Susan, Chris Ozminski, and Neiger found Trask's backpack on the shore of Diamond Lake. The pack contained, among other things, a pair of snowshoes, a painted cow skull, boxer shorts, and a live green snake.

"How do you know about the Trask case?" the officer asks.

"I'm the guy who found him," Neiger says. Late May 2015, another trio of MiBSAR volunteers, including Neiger, Ozminski, and Todd Theoret, located the man's remains along the east shore of Lady Evelyn Lake. Trask's skull showed signs of severe trauma— it's believed he slipped, hit his head on a rock, and died in a fall. Neiger isn't bragging, just talking cop-to-cop. That's how we ended up on this train—the OPP was impressed with his work on the Trask case and asked if he'd look into the Linklater case.

Like Susan, Ozminski, and Theoret, I'm a volunteer on this search, and I'm hoping—of course I am—that we can have similar luck in finding Michael Linklater. Or at least a clue or two that helps evolve the search. I have no skills to offer other than curiosity, and I appreciate that Neiger has allowed me to come along. If nothing else it'll be a Canadian bush survival master's course for me. Neiger loves this country, the bush. He's guided self-supported ski trips through here in deep winter. In the nineties he solo-canoed from Lake Superior to the Arctic Ocean. My favorite Henry Rollins observation is that "humans are pretty crafty but will fold quickly in severe cold." He's right, of course, but Neiger is the exception. If there's anything he's better at mitigating than the cold it's the bugs, which eat on me while leaving Neiger be.

As the train slows, we walk to the baggage car for our packs. The cargo men keep the doors open for the breeze. There are canoes and bicycles and crates full of barking dogs. "What are you doing at

Ranoke?" one of the men asks. "We don't get many people getting off here."

"We're searching for Michael Linklater," Neiger says.

The men remember Michael Linklater. "Haven't seen Johnny in a while," referring to Michael's brother. "Not sure if he's in camp or not." The train cries to a stop, we toss our packs into the weeds and jump out after them. We wave at the bag men, one of whom gives the engineer the high sign, and the train diesels back up, brakes hiss, and the Polar Bear Express slowly rolls north.

It's sunny, sixty-five degrees. There's a light breeze—too light to knock back any bugs. Neiger is militant with time and navigation, and we start walking into the bush at 1:10.

Michael Linklater was—*is?*—a highly skilled hunter, fisher, and trapper. He was also infamous as a mean drunk. Linklater's girlfriend told family he took her to a hidden bunker, a root cellar, that she probably wouldn't be able to find on her own, and wouldn't show anyone if she could for fear of Linklater's rage.

That's the key, and Neiger has a plan. He thinks that if he can find the bunker, he'll find the man. Or at least it'll be a big clue as to what's become of him.

Neiger has maps, of course, but he's also printed out satellite images that show, ever faint, lines that run across muskeg between the rail line and the Abitibi River. Those nearly invisible lines are old winter logging roads that have grown over but left a scar. At the end of those winter roads are long-abandoned logging camps, reclaimed by the bush. "Each camp had a cookhouse," Neiger says. "Most cookhouses had a root cellar. Michael would have known about every one of them." We find the ghost logging camps, we find the root cellar, we find Linklater.

We're wearing Gore-Tex waterproof boots and gaiters, but bog water still finds its way to my socks. I'm exhausted between the muskeg, a swamp of water and dead vegetation covered by sphagnum moss, and my heavy pack. The day gets hot, the bugs are incessant, and I can't imagine what exercise at the gym could prepare someone for this type of travel. "It's like walking on soaked used mattresses for miles," Neiger says. We stop to refill our water bottles—bog water that we treat with iodine and flavor with lemonade powder—and replace the full-strength military-grade DEET that I once thought was poison but now think is worth its weight in bitcoin. The water is weak-tea colored and refreshingly cool. Neiger shoots an azimuth with his wrist compass. The going is slow, but we're buoyed by the hunt for a ghost town long swallowed by wilderness.

Occasionally we come to doghair growth so thick it snags our packs and we can't see through it, let alone walk through. "If he's in there he's staying in there," Michael says. We drop our packs and do what he calls a *loose grid search*. Whenever we leave our packs, he's insistent we have on our persons fire starter, a knife, a compass, an emergency blanket, snacks, and water—he never takes for granted that we couldn't get turned around and or injured and not be able to get back to our packs. I quickly understand that he's not being overly cautious, rather wisely prepared.

Of course, I can't help but compare this to the search for Jacob. My mind's still reeling from the trip to Vancouver Island and back to the Olympic Peninsula with Randy. I don't have a connection with Linklater—I feel like I know Jacob through Randy. Jacob is a good kid; Linklater is—*was?*—not a good man. My thought is that Randy would love this, this approach to finding someone missing. I'm going to tell him about it after we find a ghost town and a root cellar.

Neiger found one of Michael's huge moose snares, made from surplus powerline cable. For a while John Linklater was leaving food and supplies in the bush for his brother, just in case he was alive and needed them. A few items—an axe, some clothing—were taken from the family camp.

One week into the initial search, a half kilometer south of the camp, indigenous searchers heard a voice goading, heckling them. It spooked some of them enough that they wouldn't go back into the bush to search. Still now, anything odd—a missing case of canned soup, a strange light in the distance—gets assigned to Michael Linklater, the missing trapper of the Abitibi.

Upriver at railroad mile 103 there's a camp, the nearest neighbor, twelve miles south. The owners reported two gill nets had been stolen. Neiger thinks it could have been Linklater—the list of suspects out here is pretty short. "I think the cellar's along the river—that's where the food is, that's where the water is," he says. "We're gonna find those gill nets, those two gill nets missing from the next camp upriver. We're looking for anything not natural, anything human in origin."

We pitch camp. I have a tent, which helps a little with the bugs. Neiger eschews a tent in favor of a self-sewn tarp shelter. It weighs about the same as a napkin but bugs have easy access. Neiger doesn't seem to be affected. We eat a dehydrated meal, plan the morning's search, read a few pages, and fall asleep to the howl of coyotes.

Weather is moving in. Rain is easier to deal with than bugs. We're flanking the river just inside the woodline, above the steep west bank of the Abitibi, looking for spoor—broken limbs that indicate a man on foot, a tin can, a beer bottle. *Socketing*, a depression in the ground that indicates rocks have moved. Bones. Neiger reminds me to look up as we bushwhack—things, or people, can be found in trees. The invisible, continuous room of surveillance is what Neiger calls the *searcher's cube*. "Can you imagine using a heli up here?" Neiger says. "Unless he's out on the tracks you're not gonna see shit." OPP used a helicopter on the original search; they didn't see shit. But a heli is how they'd have to get one of us out of here if it came to that. One of the first things Neiger did was inform me that a Huey rescue runs $5,000 an hour, his way of emphasizing that safety is always first.

Neiger, as hard-core as he is, understands that we need rest breaks. "We're living in the bush," he says. That's to say that carrying your home on your back through swamps and doghair, up and down in heat and rain, requires a different pace than if you were working shifts out of a motel room. He's an advocate of hot soup and coffee when we break. In the rain, he quickly ties up a tarp to keep us dry.

We sit underneath it, and I ask him about Jacob Gray and search-and-rescue protocols and red tape. Neiger echoes the cardinal rule I learned in Olympic National Park: Do Not Self-Dispatch. "Sometimes I work for law enforcement," he says. "Sometimes I work for the family. Sometimes I flat-out work for the victim."

I ask him why he's working so hard to find Linklater instead of, say, any other vanished person. "I like the hunt," he says. "If you're looking for the perfect case? You know what I mean. The family wants him found. They have a spot in their heart for him, even though he lived a challenging life. There're loose ends—these cases need to be closed up."

We hike along the river on day two toward the Linklater camp, hoping to catch John Linklater, Michael's brother. We find a gill net line, but just the anchor, no net—it's John's. An hour later we reach John's big freighter canoe and walk the steep trail up to the camp. I wonder why Michael Linklater didn't also take the freighter canoe with the big outboard motor.

Anything broken or no longer useful out here would have to be taken out on the train or floated down the river, so things pile up and weeds grow. The particle board and blue tarp camp is a compilation of modern and ancient, paddles and outboards, snowmobiles and snowshoes. There's a canvas sweat lodge with the door tied shut. Beer bottles, coffee cans. This is where Michael Linklater was last—positively—seen, at six o'clock in the morning, July 13, 2003, when he went out to use the outhouse. Neiger leaves a note to John on his door.

We follow moose, bear, and wolf tracks north along the Abitibi. Neiger takes lots of photos of wolf tracks and shit. He has a forensics ruler he sets beside them for scale. This is downriver from where Michael Linklater's hat was found early on in the search. We make camp at the confluence of the Abitibi and Little Abitibi, refill water, and go for a swim.

The next morning, we labor up the bluff and cross a small creek. Bam, Neiger finds an old iron cookstove with rusted hinges and saplings growing through the range top. The brand on the stove says BRANDON. A cookstove wasn't carried far from a kitchen—there may be a root cellar nearby. The buildings themselves have been salvaged, moved to another campsite for another logging operation, but with a little imagination you can see the camp. *Smart searching*, Neiger calls it. You can cover more territory with your brain than with your boots. "We'll develop it further, find the dump. They didn't haul the garbage, they just chucked it."

We drop our packs and slow-survey the perimeter of the old logging camp. The dump is indeed within bottle-tossing distance of the cook shack. The bush is well into the process of taking its land back, which is why the old stove appears as if it fell out of an airplane. We find a pile of rusted cans. Neiger turns into a little kid with history forensics. Randy would love this—he'd get so into it he'd almost forget about his troubles for a while.

I find a few green Molson bottles, labels long composted away. Chances are they were left here by moose hunters long ago, because their age doesn't synch with the logging camp. Neiger finds a teakettle and a crew-size enamel coffeepot. A moose skull with the paddles sawed off. "That wasn't a natural death," he says.

Thirty meters from our packs we get turned around. Standing in the stunted spruce I understand just how easy it is to get completely lost. Sure, there are the handrails of the river and the railroad tracks, but I'm disoriented even inside the city limits of a phantom camp town.

We find our packs, then a fifty-five-gallon barrel stove. Next we find a portable Airtight wood stove. Neiger points out earthen evidence of a graded road. But no root cellar.

"We're looking for a canoe, too," he says. He already found one the last trip up here, south of the Linklater camp. Neiger believes that Linklater could have several stolen canoes stashed along the river, a virtual trapper's navy.

Our short-term plan is to sweep a section between the ghost logging camp and the river. I'm within hollering distance—Neiger calls to me. He's found a collapsed, green cheapish nylon cabin tent, maybe bought at Canadian Tire, next to a fire ring and a rusted bucket from the logging camp to sit on. Neiger is carefully examining the area. Cut marks on a tree, two Nutri-Grain granola bar wrappers. Two foil flavor packets for ramen noodles, opened. A tent bag that says *JOHN LINKLATER MILE 115* for the baggage handlers. Michael was here, but it's been a while.

Neiger takes photos, and I walk a few paces away, where I find a complete skeleton of a gray wolf, five feet long, and curled, stomach down. There's no pelt, no sign of fur near the skeleton. The bones are so white they look plastic. Critters should have twittered away the vertebrae or little leg bones, but no. The largest canine predator in the world. The wolf seems to be on a restful watch, surveilling the campsite. The skeleton looks like a museum display—its quality is unsettling. "Hey, Michael," I call.

Neiger figures the skeleton and the tent camp have similar

dates—he's chewing on a possible connection. The Linklaters certainly shot wolves, but this one hadn't been shot, and it's bizarre that the skeleton had not been disturbed for at least several years. A million square miles of Canadian bush and the wolf is literally twenty feet from the Linklater tent.

We want to ask John about it, so we trek back to the Linklater camp. Neiger calls out, but John doesn't answer. The note is still on the door where Neiger left it. Neiger stops to listen. He looks at me and points to the sweat lodge. The canvas door is tied open. It was tied shut when we were here two days earlier. Neiger walks up and respectfully, cautiously looks inside. Nobody. He's quiet for a few beats longer than I expect, then says, "Maybe Michael needed a sweat."

My neck and forearms are welted with fly bites. It's 5:30 p.m., we're waiting for the southbound Polar Bear Express, but not to get out of the bush; we're using it as a shuttle. The plan is to hop off at mile 103 and camp at the river, near the camp where the two gill nets were stolen. Eventually the slow train's headlight appears on the horizon. It's hot. We stand in the tracks and cross-wave our arms over our heads. "What if the conductor is dozing off and doesn't see us?" I ask.

"Then we're walking again," Michael says.

We throw our packs into the boxcar and climb up after them. The passenger car is cool with air conditioning, which feels unnatural, but I'll take it. No bugs. Twelve miles on the train costs us seven Canadian dollars each. It cost more than that in diesel fuel to stop a twenty-car train with 125 people and twenty dogs aboard.

We hadn't seen another person in five days, and we're starved for conversation. The conductor tells us the train is the main drug conduit to the Far North. In many ways it's the only conduit to the Far North.

The freight man in the baggage car introduces himself as Robert and we find he's a cousin to the Linklaters, who are multitude up here. Robert's curious that we're here, and it's apparent he hasn't thought much about Michael's case in some time.

"It's slow going, but we're moving the search forward," Neiger says. A boot foot, a railway mile at a time. It's obvious that if Neiger wasn't on it, the search wouldn't exist.

We camp by the railroad tracks, mile 103. The night is full of bugs and a big moon. The next morning we head east, toward the Abitibi. A bear had eaten the north wall off the camp where the gill nets had been reported missing. We found blackflies and deer flies and another old Airtight stove, but no logging camp. The clouds clear, and it's shaping up to be hot again.

Neiger has found a blue tarp cut in half with a hole in it to make a poncho. John Linklater put the uncut tarp out for Michael. John also put out MREs, hiking boots and socks, cans of food in a food cache. "He was there, 'cause he took it down," Neiger says. The Linklater tradition is to open cans by holding the can at your chest and spinning it against the blade of a bowie knife. Neiger found two cans opened that way. "I've found a lot of MRE wrappers that are ripped open. I found a wine bottle that makes no frickin' sense." Steel traps. A black snowsuit that was taken out of the cabin. "His jeans—they were the same size, same brand his mother bought him. That was right by a huge moose snare that was classic Michael." He thinks of other items. "I found a logging camp the family didn't know about."

In the middle of the bush, Neiger shows me a hole in the earth, created by a root ball—the hole is the size of a washing machine. "There ya go, Missing 411," Michael says. "That's the portal for this area." Then he says about Paulides—"That cluster of missing persons on his map in the U.P.—those are all my cases."

* * *

"Time to break out the pic," Neiger says several times over the week. Pic is a brand of mosquito coil. Neiger showed me this survival trick last year when we spent a few days in the bush of the Upper Peninsula on the search for Paradise resident Chris Hallaxs, a survivalist who was thirty when he vanished on snowshoes in March 2004. The bugs are nearly as bad in the Lake Superior State Forest, where Neiger is still searching.

The coils, invented in Japan in the late nineteenth century, are made from dried pyrethrum powder. We light two ends with a disposable lighter. The smoke smells good to me, burning chrysanthemum, but mosquitoes and flies avoid it.

"What most people don't like are the bugs," Neiger says. "They're an acquired taste." I would add to that sleeping in your clothes, which Neiger prefers because it allows him to economize and make-and-break his bivy faster. He sews his own bush clothing, which he soaks in Permethrin, another flavor bugs don't like.

Six days in, I am starting to acclimate, although my legs are still heavy. I think about the search for Jacob and what I've learned from Neiger on this trip—searching is immensely difficult, though there are a few good people doing it.

On our last night in the bush—unless we miss the train—we camp along the river, nine kilometers—*klicks*—south of Williams Island. It's warm. I swim and wash out some clothes. My tent is five feet from a wolf track in the clay bank. Neiger finds a heavy antique logging chain with a choker at the mouth of a little creek. Dinner is hot Thai tuna in ramen noodles. Tomorrow's plan is a single-klick bushwhack to the train and back to civilization.

It's still very light at nine p.m. when I hear the southbound running three hours late. "I'm gonna miss the bush," Neiger says. "This is good bush." That's a Neiger saying. From my vantage, good bush entails mosquitoes so bad I have to stick my bean out my tent to piss and I still get eaten.

Neiger has long ago given in to Stockholm syndrome with the mosquitoes and blackflies. He spends more than a hundred nights a year in the bush. He posts $1,000 rewards out of his own pocket. Though he works with some he trusts and is a believer in their value, he's suspicious of most dog teams. "They're not team players," he says. "They hoard it. [Dog] people are territorial and people go unfound because of that. A lot of cases could be solved with more work," he says. "For families, these cases deserve that." For dogs and handlers, it's a real-world application. "And it's damn-good training. The most seemingly insignificant detail could be huge." He pauses for a moment to look at the stars that have begun to appear in the clear sky. "It's a good thing to find missing people."

The next morning when we're packed up and begin walking, we see tracks—two wolves have followed us. Mile 105.5. We have time to wait; Neiger takes a nap in the weeds—the little cloud of smoke around him is mosquitoes.

The train comes toward us—flagging down a whistle-stop locomotive is one of the most satisfying things I've ever done. The engineer sticks his head out of the cab: "You guys lost?"

"Not anymore!" Neiger hollers.

We ride in the open boxcar chatting with the baggage crew before heading to the dining car for pepper steak and beer. Like backpacking, simple food tastes so much better on a train. We're the only non-indigenous passengers going to Cochrane.

On the drive back we stop at the OPP office in Cochrane to inform them about the tent found along the river. The OPP officer seems surprised anyone is looking for Michael Linklater at all. We rendezvous with John Linklater in a Tim Hortons in Timmins, the biggest city in northern Ontario, where John lives more permanently these days.

John, freckles, brown eyes, and red hair, walks in and begins speaking Cree with a young man; many people up north don't speak English. Neiger eagerly informs John the tent was found three and a half kilometers downstream from his camp.

"I put it up," John, now in his mid-sixties, says. "A week or two after he went missing. I left canned food, six or seven sardine cans." Nutri-Grain bars too.

Neiger asks John what the wolf skeleton could mean. "Hard to say," John says. He tells us Michael shot a wolf near the confluence of Abitibi and Little Abitibi, but this wasn't it. The wolf skeleton didn't impress John much; he was more interested in an outboard motor that disappeared. "We lost an engine—Yamaha. My buddy hid it—we figure Mike found it."

"Say, John," Neiger says, "when we first tried to catch you at your camp everything was shut. When we came back through a few days later the door to the sweat lodge was tied open."

John is unimpressed with this information, too, as if he's thinking no big deal, *my brother needed a sweat.*

Daniel Linklater, John and Michael's older brother, has seen snowshoe tracks from the train. "Yeah," John says, present tense, "he knows how to trap." John has seen lights and says people on the train have seen lights. "But they don't tell us 'til after so many months." That's the speed of the "muskeg wireless."

I check in with Neiger now and then for updates—he's in the bush as often as he's at home. Linklater is still missing.

Neiger donated his significant website-building talent to Jacob's case. He also consulted with Randy and provides me with countless resources, including swiftwater authorities, K9 handlers, SAR and law enforcement contacts. I appreciate that I can run a wild hare by him at any time and he's willing to patiently hike me through the scenario—*Hey, Michael, could Jacob, cold from the river, have covered himself with forest duff and died of hypothermia? Could he have kayaked to Canada?* Many such cans of worms.

Neiger will never run out of cases. As I write this he just got back from northern Wisconsin. There's a twenty-two-year-old man named Nicholas Hietpas missing in the wilds of Oconto County. Hietpas is an experienced outdoorsman. His camping gear was found laid out at his vehicle, April 18, but Hietpas and his dog are gone.

CHAPTER 26

OLYMPIC NATIONAL PARK

*Rigid, the skeleton of habit alone upholds the
human frame.*

—Virginia Woolf

SUNDAY EVENING, AUGUST 11, Randy calls. I'm expecting
him to tell me about a new search plan. I've come to look forward
to Randy's calls, a fresh approach to the search, Randy Gray's optimistic possibilities. I keep my bag half packed at the ready. I pick
up, happy to catch up with Randy, whose energy and excitement
are like a shot of vitamin B. "They found Jacob," he says. I can tell
from his voice they found a body, not a live young man. "I'm on my
way to the Sol Duc now," Randy says. "I'll be there tomorrow."

I can hear Randy is in his truck, driving. *Jesus, where did they find
him?* "Hoh Lake, up on the High Divide," Randy says. "I'm gonna
try to get up there to help bring him down."

Jesus, Randy. I drive to my small regional airport knowing I
missed the last flight out, but they got me on the first plane Monday
morning. I know I'll be racing Randy, trying to get there before he
takes off into the mountains unprepared with the gear, food, and
water he needs to take care of himself—I know Randy by now. I
also know he'll need someone to talk to, someone to talk him out of

doing something rash, foolish, and dangerous. Randy is wired for action, a plan, not terminal news.

I call Bob Chung in Port Townsend, and he agrees to meet me in Sequim and bring extra backpacking gear for Randy—Bob knows Randy well, too, knows that he'll bust up the mountain with nothing but a hoodie and a Snickers. We'll race to the Sol Duc and try to head him off at the trailhead.

Two days before I come through Sea-Tac, the Seattle-Tacoma airport, for my last trip to meet Randy in the Olympic Mountains, a twenty-nine-year-old Horizon Air baggage handler named Richard Russell stole an empty seventy-six-seat twin-turbo-prop Bombardier Q400, took off, and did impossibly difficult aerial stunts over Puget Sound. He was married, a well-liked man with a lot going for him. "I'm just a broken guy," he told air traffic controllers, who calmly tried to talk him out of doing something even more rash than stealing a commercial aircraft. Russell said he didn't want to hurt anyone, but also didn't want to land at Joint Base Lewis-McChord, the nearest runway. He augered into Ketron Island, a sparsely populated island in south Puget Sound. No one other than Russell was killed.

It appears Russell had the skills to land the plane if he'd wanted to; he reportedly practiced on video games and flight-simulator videos. I chatted with an Alaska Airlines pilot certified on the Q400. "I'm impressed, actually," he said. "That's a two-pilot aircraft. It wasn't designed to do those aerials."

It's been sixteen months since Jacob vanished. In that time Randy has been back and forth, searching the forests and rivers of the Olympic Peninsula, the small goat-and-spinach farms of the San Juan Islands, the yoga communes of the Gulf Islands of Canada. Northern California on the Oregon border, religious compounds in southern British Columbia, the forests and beaches of Vancouver

Island across the Strait of San Juan de Fuca from Olympic National Park. Parts of Idaho where people on self-discovery missions were said to congregate, Eastern Oregon and Eastern Washington, which is a world away from the Olympic Peninsula. He's driven tens of thousands of miles and hiked hundreds. He's swum dozens.

On Friday, August 10, a team of volunteer biologists who made a trip into the mountains to study marmots found Jacob's clothing, some gear, and a wallet with two driver's licenses inside, on a scree field near a ridgeline above Hoh Lake, 5,300 feet above sea level and at least fifteen miles from where he left his bike. His body wasn't found near a trail; in April the terrain would have been snowy and prone to avalanches, rotten snow bridges, damp with hypothermic, below-freezing temperatures.

"Can I go with you to bring the remains down, bring Jacob down?" Randy, still in California, says to Ranger Brian Wray.

Ranger Wray tells Randy, "No. Because the remains have not been positively identified yet. Let us do our job."

That's the phrase Randy and Laura have heard since April 2017. *Let us do our job*.

Wray makes a rendezvous arrangement for Monday, in Port Angeles. It's clear that Wray cares about Randy. Randy would always try to get Wray to take him target practicing with his government-issue pistol. One time he showed him proper stun-gun technique, and I thought Randy was gonna volunteer one of us to get tased. The two had become friends through Randy's nightmare.

But, of course, Randy isn't going to listen to Wray when he's told to let him do his job. Wray isn't surprised when Randy blows off the meeting on his way to the river and up to the trailhead.

"What would you do?" Randy says. "When does a dad stop being a dad?"

Monday afternoon, Jack Reagan, a friend of mine in Sequim, picks me up from the Bainbridge Island ferry and once again loans me his Chevy Yukon. The Yukon is enormous, and I can sleep comfortably inside. I pick Bob up at the bus station and we grab a few groceries and book it toward the Sol Duc Trailhead. Bob is recovering from an eye injury and can't drive and isn't up for back-packing into the Olympics, but he is invaluable with logistics and support—it's good to see Bob, who has become an old friend in a very short time.

It's late dusk when we get to the trailhead lot at the end of the winding Sol Duc Road. I'd forgotten to look when we passed the place where Jacob's bike was found sixteen months ago. Bob has been all over here, too, combing the forest and riverbanks. It's hard to believe they found Jacob up-country—I'd have been less surprised to hear they found him in Australia or Argentina. We see Randy's truck in the parking lot and three Olympic National Park Ranger vehicles and uniformed rangers looking at maps spread out on vehicle hoods and talking on radios.

I ask a ranger I hadn't met before if Randy is up there, on the mountain. Is he with a group of rangers or alone? Does he have gear? Is he spending the night?

The ranger looks at me confused. *Who?*

"Randy Gray. Jacob Gray's dad," I say.

"Who?"

"They found Jacob's remains, are bringing him out?"

"Oh, right—we're working a different situation," he says. "There's another emergency going on." I hear the word *heli* on radio traffic.

He won't—or can't—tell me what the emergency is, but it's obvious Randy is up there, somewhere in those million acres. It'll be full-on dark very soon. Now I'm thinking that no one knows any-thing about Randy being on the trail, that he's up there stumbling through the dark, and the next emergency might be him.

I see Ranger Brian Wray and tell him we're concerned about

Randy. "I think he went up there thinking, I'm gonna carry out the remains of my son," Wray says. "I told him they were already brought out."

We try calling Randy on his cell phone, no luck. If we try hiking up the Sol Duc Trail with headlamps it would be unlikely we would run into him. We leave a note on his windshield, *RANDY! BOB AND I ARE WORRIED ABOUT YOU. WE ARE AT THE BARN ON 101. TALKED WITH RANGER BRIAN WRAY @9:30, CALL BRIAN. MICAH, MALLORY, DAVE, ETC. WILL BE HERE TOMORROW.* Even in this digital age, so much happens via windshield notes. Of course, Randy would be stopping by the barn even if we weren't there, but I wanted him to know there were friends on the ground and distract him a little for the half-hour drive down the mountain.

Nothing is left for Bob and me to do but head down to the barn and worry about Randy. He'd shown me where the key is hidden, which is a place Bigfoot might look if he wanted inside bad enough, but maybe that's the idea. We push the big bay door open to let in the night air. Bob and I make pasta, organize gear, and cool our heels. There is no moonlight, it's a new moon. If he doesn't show up, we'll head back up at dawn.

Dammit, we must have just missed Randy, we're saying. I do the math story problem in my head, drive times and airlines and time zones and ferries. A diesel pickup thrums into the barnyard, headlights sweep the bay. *Randy!*

He stumbles into the barn dragass at eleven p.m., in a cotton hoodie and cargo shorts. He's limping. We get the story. Randy isn't sure of the exact location where Jacob was found. Rangers purposely didn't give him a GPS coordinate, knowing he'd head straight for it, but then Randy Gray isn't a technology guy, is more comfortable with a map and compass. Or nothing at all.

He missed the rangers who were packing Jacob's remains out—it appears Randy hiked past the ridge where rangers were recovering Jacob. Like a cartoon missed connection, Randy kept going southward down the trail and dropped a thousand feet into the Hoh River Valley to Hoh Lake while the rangers slipped in behind to head back to the trailhead.

Randy got a cell signal at Hoh Lake and called Ranger Wray, who tried to talk him into hiking down to Deer Lake, where he could spend the night with backpackers and not try to scramble out in the dark.

With no information and nothing else to go on—and no gear for a comfortable overnight stay—Randy decided to head back to the trailhead. On his way down, above Deer Lake, which is at 3,600 feet and four miles from the trailhead, Randy could see someone lying across the trail with people around. Strange, he thought. When he arrived at the spot he found rangers administering CPR to a twenty-nine-year-old woman from Iowa who had suffered cardiac arrest.

Randy stayed and helped the rangers, taking turns with the chest compressions. "It's exhausting," Randy says. "They showed me how to do it." After the Navy helicopter arrived to take the woman away, Randy learned one of the rangers he shared CPR compressions with had been part of the small team who'd just brought Jacob off the mountain. There would be no storybook ending, where the sacrifice of Randy's son brings him to the mountain so he can help save another person's life. The woman died.

Bob makes sure Randy gets fed with pasta, hydrated with Gatorade. He ices his Achilles on the couch—he injured it rock-hopping on the beach, but I know that all the miles in the river and mountains here in the Olympics have worn Randy bone-tired, his cartilage and ligaments thin. He even has a crutch in his truck rattling around with his other tools. "I'm not really a crutch guy," he says. Randy might have the highest pain threshold of any person I've met.

Micah is flying out from Vermont and will be here tomorrow; Laura and Mallory are headed up from Santa Cruz and will be here in a couple days. Randy makes plans to collect Jacob's gear and clothing from the ranger station in Port Angeles. Arrangements will need to be made with the funeral home, even though we think Jacob's remains have been sent to the coroner in King County. There is much room for logistical confusion when skeletal remains are recovered in the mountains.

Electrical power in the Bigfoot Barn had gone out at some point, and someone makes the mistake of opening the chest freezer. Rotten fish—many pounds of it—that Derek had caught overtakes the barn. That would have to be dealt with now, too. Randy ices his Achilles on the couch some more, an hour, making phone calls the whole time. He doesn't seem to mind the fish smell. Bob lays out a backpack and sleeping pad for Randy—there's talk of hiking up to the spot where Jacob was found. Randy wants to see if the rangers collected everything, but mostly he wants to see the last place on the planet where his boy was alive.

Randy is thrilled to see his oldest. Micah is anxious to see if he can get his head around what happened to his little brother, square things before he has to go back on duty on Lake Champlain. The next morning the four of us drive to Sequim to take Bob back to the bus station. We get breakfast burritos, and Randy ducks into a pharmacy for an ankle brace and some inserts for his shoes. His knee is still tender from surgery. Just two weeks ago he had knee surgery. "It was Joe Montana's surgeon," he tells us with no small amount of pride and excitement. "Dillingham. Dr. Michael Dillingham." Team physician for the San Francisco 49ers—some of their knees probably didn't look as bad as Randy's. Now he's thinking he'll go straight from crutchworthy to a thirty-mile round trip in the mountains with a pack. The pharmacy assistant tells him he shouldn't be hiking anywhere on that Achilles. "I'll take it easy," Randy says. "And I got some new hiking boots."

It pains Bob to have to go back home and attend to his bike shop and eye injury. On the way back to the barn we stop by ranger headquarters to pick up everything else, as well as a backpacking permit and bear-proof food keg. Ranger Peter Maggio waives the permit fee and keg deposit. I buy some maps because I don't trust a GPS and batteries alone.

I'm not sure the rangers are supposed to give us the GPS coordinates, so I take a screen shot of the computer with a photograph of the scree field that includes the coordinates. Maggio either doesn't mind or pretends he doesn't notice. Here's the thing: All the ONP employees feel for Randy and the entire family. I'm convinced some of them lose sleep at night. I'm convinced they go home and see Jacob in their own families.

I make a pen dot on the paper map, but it's only a ballpark, a pirate map. We'll get close, but we need the GPS if we want to be spot-on.

Later I'll learn from the official final report that I received through a Freedom of Information Act request that rangers collected *1 human skull* they bagged separately from various skeleton parts listed, collectively with *misc. bones*, as to pretty much make up a whole. The bones were scattered along the slope in a pattern described by rangers as *upper field* and *lower field*.

Maggio respectfully made sure that Jacob's things made it into Randy's truck. It's surreal driving the half-hour back, as if he's with us. The gear makes a big colorful puzzle laid out in the Bigfoot Barn. Here's what rangers cataloged on the mountain in their official report:

tarps (2)

poncho liner

bike gloves

knife pouch

Pagosa (brand) backpack and contents

socks ("lots")

winter Santa Cruz cap

fleece neck gaiter

blue Montbell jacket

netting with carabiners and p-cord

hiking pole

Keen boots (1 pr)

hammock

wool jacket gr

belt

compass

wallet and contents (2 IDs, SS card, bank cards, AAA card, ins. cards)

Zippo lighter

Leatherman and pouch

Bible

Carhartt pants

Montbell rain pants

The canvas pants are torn and tattered, but everything else looks surprisingly good, if a bit faded. His clothes are laid out like a magazine fashion shoot display—garments bent and folded to suggest animation, but no mannequin, no body there. *Here's what Jacob had with him on the mountain.* But I know that Randy and Micah are thinking what I'm thinking—what did Jacob *not* have with him on the mountain is every bit as important. And just because it's not here, that doesn't necessarily mean Jacob didn't pack it up there with him and the gear is lost to slides and wind and wildlife.

The backpack looks almost brand new, which is remarkable, having been exposed to intense sunlight and all other elements for so long. It's not a full backpacking-size pack—a savvy hiker could overnight from it in mild weather, two nights at best, but it certainly isn't intended for a foul-weather expedition. "I can use it," Micah says. Randy is as quiet as I've ever seen him as he very carefully lays out Jacob's gear and tattered clothing and unpacks the backpack.

Contents include a silver emergency blanket, opened. A big bag of trail mix (it still appears edible), a headlamp, fire starters, fishing line, hooks, water filter, toilet paper, more socks, a notebook.

Randy picks up everything and studies it. "Look at this," he says. In the wallet there's a business card: *Bob Chung, PT Cyclery, 252 Tyler Street, Port Townsend, WA 98368 (360) 385-6470.* "He was supposed to call if he had trouble. I gotta give this to Bob."

Rangers said Jacob's boots were found wrapped in trash bags, individually, with paracord. "That could be a sign of suicide," Micah says. Micah is a true Coastie and doesn't speak with emotion, rather is matter-of-fact, even with issues involving his little brother. He reads his father's face and reels it in a bit, decides not to push that theory. "Have your things neatly wrapped up," he says, trailing off. "People do crazy things before they commit suicide. Why would you care about your stuff, you're gonna be dead."

The suicide theory hangs in the air like a cloud off the Strait, but I'm not sure that's why the boots were wrapped up. It may be more likely that he was shedding clothes in early signs of hypothermia—feeling uncomfortable warmth—and thought he'd still need them, wanted to keep them dry. Using the paracord could have been an overkill that came with the irrationality of hypothermia. I shiver to picture Jacob walking through the April snow in soaked and frozen socks.

"Hard question," Michael Neiger says. "He was obviously trying to keep his boots dry, *unless* he was trying to keep them from freezing by putting them in the foot of his sleeping bag. We often do this in cold weather, first sealing them in a stuff sack or plastic bag to keep dirt or moisture on boots from soiling or wetting the inside of the sleeping bag, but still keep them warm. He could have been getting hypothermic, and a habit/routine led him to package them."

Jacob didn't appear to have his running shoes with him—no footwear besides the boots. And—this is most disturbing to me— Jacob didn't appear to have carried a sleeping bag up the mountain with him. His bag (*a* bag, if it can be assumed he only had one) was found with the items at the bike along the Sol Duc—was he trying to save weight and pack space by only carrying the flyweight emergency blanket? Was he only intending to sleep out in his hammock for a night or two? I can only imagine how bone-chilling an April night at 5,000 feet in the Olympic Mountains would be after hiking and sweating all day; you'd never truly be dry, you'd never truly be warm. The idea that a wool coat and a foil blanket could suffice is not by any stretch rational. But then, at twenty-two, I made bushels of poor choices.

I ask Neiger what it could mean, that Jacob left his sleeping bag below. "If it was not real cold out, he might have tried a bivy without a bag," he says. I tell Neiger that he was carrying everything in a backpack too small for the journey, that time of year. "That fits," he says. I can see Jacob saying, *I don't have room, I'll just tough it out with the emergency blanket.*

At any rate, if Jacob's sleeping bag had been missing from the gear found at the bike, it would have been a solid clue that he'd gone *up*, that he intended to stay out in the wild. Perhaps it would have taken the focus off of the Sol Duc River and led searchers into the mountains sooner, with more resources. It's always the second-guessing that weighs so heavily on the hearts and backs of searchers and family.

"He wanted water for his trip [up the mountain]," Randy says. "That's what I'm thinking now. He told me, 'Dad, if they find my bike, I'm coming back for it—I'll kind of hide it off to the side of the road, Dad.'" Randy looks as if he's thinking the thoughts into the air and watching them, see if they fly. "He didn't quite hide it here."

If that was true, that Jacob had spoken his plan to Randy like that, maybe the trackers were right, that he'd gone to the river for water. But instead of slipping into the Sol Duc, he bottled some of it and went up.

The orange Coast Guard Eurocopter HH-65 Dolphin from the Port Angeles station flies over, westbound, railing the park boundary, low enough to shake the roof on the barn.

Jacob's skull came down the mountain and out of the park first—Ranger Wray drove it to Port Angeles to process it for transfer to the funeral home. The remainder of Jacob's bones they'd recovered were held up due to the emergency involving the woman from Iowa. Jacob's skeletal remains were taken to Harper Ridgeview Funeral Chapel in Port Angeles, from where they would go to the coroner's lab in Seattle.

I have no doubt we'll be packing up to where Jacob's remains were found—I've already started making a grocery list on my phone because Randy is wildly liable to stick a granola bar in his pocket and say *Let's go*. I have some guilt—the ambulance chaser—that I'm here at this time. Randy, always the considerate soul, invites me into the meeting with the funeral director, but I opt to wait outside. I've convinced myself if I have a purpose on this trip it's to make sure Randy is fed and comfortable when he dives headlong back into those mountains. I can Sherpa for him, though on a very humble scale. At least he'll have hot coffee and warm rehydrated dinners-in-a-bag.

Mallory—who is pregnant with her third child—and Laura feel like Mexican food following the meeting with the funeral director, so we grab lunch at Sergio's Hacienda. Then Randy, Micah, and I hit Swain's for supplies. Randy is a kid in a toy store in Swain's. I am, too. Swain's is, well, everyone's favorite store. Think an REI without the urban-chic design that also sells PVC pipe and potting soil and makes keys. There's a big popcorn popper and bags of circus peanuts for sale. Swain's has a section devoted to Bigfoot. Randy has spent literally thousands of dollars here—Swain's knows him, why he's here, and has for sixteen months given him a significant discount on all his gear, from walkie-talkies to merino-wool underwear. I don't know the world of retail, but my hunch is they trade to Randy at cost.

Micah picks out a backpacking water-purifying filter pump, and I grab more stove fuel and Mountain House dinners: chicken teriyaki, beef stroganoff, chicken à la king, chicken and dumplings. "Are these okay?" I ask Randy and Micah. "Let me see," Randy says, and studies the bright packages with impossibly handsome and happy models spooning hot entrees into their mouths in perfect weather—outdoor models never seem to have to dress for mosquitoes or blackflies. "Oh, this is gonna be *gooooooood*!" he says. "After dinner we'll lie out and watch the stars." He hasn't forgotten why we're going—but I'm glad the old Randy is still gonna make the trip. "This is gonna be *gooooooood*."

CHAPTER 27

HOH LAKE

Life is not separate from death. It only looks that way.

—*Blackfoot proverb*

LOUISE ERDRICH'S CHARACTER Fleur Pillager in the novel *Tracks* walks a *death road*, an unmapped path not seen by everyone; Fleur carries the bones of ancestors with her. Jacob followed a similar road when he veered from his plans to go to Vermont, then a mountain path unseen because it was under snow, but also not seen because only he could see through gauze to a place special to him, a place off the sanctioned trail. He abandoned his bike for the lure of *walking on.*

Randy removes a laminated MISSING JACOB GRAY poster from the shack at the park entrance on the Sol Duc Road—Randy expresses appreciation that they kept it up for the duration of his disappearance.

The trailhead is sleepy when Randy, Micah, and I arrive and park the truck, ready to hike in as, well, backpackers. That's what we are. We're not park rangers. We're not marmot biologists. We're not mourners exactly. Rather, backcountry tourists to this grand park, but with a mission. If anything, the mood is quietly upbeat—

I know Randy loves this park and Micah loves being outdoors. It would be presumptuous of me to say it feels like Jacob is with us there in the parking lot at the trailhead as we gobble a last banana and tie bootlaces, but it does feel like we are going to rendezvous with him.

Randy never mentions his mission to fellow hikers we pass or meet on the trail, just points out blueberry patches and what a beautiful day it is. "Have ya seen any bears?" Randy says; bears always make for good conversation.

The trail rises through mossy lowland old-growth Douglas fir, western red cedar, Sitka spruce, Western hemlock—trees more than two hundred years old. We pass Sol Duc Falls, where most of the day-hiking tourists snap photos before turning around and heading back to the rental car.

At Deer Lake the vegetation slowly transitions from montane to scrappy subalpine forest—mountain ash, beargrass, rhododendron, and subalpine fir. We filter water and make coffee at Deer Lake, and Randy shows us where they administered CPR to the woman from Iowa. "I thought someone had just decided to sleep across the trail," Randy says. "But then I see they're doing chest compressions." Randy pops almond M&Ms like a bear on blueberries. We eat plenty of those, too.

We continue up. My pack weighs about sixty pounds—I'm carrying extra everything just in case. I'm grateful now for the June trip into the northern Ontario muskeg with Michael Neiger—the bush was flat, but there was plenty of it, and it helped with whatever pack fitness I have now. The trails are not busy, nothing is crowded. Most of the backpackers we meet seem to be from Europe or Asia. I note the lack of mosquitoes—a year ago in the Olympics the mosquitoes were ferocious; after the summer northern-Ontario bush, I'll never take a lack of mosquitoes for granted again. Give me black bears over biting bugs any day.

With binoculars we glass the face and ridge where Jacob was found. "That's it," Micah says. We don't know exactly where to look, but the contours match the photo I took with my phone from the computer screen in the rangers' office. We know we're looking in the right area, a couple miles away, across the Bogachiel River headwater cut.

"I walked past it the other night," Randy says. "Hoh Lake is on the other side, down. I walked right past the spot." This means he walked past the spot where we'll need to leave the trail and tie into the ridge underneath Bogachiel Peak. It's easy to see how the rangers packing Jacob's remains out could have stealthily slipped back onto the trail to head down. I think about what it must be like, packing-out human bones. They wouldn't weigh much in a literal sense, but emotionally, I imagine, they'd weigh a ton. Randy wanted to feel that weight, tried his damnedest to get under it.

We continue toward the High Divide in the bluebird sunshine filtered by a thin veil of wildfire smoke out of Canada. We can see Mount Olympus and the glaciers to the southeast. I think of the missing there and can understand why they were attracted to the place. To the south, down-mountain, is the Hoh Rainforest, where Randy and I found the quietest square inch and the spawning salmon. Who knows—Jacob may have been planning a loop, a Great Circle Route that would have brought him back to his bike along the Sol Duc. From where he was found, he woudn't have been terribly far from the snowline, had he walked down toward the rainforest.

I miss the possibility that Jacob's still alive, out there in TROTW on a walkabout. I'm sorry that Randy doesn't get to keep hoping anymore, and don't think *closure*—whatever that means—is gonna fit him well. I can't picture Randy Gray in repose.

Micah points toward the ridge where they found Jacob, but it's late enough into the day that hiking up now would be neither safe nor productive. We decide to continue on the main trail and head down, toward Hoh Lake, make camp, eat a hot dinner, and get a fresh start in the morning—we still have a couple miles to go to get to the lake.

Two backcountry rangers in uniform check our camping permit, which is tied to my pack—I swivel without taking it off to let one of them grab it and verify our officiousness. "Hoh Lake," one of the women says. "Nice, but watch for the bears down there."

Worse than black bears, a group of Boy Scouts are camping there. Glad they're enjoying the mountains, but they're likely gonna be loud late. At any rate, we swim, wash our socks, and slap them against a warm rock to dry. Randy stands in the lake, submerging his leg in the cool water against the swelling. He's remarkable— hasn't complained once about his leg, as if that would be enough to stop him from being here.

Hoh Lake television: For a couple hours we watch two fat black bears eat blueberries on the hillside north of the lake, then flop and logroll into the lake. They swim lazily, then climb back out and up the hillside, eat more berries and roll into the water again. A couple times a bear would swim seemingly toward some Scouts, and we would watch with a little excitement that they could send them running, but with all the berries and salmon, Olympic National Park bears live like gods and have little use for Scouts or anyone else.

That night, after dinner, I hide the bear keg and cheat a pull from the flask of Monkey Shoulder. We'd picked up flasks at Swain's. It's sweet and not very hot, exactly the Scotch blend a twenty-two-year-old kid should like, especially with the silly name. Laura and Mallory had called all over the Olympic Peninsula to find it, finally locating a bottle in Forks that Randy drove over and picked up. I should have saved it all for a toast, but the shot helps me sleep—I'm anxious, as I know Randy is, maybe Micah, too.

Randy and Micah opt to sleep right along the lake, near the Scouts, on tarps, under the brilliant stars. Sometime after dark they come stumbling toward my tent and ask to sleep inside. Bugs, Scouts, or both. I'm glad I packed a three-person tent.

In the morning we have oatmeal and coffee. Hot chocolate mix for Randy so he can get his mocha here with the spirit of Jacob. Randy enjoys that Micah is here—even under the most unfortunate of circumstances, it's a little like old times. His firstborn. Micah tells us stories of the Coast Guard and about the trip he and Jacob took to move Micah's family from Alaska to Vermont when he was transferred there. None of us lose track of why we're here, but Randy and Micah are enjoying themselves. A quick wash-up of dishes, and we're headed up the trail to Jacob's ridge.

Sunny and warm again. Micah gets us on spot where we need to exit the trail and scramble up to the High Divide Ridge. We sip water and survey the area so that we can sneak onto the ridge unseen by hikers and backcountry rangers. It takes some effort to hump it up the slope with heavy packs on, but soon we're above the trail and out of sight.

We're right at the treeline; trees are scarce. I have to remind myself we're only at about 5,000 feet—in the Sierras, a few hundred miles south, the treeline is twice that height. It's because of the heavy snows and weather off the ocean here. The footing is tricky and treacherous enough in the scree—I imagine Jacob cat-walking out here in the April snowpack.

We come across an old weathered spruce tree, boughs hollowed out, so that it makes a natural teepee. Jacob may well have camped there, a natural hideout. Spread out his tarp like Jeremiah Johnson. Maybe hung his hammock. If so, he'd have been packed up and moving out when he perished. So close to his bivy, if indeed he bivvied in the tree. Maybe he couldn't get truly warm in the tree and was on the move to get out of the mountains when hypothermia affected his reasoning skills. He most certainly would have been wet from snow and sweat. I think about the boots bagged individually, wrapped with paracord. Randy carefully checks the ground inside the tree, looking for anything. I know *anything* includes everything from candy wrappers to bones.

We drop our packs, careful to position them so they don't slide— they'd roll a couple hundred feet before stopping, maybe all the way into the Bogachiel River. I chock my pack with a couple head-size rocks just to be safe. Micah homes in on the GPS coordinate with exactitude. "We're looking at it," he says. "We're here."

Randy and Micah sweep the slope close to the ridgeline, travers- ing in tight Z patterns, looking for anything. The wind makes it difficult to communicate with voices.

Randy heads down the slope in that sure-footed athletic lope of his, toward the trickling headwaters of the Bogachiel River. He wants to see if any of Jacob's things washed downhill in what would be two spring melts now, including the April thaw the month he went missing. It's steep and the scree is crumbly, and Micah and I are concerned that he'll keep going, follow the watercourse too far down—he doesn't have food or water with him and that's never stopped him before.

Micah and I sit for a minute and wait. We're both wondering if we're gonna have to go after Randy, take him some food and water and coax him back up the mountain. It's windy; the sun is intense. I of course think about the irony of a father gone missing in search of his son's bones. But then he appears below, slowly making his way back, picking his way through the moraine and up toward us.

We spend several hours combing through the scree. Every now

and then Randy and Micah pick up a rock, examine it, then pitch it. Every now and then I look across the valley and see backpackers the size of picnic ants headed toward or away from the High Divide. I wonder if they can see us, wonder what the hell we're doing out here in an open face of nothing rock. An occasional jet passes over, leaving a contrail. I taste a hint of wildfire smoke.

The rangers did a good job of recovering Jacob's things—there's no sign a human being had ever been here. I walk the ridgetop, and I'm looking at insects and rodent tracks and plants I can't identify when I find what I think is rock shaped like a bear bone, a paw phalanx. I pick it up to feel it's indeed a bone. A skinned bear paw looks eerily like a human hand.

"Hey, Micah," I call. He's down the ridge from me, maybe twenty yards, and can't hear me against the wind. I'm a little glad he can't hear me. I walk to him, hoping he'll tell me it's bear. Of course it's bear, they're all over these mountains. But then bear don't make a habit of dying on ridgetops and not leaving more of a skeleton.

"It's bone," Micah says. He holds it close to his eyes to examine it. He nods. "Finger bone." He holds the phalanx next to his hand to verify where it fits—it's a match. He clutches it in his fist. "Hey, Dad!"

"Are you sure it's not from a bear?" I say. My question is awkward and redundant.

Micah nods. Soon he finds another small bone. He keeps them in his shirt pocket.

Micah makes a cross of tree limbs tied together with parachute cord. The cord is rescue-orange, so I busy myself with tucking vegetation in it, juniper twigs mostly, so someone glassing the ridge from the main hiking trail couldn't see it, unnatural Day-Glo. Randy chips a marker into a chunk of granite with a hatchet. With the hatchet he digs a small hole on the ridge.

At dusk Randy calls Mallory and Laura, who are back in Santa Cruz, and puts the phone on speaker. Mallory plays some music Jacob liked, including the band The Devil Makes Three, sort of gothic bluegrass.

We toast Jacob with the Monkey Shoulder, each pouring a share on the ground for him; Randy shares most of his with Jacob. And then, at dark, by the light of stars and a flash of phone, an owl sweeps by, buzzing us within a couple feet so that we can feel the wind it makes. The timing is so odd as to make it not seem a coincidence. An owl! It circles and buzzes us again, then again. Micah and Randy laugh! *Jacob!*

We camp illegally in a notch on the ridge. It would have been possible to see us from across the rift, on the trail in, but only if you were looking with intent. "What are they gonna do?" Randy says. He says it not like a rhetorical question, but a literal one. *What are they gonna do?* We do not make a fire, which really would have been pushing it. But even then, what are they gonna do. Me in my yellow tent, Randy and Micah on tarps under the Milky Way. We get to spend the night camping with Jacob.

As we're coming out the next morning, three black bears race out of a huckleberry thicket and up the trail. Randy yells, "*Hozzzza-hazzza, bear!*" Bears don't see well, and they sort of buck like a bull when they panic—they don't have any truck with us, either. Randy makes a bullfighter's sidestep and they charge up-trail toward me—*thanks a lot, Randy*, I think—before exiting up the mountain to another berry patch away from smelly, noisy backpackers.

The spirit of Jacob is everywhere—I know him enough by now to know he'd love this bear interface, he'd love eating these blueberries and a soak in Sol Duc Hot Springs afterward. He'd love the tacos at the Bigfoot Barn.

Randy's knee gets him into and out of the mountains. He

lies on the couch in the Bigfoot Barn one last time, ice on his leg. Randy doesn't see it anymore, but I look at the big papier-mâché Bigfoot, the jumbo plaster-of-paris feet molds, the Sasquatch conference posters, the David Paulides Bigfoot books, the newly bleached-out empty chest freezer. It again floors me that this is the headquarters of the search for Jacob, this clubhouse for mountain people who subscribe so passionately to cryptozoology and hiked themselves to the bone in search of a stranger's kid, an even deeper enigma.

I sleep in my tent in a thick Washington fog and awake in the morning to the smell of hot coffee. Randy had made it, unzipped my tent, and set it inside. It's still warm when I wake up.

What happened to Jacob will forever remain a mystery. The autopsy work was done in King County, Seattle, but the Clallam County Coroner's Office told me the official cause of death is inconclusive— they positively identified Jacob through dental records.

It's likely Jacob succumbed to hypothermia, but that can be a catchall for people who perish in the mountains. When a snow-mobiler dies in the Upper Peninsula, which happens at least every week in winter, my Yooper neighbor Richie says it wasn't speed and alcohol that killed him, "It was a tree." Something led Jacob away from his bike and deep into the mountains. Something caused him to succumb to the cold. Something made him decide not to pack his sleeping bag. Did he see God up there? Jesus. The Devil. All three.

While commuting on my bike to work I heard a woman on a podcast refer to a tarot card, the Four of Arrows. I looked it up in the card book *The Wildwood Tarot* by Mark Ryan and John Matthews. It's not known that Jacob was into tarot, but, again, there's so little to go on. "He may have read tarot with Wyoma," Mallory told me. But then many, if not most, of my college-age students are into tarot, at least in a cool-thing-to-do way—one of them has the High Priestess card tattooed on her arm.

The tarot book shows a figure lying on their stomach, eyes closed, surrounded by four arrows sticking into the ground. It appears to be a green meadow. There's a colorful butterfly flying over the scene. *Rest. Recharging after a period of stressful activity, work, or emotional trauma. Allow time for the imagination to sojourn into the Otherworld to renew and rejuvenate vitality.* The number four is also a sacred number to some Native peoples, but that seems even less to draw from than a tarot card.

Lost-person behavior holds that most adults tend to go down when lost in the mountains. But Randy's hunch early on was right. "Jacob would have gone *up*," Randy said. He told me this months after the paddle-out in Santa Cruz when more than a hundred surfers and boaters saw Jacob's ashes off, his embarkment into the Pacific Ocean.

Family, friends, and others wonder if Jacob could have been found alive if ONP officials had gotten a helicopter in the air and dogs into the backcountry within a day or so of finding the abandoned bike. Jacob's remains were found on a treeless ridge and might have been seen from the air.

But perhaps Jacob didn't want to be seen.

"He wanted to return to the earth," Laura says. "He went up. I'm sure those were his tracks on the Aurora Trail."

Robert Koester, Professor Rescue, says, "Children will often go up. So will people on a vision quest. Depending on what message they get from God, I have seen people climb mountains."

Some will say the psychic was right; I think there's more evidence in the fossil record that Bigfoot could exist than proof that psychics can see missing persons, but I respect the people who believe they're helpful. Jacob was near the headwaters of the Bogachiel River, but few places in Olympic National Park are far from water. Jacob would have liked that a psychic had a vision with him in it—Jacob would have said the psychic nailed it.

Randy was right, too, about the two sailors missing on Vancouver Island, Dan Archbald and Ryan Daley. They were killed by drug traffickers when they kept some of the cocaine for themselves. Ben Kilmer committed suicide—his disappearance and death do not appear related.

I still get updates from Randy. He talks his texts into the phone and there's much lost in translation, but I've become something of an interpreter. Here's what I learned this week: *They make this parachute with a motor on it—would be perfect Search & Rescue, don't know why they're not using it now, I'll get more information, see what you think! I'm going to get certified. You can take off on a 50-foot runway, can cruise above the treetops and goes at least, if not faster, than 20 miles-per-hour—can cover a lot of territory for Search & Rescue.*

A powered paraglider, PPG, or paramotor. With Randy strapped in, a propeller on his back, that would be better than a drone. (Though I know a guy who died in a paraglider accident, which can be dangerous in winds and mountains and trees.) But for Randy the coffee cup is always half full, a propellered parachute another tool; I have an image of Randy Gray floating over Olympic National Park, rangers having a conniption on their radios.

Every day I recall a simple thing Randy Gray told me while we searched for Jacob in Olympic National Park four months after he disappeared. We spent a lot of time staring into the Sol Duc River, tossing stones into it, swimming. Randy would read the water, the hydraulics, and talk with me matter-of-factly: *A body could get caught in that, but I checked it. Twice.* Randy's is a simple surfer's koan, a surfer-father's philosophy: "You think you know, but you don't."

The other thing I can't vanish from my mind is a thing Randy said in the shadow of Mount Rainier, a thing he said to A—, the Sasquatch feeder. We were sitting in lawn chairs on a damp evening around a small fire, waiting for the Sasquatch to come grab some donuts and maybe tell us what happened to Jacob. "I've hiked more miles in the last two years than the rest of my entire life," Randy said. "It's a sad hike. But it's a beautiful one."

ACKNOWLEDGMENTS

I am grateful for the trusting generosity of the Gray family, especially Randy—thank you for letting me hitchhike along on your journey. Randy's sister, Judy Baldwin, allowed me to stay at her home in Santa Cruz multiple times. Dani Campbell, besides working tirelessly searching on the ground and in the water, kept an exacting timeline, on which I relied when writing the narrative of the first couple of weeks after Jacob disappeared. If someone goes missing in the wild, you need a Dani Campbell to take notes.

My family at home, Hilary, Avalyn, and Sam, have been my support crew for this project. Hilary read countless drafts. My daughter Hailey Brey designed and drew the maps.

Thank you to my indefatigable agent, Julia Masnik, who deftly delivered this project into the right hands. I am indebted to Maddie Caldwell for acquiring the book and editing it with such care for the story and patience with me. Thank you to Rebecca Maines and Jacqui Young for the intrepid edits and fact checks. Brian

McLendon and Luria Rittenberg for their production and publishing prowess. And Jarrod Taylor for making sure the forest on the cover is actually in the Olympic Peninsula.

This book started with feature articles in *Bicycling*, *Runner's World*, and *Outside* magazines. Thank you to Emily Furia and Taylor Rojek at *Bicycling*. Nick Weldon and John Atwood at *Runner's World*; Howard Bryant chose to include my story about Amy Bechtel in *Best American Sports Writing 2017*, for which I'm humbled. Two of the best fact checkers in the business, Jan McLeod and Nicholas Hunt, pored over the Amy Bechtel and Joe Keller stories respectively. Thanks to Alex Heard, Chris Keyes, Axie Navas, Mary Turner, and Abigail Wise at *Outside*. Special thanks to my longtime *Outside* editor and good friend, Elizabeth Hightower Allen.

For assistance and friendship on and off the page, thank you to Tanya Barba, Nathan Bay, Rus Bradburd, Bob Chung, Scott Dorsch, Alan Duffy, David Francis, John Gookin, Scott Jordan, Jeff Kerby, James Million, Michael Neiger, Monica Prelle, Derek Randles, Chris Solomon, Tracy Ross, and Heidi Streetman. Lindsay Ginest at Suite Vans Maui loaned me her ProMaster when I didn't have a place to stay for the night. Jack and Janice Reagan are my fixers on the Olympic Peninsula, who time and again fed me, loaned me a Yukon and a camper in which to sleep and write, and shuttled me to and from the Bainbridge Island Ferry.

Local newspaper journalists make the world go round. Jesse Major at the *Peninsula Daily News* was invaluable from the day I learned about Jacob's disappearance. Jesse is generous to a fault.

I am fortunate to be employed at Northern Michigan University, whose support is remarkable. Thank you to my colleagues, the Department of English, and the College of Arts and Sciences. Special thanks to Angie Rasmussen and Lori Rintala in the Department of English for organizational and logistical assistance that helped make time and travel possible.

Twenty percent of author royalties generated by sales of *The Cold Vanish* will be donated to the nonprofit Jon Francis Foundation.

INDEX

Page numbers of photographs and illustrations appear in italics.

Key to abbreviations: NPS = National Park Service; ONP = Olympic National Park; SAR = Search and Rescue

INDEX

INDEX

ABOUT THE AUTHOR

JON BILLMAN is a former wildland firefighter and high school teacher. He holds an MFA in Fiction from Eastern Washington University. He's the author of the story collection *When We Were Wolves* (Random House, 1999). Billman is a regular contributor to *Outside* and his fiction and nonfiction have appeared in *Esquire*, *The Paris Review*, and *Zoetrope: All-Story*. He teaches fiction and journalism at Northern Michigan University in the Upper Peninsula, where he lives with his family in a log cabin along the Chocolay River.